D0613175

Transformational Philanthropy

Entrepreneurs AND Nonprofits

Lisa M. Dietlin
President and CEO
Lisa M. Dietlin Associates, Inc.
Chicago, Illinois

JONES AND BARTLETT PUBLISHERS
Sudbury, Massachusetts
BOSTON   TORONTO   LONDON   SINGAPORE

World Headquarters

Jones and Bartlett Publishers	Jones and Bartlett Publishers	Jones and Bartlett Publishers
40 Tall Pine Drive	Canada	International
Sudbury, MA 01776	6339 Ormindale Way	Barb House, Barb Mews
978-443-5000	Mississauga, Ontario L5V 1J2	London W6 7PA
info@jbpub.com	Canada	United Kingdom
www.jbpub.com		

Jones and Bartlett's books and products are available through most bookstores and online book-sellers. To contact Jones and Bartlett Publishers directly, call 800-832-0034, fax 978-443-8000, or visit our website, www.jbpub.com.

Substantial discounts on bulk quantities of Jones and Bartlett's publications are available to corporations, professional associations, and other qualified organizations. For details and specific discount information, contact the special sales department at Jones and Bartlett via the above contact information or send an email to specialsales@jbpub.com.

Copyright © 2010 by Jones and Bartlett Publishers, LLC

All rights reserved. No part of the material protected by this copyright may be reproduced or utilized in any form, electronic or mechanical, including photocopying, recording, or by any information storage and retrieval system, without written permission from the copyright owner.

This publication is designed to provide accurate and authoritative information in regard to the Subject Matter covered. It is sold with the understanding that the publisher is not engaged in rendering legal, accounting, or other professional service. If legal advice or other expert assistance is required, the service of a competent professional person should be sought.

Production Credits
Publisher: Michael Brown
Associate Editor: Megan Turner
Editorial Assistant: Catie Heverling
Editorial Assistant: Teresa Reilly
Production Director: Amy Rose
Senior Production Editor: Renée Sekerak
Senior Marketing Manager: Sophie Fleck
Manufacturing and Inventory Control Supervisor: Amy Bacus
Composition: Tolman Creek
Cover Design: Scott Moden
Cover Image: © Liga Lauzuma/ShutterStock, Inc.
Printing and Binding: Malloy, Incorporated
Cover Printing: Malloy, Incorporated

Library of Congress Cataloging-in-Publication Data
Dietlin, Lisa M.
  Transformational philanthropy : entrepreneurs and nonprofits / by Lisa M. Dietlin. -- 1st ed.
    p. cm.
  Includes bibliographical references and index.
  ISBN-13: 978-0-7637-6678-8
  ISBN-10: 0-7637-6678-X
  1. Charities. 2. Entrepreneurship. I. Title.
  HV48.D45 2009
  361.7--dc22
                          2009017810

  6048
Printed in the United States of America
13 12 11 10   10 9 8 7 6 5 4 3 2

To my dad, Robert, known as Bob to his friends; he was a welder, big game hunter, fisherman, taxidermist, and the consummate entrepreneur. He taught me to dream!

And to my mom, Shirley, who gave me wings to fly!

Finally, to my nephews and nieces: Michael, Anna, Benjamin, Nathaniel, Caitlin, and Robert . . . may you find the courage to explore the entrepreneurial and philanthropic worlds. May you dream big dreams and have the wings to fly!

Contents

Foreword

It is a pleasure to write the foreword to Lisa Dietlin's book, *Transformational Philanthropy: Entrepreneurs and Nonprofits*. I have known Lisa for a number of years going back to when I was a visiting professor at University of Illinois at Chicago (UIC), teaching my Nine-Step Success Process™ to business students. She was the Assistant Dean of Development for the College of Business Administration at UIC. She was dynamic then and is dynamic now—especially after writing this wonderful research document that provides so much detail and valuable information. Having worked in the nonprofit area for a large part of my life, I have found that it takes years to learn what Lisa has given us in this work of art. She covers every angle and provides us with a road map for success. Her insights into the entrepreneurs' world cannot come at a better time while we are going through this transformation in the twenty-first century.

Our future generation may not have Social Security, a pension, or other means of taking care of themselves long term. Entrepreneurship is a viable option that needs serious consideration in this age of reinvention and recreation. As we live longer and our world becomes smaller, we need many ways to look at diversifying our opportunities. This book gives great insight regarding the importance of giving back, the importance of charity, and the true meaning of philanthropy. It defines major gift giving, and puts this subject in perspective where each of us can be encouraged to be a productive member of the community. The weaving of entrepreneur and philanthropic giver teaches us how to be more productive on the business side and enhances our spirit of giving. It is remarkable how this book will create a deeper meaning of how to be a better human being.

Congratulations, Lisa for going to the next level and taking the risk to make it happen for so many people. You make us better!

Stedman Graham
Author
Entrepreneur

Acknowledgments

I recently realized by inadvertently opening the wrong Word document that the dream for this book began in November 2005. Six years after finishing my master's thesis, I put a pen to paper to continue documenting my research on entrepreneurs and why they give their money to philanthropic organizations and endeavors. It has been a wonderful journey to discover why successful entrepreneurs decide to give back and to share that knowledge.

In writing this book, I also realized it truly takes many people to make it happen. First, the work of Hank Rosso's *Achieving Excellence in Fundraising* was instrumental in my developing the thoughts and ideas shared in this book. In particular Eugene R. Tempel's work in defining the multiple roles of philanthropy was the basis for developing the "Individual Philanthropic Audit" found in this book as an appendix. I was also introduced to the idea of transformational philanthropy by reading James M. Hodges's chapter titled, "Gifts of Significance." I am indebted to Mr. Temple and Mr. Hodge for sharing their thoughts on philanthropy and allowing me to stand on their shoulders to move philanthropy forward. Second, my personal thanks and appreciation go out to everyone who listened to me share the story about this book and its importance. Many hours were spent talking to friends and family about this dream. In particular, I would like to thank my best friend, Mary Ann Beckwith, for her unconditional support in this and all my life's endeavors as well as friends Renee Torina, Margaret Soffin, Karen Hynes, John Jones, Valerie Ingram, Aimee Daniels, Caroline Coppola, Suzanne LeMignot, Esequiel Sanchez, Julia Koch, Charles Katzenmeyer, Suzanne Jurva, Hope Ross, Erin Minné, Kristyn Hartman, Yasmin Bates, Emilia DiMenco, Wim Wiewel, Margot Pritzker, Denny Cummings, Stedman Graham, Kathryn Tack, and many others. It has been a long road, but well worth it!

Thanks to my clients and those in the nonprofit world as well as the entrepreneurial world who were willing to share their stories. I appreciate all of your support to see me through this project especially Jan Pruitt, Sherry Hooper, Jaynee Day, Rob Acton, Christine Bork, Ann Alvarez, Lanetta Haynes, Melanie Nowacki, Art Taylor, Julie Rizzo, Cathy Brod, Katherine Sawyer, Christel Kedzie, Cindy Zimmer, and Melissa Schmitz.

I also thank the entrepreneurs who sat for interviews. I was humbled and amazed by their willingness to share their thoughts and feelings about the philanthropic world and why they give away their hard earned money. I am indebted to Julie Azuma, Suzy Bogguss, John and Rita Canning, Richard Driehaus, Garth Fundis, Carolyn Gable, Deborah Gibson, Leticia Herrera, Bill Imada, Al Johnson, Suzanne Jurva, Janet Katowitz, Marsha McVicker, Alfredo Molina, Carole Mundy, Stephan Pyles, John W. Rogers, Jr., Cibeline Sariano, Peter Thomas, Art Velasquez, David Weinberg, and Chad Willis for their candor and willingness to participate in this project.

Thanks to Stacy French Reynolds and Stephanie Radkay for reviewing the manuscript before it was submitted to the publisher. Thank you to Kristina Kolerich, Lorena Alonso, and Valerie Ingram for conducting research for this book when I found myself at wit's end.

Thanks to my former staff member, Lindsey Nathan, for providing outstanding assistance and encouragement on a daily basis during the course of writing this book. I couldn't have done it without you!

Thanks to my current and former staff members for their constant and much needed support during the writing process especially Kristie Walstrum, Julie Fregetto, Barbara Figgins, Lisa Guzman, Jennifer Smith, Tara Sullivan, Sara Davenport, and Suzanne Zbylut as well as interns Karen Aw and Laura Sevo.

Thanks to my editors for their support of this project. I appreciate your efforts as well as the entire team at Jones and Bartlett, including Megan Turner, Catie Heverling, Renée Sekerak, and Sophie Fleck for making this dream come true.

Finally, to my family, my mom, Shirley, my sister, Linda, my brother, Jeff, my sister-in-law, Danielle, and Aunt Phyllis who heard numerous times about this process and still are willing to talk to me about it! It truly does take a village.

Introduction

en·tre·pre·neur—noun, translated from its French roots, means "one who undertakes." The term entrepreneur is used to refer to anyone who undertakes the organization and management of an enterprise involving independence and risk as well as the opportunity for profit.

In 1985, there were 13 billionaires in the United States. A little more than 24 years later, there are more than 1,000 billionaires with 236 of them being Americans. Their wealth comes from all areas of the business world, and they are generally very generous individuals.

Today, we find more and more information in the news media about the philanthropic sector, sometimes called the independent sector. There are articles in newspapers on a daily basis, and almost weekly you can learn from a television news program of some charitable endeavor done either by everyday Americans or celebrities. There are Internet Web sites wholly dedicated to providing information as well as blogs and podcasts.

The nonprofit sector accounts for nine percent of all those employed, and the numbers are still going up. However, the philanthropic sector is still not thought of as an automatic or sometimes even a viable career choice. Just think back to when you were growing up. My guess is that you were told you could be a doctor, a lawyer, a businessperson, an engineer, a scientist— even an astronaut or the president of the United States. However, my guess is you were not told about the careers that could be found in the philanthropic world. Working in the nonprofit world is not something that career counselors advocate, let alone raise as a possibility. However, there are many jobs available in the nonprofit sector beyond those involving fundraising, including working as a doctor, social worker, information technology staff, engineer, or chief financial officer for a nonprofit organization; even security personnel, chefs, teachers, and others are needed. But here's a piece of advice for those looking for new careers: if you can raise funds, meaning that you can ask someone for a charitable donation in such a way that they are left with a good feeling that they have made a difference in someone's life or in their community, you will always have plenty of job opportunities. I nodded knowingly this year when *US News and World Report* listed fundraiser as one of the best careers for 2009.

Many entrepreneurs, after having built a successful business and selling it, are looking for an "encore" career. This situation is a prime opportunity for entrepreneurs to explore the nonprofit world as an encore career choice or activity and for the leadership of nonprofit organizations to seriously work to engage these very talented individuals.

I am often asked when I decided to become involved in the philanthropic world primarily as an active fundraiser. My immediate response is that I have always been involved in raising money for a worthwhile cause and have been willing to ask others to support a cause, a candidate (for a while I did political fundraising), or a nonprofit organization. I fondly recall that while taking a step aerobics class at a university for which I worked, a colleague of mine commented, "Your workout t-shirts always have a cause on them; you are a walking advertisement for the causes you care about or those you are involved in." I thought about this statement and realized it was true. My entire life has been dedicated in one way or another to supporting causes I care about and asking others to consider being supportive, too.

I am, therefore, very excited to share this book about entrepreneurs and nonprofit organizations. My actual research in this area began over 10 years ago while I was working on my master's degree, but my work with entrepreneurs has been ongoing since I began fundraising. Entrepreneurs, better known as small business owners in many communities, were the ones I found always willing to consider new ideas, new candidates, new projects, or new nonprofit organizations. What I found amazing is that most of my colleagues overlooked this part of the business sector when seeking charitable donations. And, according to an article published in 2008 in *The Chronicle of Philanthropy*, a study revealed that most charities do not seek out donations from small businesses.

Entrepreneurs are the individuals most likely to make a transformational donation. By *transformational*, I mean a philanthropic donation that changes the course of or has a tremendous impact on a nonprofit organization. However, most entrepreneurs do not have a plan of action or strategy for their philanthropic activities. They tend to choose charities and charitable activities because of their own personal interests or those of their employees. For example, if an employee is diagnosed with a particular disease, the nonprofit organization associated with that disease might be the company's charity of choice.

Additionally, entrepreneurs, especially young entrepreneurs, are beginning to incorporate philanthropy into the plans of their company from the beginning. They see a value in combining their business strategy with their philanthropic strategy. The interviews with Suzy Bogguss, Cibeline Sariano, and Chad Willis highlight how they incorporate their charitable efforts into their businesses. Business owners are also working to include their employees in the decision making regarding the company's philanthropic endeavors. The interviews with Alfredo J. Molina, Carolyn Gable, Bill Imada, and John W. Rogers, Jr. (see the section "Entrepreneurial Stories") detail some of the ways they include and encourage their employees to become involved in philanthropic activities. At the beginning of each entrepreneur's story is their personal bio. My interview with them follows their bio. I think you will read that the key to success in engaging entrepreneurs is for the leadership of nonprofit organizations to be patient as the company grows.

In these tough economic times, I am often asked if Americans will continue to be generous. The answer is yes. Research has shown that during every recessionary period the United States has gone through since 1967, giving has only decreased on average by 1.3%, whereas in good economic times, giving increases by 3% to 4% annually. These are pretty good odds. Through reading this book and the interviews I conducted with entrepreneurs, you will come to realize that it is individuals, especially entrepreneurs, who will help the nonprofit sector survive these tough economic times and thrive!

It is my hope that in the following pages entrepreneurs as well as the leadership and staffs of nonprofit organizations will discover a means for creating a win-win situation for everyone involved in the philanthropic world. It is a wonderful and amazing place in which to work and become involved. It is the place where dreams *do* come true.

Chapter 1

Philanthropy Versus Charity

Before attempting to understand the philanthropic world, a common definition for entrepreneur should be articulated. Many definitions can be found, and they are all fairly similar. According to Merriam Webster's online dictionary, an *entrepreneur* is one who organizes, manages, and assumes the risks of a business or enterprise. The Internet site Wise Geek defines an entrepreneur as "an individual who accepts financial risks and undertakes new financial ventures." The word itself is derived from the French words *entre* (to enter) and *prendre* (to take).

The term *entrepreneur* is therefore often used to refer to any person who undertakes the organization and management of an independent enterprise involving risk as well as the opportunity for profit. In the following pages and chapters, the great value added to society, communities, and the world by the presence of entrepreneurs will become apparent.

UNDERSTANDING THE NONPROFIT WORLD

I am often asked, "What is a nonprofit organization?" Although I would like to give a specific and definite answer, that is still not possible. Nonprofit organizations can be defined in many ways, but most are defined by their tax-exempt status. There are even many different names to describe the nonprofit sector, such as the following:

- Not-for-profit
- Nonprofit
- Nonprofit organization
- Tax exempt

- Civil
- Independent
- Charitable sector
- Social sector
- Third sector
- Voluntary sector
- Charities
- Foundations
- Nongovernmental organizations (NGOs)

One of the first things to know is that organizations in the nonprofit sector are simply trying to create a better world. You only have to read the mission and vision statements of nonprofit organizations to see that this is the ultimate goal. However, they don't always agree on what makes a better world. Two nonprofit organizations may have completely opposite mission statements, such as Planned Parenthood and National Right to Life, two nonprofit organizations with contrasting ideas of what would constitute a better world. Nonprofit organizations with completely polar opposite missions coexist in this world. Using the same example, it can be noted that nonprofit organizations, such as Planned Parenthood and National Right to Life, exist along the entire ideological spectrum from liberal to conservative. Each has very different agendas, each is on opposite ends of the liberal/conservative spectrum and each is a nonprofit organization.

Also, multiple nonprofit organizations may be doing the same type of work. One only has to think of the more than 200 food banks that constitute the network of Feeding America (formerly America's Second Harvest). Each one is dedicated to feeding hungry people in America, but each does it a little bit differently in a specific geographic area. That said, there are many more nonprofit organizations that exist to feed hungry Americans than these 207 organizations, with some even coexisting in the same geographic service area. It does not mean that one is better than the others, but simply that each nonprofit organization when it began had a mission to feed hungry people. However, the methodology for achieving the mission for each might be either subtly or drastically different.

Feeding America feeds more than 25 million people annually. Think about it this way: the number they feed is more than the population of many states, including Texas. However, there are 35.5 million Americans who are food insecure, meaning they do not know where they will get their next meal.

HISTORY AND INFORMATION

I think it is important to remember how philanthropy began in this country. When the Pilgrims and first colonists arrived, there were no hotels, supermarkets, or businesses waiting to greet them when they disembarked from their boats. They got off the ships and began building a community, which turned into a colony that was governed by England. As we all know, that first winter was rough and half of the colonists died. But those who survived were determined to make a new world.

While they built their homes, stores, and businesses, they recognized there were no hospitals, libraries, schools, or universities. The individuals living in the "New World," as it was called, needed to develop a system whereby things that were commonplace back home—hospitals, schools, libraries, poor houses, orphanages, museums, and soup kitchens—would come into existence for the benefit of the population. Although all of these things could be found in the countries they had left, these entities and institutions were founded and funded primarily by monarchies ruling those nations or by established churches such as the Catholic or Anglican Church. The new colonies, whether settled by the English, the Spanish, the Dutch, or the French, were far removed from their homeland, and the hopes of having a king or queen build a school or hospital in the new land were small. The colonists had to become entrepreneurial in thinking of ways to develop medical care infrastructure, educational systems, and religious establishments without a monarchy or national religion to provide the funding.

Out of this chaos, a nonprofit sector was born—a sector that now employs more than 12 million individuals and accounts for 9% of the workforce in the United States. Neighbor helping neighbor, friend and foe working side by side to accomplish a shared goal, whether it be providing medical treatment, building schools, restoring homes, or ensuring an adequate food supply, Americans have always been philanthropic. They have always been willing to jump in and help their family, friends, and strangers and, yes, even their enemies.

Think also of the great western migration in the mid-1800s of families looking for a better place to live and work. Quilting bees, barn raisings, and harvest days became a tradition, but they were really born out of need—a need allowing individuals from all over to come together to resolve. American history has many examples of the philanthropic tradition, but the important thing to note is that this philanthropic spirit still exists today. Although the nonprofit sector and the individual charities within it might appear to lack a cohesive strategy that will achieve the outcomes desired, there is a long track record and history of success throughout the past 400-plus years of documented civilizations in this hemisphere.

The reasons nonprofit organizations continue to exist today are the same as in the past: the community—in this case the American people and society—wants things that businesses and the government cannot provide. Citizens take action recognizing that what businesses cannot profit from and governments do not provide still need to exist for the benefit of humanity. Surprisingly, not a lot has changed in almost 400 years. Citizens, meaning everyday people, are still the reason the majority of nonprofit organizations are created today.

The nonprofit sector provides societal benefits that are large and varied. Just think of all the different types of individuals, corporations, and foundations involved in philanthropic work. There is no stereotypical nonprofit organization or constituency either in terms of services provided or of donors aligned with it. This lack of stereotypes—in other words, its diversity and differentiation—is what makes the nonprofit world exciting, dynamic, interactive, and vibrant.

From these humble beginnings to today there are more than 1.5 million nonprofit organizations in the United States, and as stated earlier, employing millions of individuals. Another way to look at it is that one in ten workers in the United States works in the nonprofit sector. And it is important to remember the nonprofit sector employs more than charity leaders and fundraisers. Nonprofit sector jobs and positions include accountants, bookkeepers, case workers, janitors, attorneys, marketing directors, communications and public relations staff, information technology staff, chief financial officers, receptionists, security personnel, cooks, social workers, program managers, administrative assistants, nurses, doctors, engineers—the list goes on and on. I often tell the groups to which I am speaking that every position found in the business world can usually be found in the nonprofit world.

Further, in 2007 while nonprofit organizations raised more than $300 billion for the first time, they had more than $2.9 trillion in assets, which is equal to one-third of the U.S. gross domestic product, according to "The Idealist Guide to Nonprofit Careers: What Exactly Is a Nonprofit?"

According to Idealist.org, here is a picture of the nonprofit world:

- 70% of the nonprofit organizations that exist have operating budgets under $500,000.
- Approximately 4% have budgets over $10 million.
- 31% of the funding for nonprofit organizations comes from government contracts and grants.
- More than 100 new nonprofit organizations file daily with the Internal Revenue Service (IRS).

It is also important to remember that nonprofit organizations work in both urban and rural communities, providing the support—and often the infrastructure—needed to deliver services, programs, and activities that otherwise would not happen.

> **LIFES (Lisa's Instructions For Entrepreneurial Success) Tip**
> The larger budgets in the nonprofit world tend to belong to universities, colleges, and hospitals, whereas the smaller budgets are often aligned with nonprofit organizations in the arts, culture, environment, and social services areas.

DEFINITIONS

In the nonprofit world, the words *philanthropy* and *charity* are often used interchangeably. Although there are a lot of similarities, there are some definite differences of which the reader needs to be aware. Both words are nouns describing the act of helping or goodwill to people. They are also defined as an act or a gift of supporting or of distributing funds to help others. The biggest difference often lies in how they are perceived by individuals in the community. *Charity* is often thought to be helping someone or something right now by giving directly to solve the problem, not necessarily through financial contributions. It could be direct aid and is generally aimed toward the needy or suffering. *Philanthropy*, on the other hand, is love of humankind, the act of improving the situation of others through charitable aid or donations. Individuals also state that philanthropy in their opinion is long term, whereas charity is immediate and often short term in focus.

Although the difference between the two words can be perceived as subtle, I like to use the story of helping someone who is hungry. I think all of us have heard the adage that if you give a person a fish, he will eat for a day. If you teach him to fish, he will eat for his entire life. Charity at its basic sense is giving the person a fish, whereas philanthropy is teaching the person to fish.

A recent example that illustrates the difference between charity and philanthropy is the short-lived television series *Oprah's Big Give*, which took philanthropic work and made it into a reality show. Although I applaud Oprah loudly and vigorously for her efforts in bringing philanthropy into the lives of everyday Americans via a medium, television, with which they are comfortable, I am frustrated, if not angered at times, at the message that was sent. The message to me seemed to be to find someone or some organization in need, throw money and resources at it, fix it immediately for the short term, and move on. This is not philanthropy. This is charity. As long as we all understand the difference, it is all right. But I believe at times the show reinforced negative stereotypes of what constitutes philanthropic work.

One of the recipients in the first episode voiced criticism, for example. She was a homeless woman who had received a down payment for a house, a new car, and scholarships for her two children. Her comment after the interaction with the contestants from *Oprah's Big Give* was that she wished she had been trained for a job. In my opinion what she was really saying was, How am I going to keep up the payments on this house I am supposed to purchase, put gas in this new automobile, and purchase insurance for the car without a job? I am inferring this because she believed she did not have the job skills necessary to secure a sustaining job. She was given a fish, not taught how to fish. Once the show and the contestants left Los Angeles, she was on her own. Most entrepreneurs I talk to are willing to give someone a fish, but they want to be sure he or she is also taught how to fish. Sustainability in making a difference is key for entrepreneurs.

I am also often asked if there is a difference between *contribution* and *donation*. There is generally not a difference. Both terms are used interchangeably throughout the nonprofit literature.

The final word that causes much confusion is *nonprofit*, in reference to whether the term should be *nonprofit* or *not-for-profit*. Again, both words are interchangeably used and reflect an organization's conduct in working on or for something without the goal of making a financial profit. There is a social profit, however.

One might ask why there is confusion about the terminology used in the nonprofit field. Given that charity and philanthropy have been around since the beginning of time and exist in every culture throughout the world, shouldn't there be more clarity? I believe the reason the confusion exists is that the nonprofit field is not an academic discipline yet. Think about it. Nobody grows up and says, "Hey Mom and Dad, my career choice is working for a charity." There are still very few educational programs dedicated to training people to work in the nonprofit arena, especially at the undergraduate level, but they are emerging and growing, especially the master's degree programs. This is a field ripe for entrepreneurial involvement because it is not yet completely formed and is always looking for new opportunities.

HOW DOES AN ENTITY BECOME A NONPROFIT ORGANIZATION?

As stated earlier, there are 1.5 million nonprofit organizations in existence, with most of them serving different missions; however, there are some common features of which everyone should be aware. They are as follows:

- To be tax exempt, an organization must be recognized by the IRS, meaning the work the group is doing or proposing to do must fall into one of the exempt purposes of the IRS code as defined by section 501(c) (3).
- Tax exemption means the nonprofit organization does not have to pay corporate taxes to the federal government on the revenue it generates (e.g., fundraising, grant making).
- By being recognized as a 501(c) (3) organization, donations are tax deductible to the donor.
- Nonprofit organizations must file a Form 990 annually with the IRS, unless the annual budget of the organization is below $25,000.
- Churches are exempt from filing a Form 990 even though they are considered nonprofit organizations.
- Organizations with an annual budget below $5,000 do not have to register with the IRS.
- 501(c) (3) status applies to both public charities (e.g., UNICEF, American Red Cross, Salvation Army) and private foundations (e.g., Rockefeller Foundation, Bill and Melinda Gates Foundation).
- Nonprofit organizations must still pay some taxes.
- 501(c) (3) organizations are prohibited from doing anything that affects the outcome of an election for any public office.

LIFES Tip

The biggest difference between a private foundation and a public charity (although both are classified as 501(c) (3) organizations by the IRS) is that a public charity must derive at least one-third of its funding from gifts and other sources, meaning there cannot be one source for the funding. Broadly speaking, foundations differ from "public charities or nonprofit organizations" in that most engage primarily in direct service, although a few do some grant making (more on this topic can be found in Chapter 12). One person cannot create a nonprofit organization and fully fund it for his or her own purposes. Others must always be involved, with at minimum a requirement of three board members to create a 501(c) (3).

Although the 501(c) (3) designation is the most common for nonprofit organizations, there are 25 other designations within the 501(c) classification. There are also nonprofits that operate under the 501(d), (e), (f), 521, and 527 classifications. These usually belong to credit unions, chambers of commerce, labor unions, membership groups (e.g., medical societies), political action committees (PACs), retirement funds, advocacy groups (e.g., Right to Life), and alumni associations, and the donations they receive are usually not tax deductible.

> ### LIFES Tip
>
> Besides government funding, there are only three ways for nonprofit organizations to generate funds:
>
> - Providing and selling products and services (e.g., childcare operations at a social services agency or tuition paid by students at a university or college)
> - Selling membership fees (e.g., a National Public Radio campaign or the Sierra Club)
> - Raising philanthropic dollars through donations (e.g., contributions from individuals, corporations, foundations, bequests)

WHO ARE THE REALLY BIG DONORS IN THIS COUNTRY?

In the United States, the great philanthropists have first been great entrepreneurs. When one thinks about the benefactors of the 20th century, names such as Ford, Carnegie, and Rockefeller come to mind. They built the great museums, hospitals, educational institutions, and libraries of the last century. They also began small businesses that became major national and, in some cases, international corporations. All three of the individuals just listed—Henry Ford, Andrew Carnegie, and John D. Rockefeller—did philanthropy as a primary focus of their nonprofit work. I am sure each of them did charity on occasion, but they each had a strategic philanthropic plan in mind when they began working on their various initiatives.

If you work in the nonprofit world, you probably already know that approximately 82% to 85% of all charitable donations annually in the United States are made by individuals: people interested in changing the world, making it a better place in which to live.

In 2007, $306.39 billion was given in America to 1.5 million nonprofits, including international causes (Figure 1–1). It was the first time annual donations surpassed the $300 billion dollar mark. I believe more important to note than the large aggregate amount donated to this sector is that individuals donated $252.18 billion, or 82.4% of the total amount when you include bequests, which totaled 7.6%. Think about it this way: If you knew 82% of your sales base for your company was in one sector, I assume you would spend the majority of your time cultivating and working that sector.

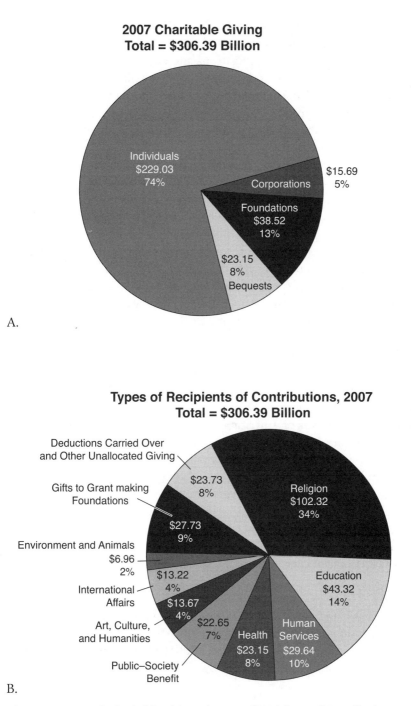

A.

B.

Figure 1–1 2007 A) Charitable Giving; B) Types of Recipients of Contributions

You would not ignore the other 18% of potential customers, but you would certainly focus your time, energy, and strategy on where your bread was buttered. For both nonprofit organizations and entrepreneurs, it is key to remember that individuals do contribute when asked and are making a significant difference in the lives of many through their financial support of nonprofit organizations.

But what about the donations from corporations and foundations? Are they charitable? The answer is yes, they are charitable, but not to the degree or significance of individuals. Although there is an expectation in society that corporations will be good corporate citizens supporting the community through charitable contributions, on average they contribute 4% to 6% of the total amount donated annually in the United States. In 2007, corporations donated 5.1%, or $15.68 billion, of the total given to charitable entities. Foundations on average account for almost double that annually, with their donations totaling approximately 11% to 12%. In 2007, foundations donated 12.6% of the total dollars given, or $38.52 billion. Although corporate- and foundation-donated dollars are very important, it is imperative for all to remember that individuals provide the large majority of the charitable dollars contributed in this country. Individuals and their financial donations are needed to make the philanthropic sector work. It might even be said they are the drivers of the philanthropic world.

Another interesting fact is that whereas we often assume that those with inherited wealth are more likely to make large charitable donations, a study commissioned by Bank of America proved otherwise. According to the study, entrepreneurs are especially generous, giving on average $232,206 annually, while those with inherited wealth contribute $109,745 annually. Both are truly significant donation amounts, but it is important to note that people who start their own businesses give $120,000 more on average annually to charitable organizations. Although almost two-thirds of household giving in the United States comes from the wealthiest 3% of Americans, everyday Americans (those with household incomes of less than $100,000) donate a larger percentage of their income to charity than those with wealth.

> ### LIFES Tip
> Individuals who have household incomes ranging from $50,000 to $100,000 on average gave a larger percentage of their income to charity than those with incomes above $100,000, according to research done by the Center on Philanthropy at Indiana University in 2005.

Individuals can and do make a difference in the daily life of nonprofit organizations. They ensure that schools remain open, museums are accessible, society's poorest members are fed, the unemployed are trained, medical services are available, art is preserved, policy discussions are possible, legal aid services are available, diseases are researched, wishes are granted—the list goes on and on.

Although most of us will respond to the needy by providing charity to help ensure they survive, most of us want to practice philanthropy. Individuals, especially entrepreneurs, want to ensure that the problem or challenge is resolved and that the resolution is sustainable.

WHAT ABOUT WOMEN ENTREPRENEURS?

Any discussion of entrepreneurs and philanthropy must also include a discussion about women and their philanthropic activities. In 2006, according to the National Women's Business Council, women owned or had a majority interest in 10.4 million businesses. Between 1997 and 2002, the number of women-owned businesses grew at almost twice the rate of all U.S. privately held businesses. This means women entrepreneurs are creating their own wealth and have the means to be philanthropic if informed, approached, and engaged.

Overall, single women are significantly more generous, by a 13% margin, than single men, after allowing for income and education, according to a 2005 study by Dr. Patrick Rooney, director of research at the Center on Philanthropy at Indiana University. Tom Stanley's research, published in the book *Millionaire Women Next Door*, stated that women had helped raise funds for at least one charity during the preceding 12 months by a 10% margin over men and were more likely to have attended fundraising galas and balls by a 14% margin. These numbers hold true with the women entrepreneurs I have spoken with and interviewed. Women business owners want to make a difference and are more likely to be even greater risk takers in supporting nonprofit organizations that are taking on new initiatives and programs than their male counterparts.

DON'T FORGET THAT NEXT DOOR IS A POTENTIAL MILLIONAIRE

In any list of the largest gifts made in the United States by entrepreneurs, a few names will be recognizable, but most are not household names. Nonprofit organizations' executive directors, directors of development, and boards of directors should make note of this fact and realize there are people of great wealth living in their communities. As a resident of Chicago, I am often told by a nonprofit organization's leaders that if they could only get Oprah Winfrey as a donor, Michael Jordan, or even Bill Gates, then all their financial and fundraising worries would be over and everything would be great with their nonprofit organization. At this point in a discussion, I then ask, "Who here knows Oprah Winfrey, Michael Jordan, or Bill Gates?" The answer is usually that no one in the room knows any of the famous people mentioned, but they believe that if Oprah, Michael, or Bill just knew about the nonprofit organization's mission and the good work being done, they would be sure to get involved and make a donation. Again, I gently remind them that the best future donors for nonprofit organizations are past donors and those in their network or circle of influence. The likelihood of Oprah Winfrey, Michael Jordan, or even Bill Gates becoming your donor is slim, especially if you do not know them!

In order to survive the challenges that most nonprofit organizations will face in the 21st century, it is, however, imperative to engage entrepreneurs in the life of their organizations.

EDUCATING ENTREPRENEURS

Entrepreneurs know very little about philanthropy or charity and have little time to educate themselves. Leaders of a nonprofit organization must listen closely to the language of entrepreneurs. Often in conversations, entrepreneurs talk only about those things they know or understand, and although their knowledge is often vast, it very rarely includes an understanding of philanthropy or philanthropic endeavors. They have been too busy building their businesses to pay a lot of attention to this part of society. Now don't misunderstand me—entrepreneurs know the basics of charity, as do almost all of us, but because entrepreneurs have been so successful in their businesses and what they have done, leaders of nonprofit organizations often assume that the entrepreneurs will have the same expertise and knowledge when it comes to philanthropic work. Those who work in the philanthropic world often place these types of expectations on entrepreneurs, insinuating through our interactions and discussions that they should know what we are discussing.

It is important to recognize that philanthropy is not usually part of an entrepreneur's culture. It is not an issue entrepreneurs think about regularly or even, for that matter, talk about sporadically. Although contributing financially is something most would be willing to do at some point in their lifetime, entrepreneurs need to be educated about the various methods and instruments available for making a charitable donation. Currently, many entrepreneurs feel ill informed and thus unable, unwilling, or hesitant to participate. When entrepreneurs do choose to be involved, it is often once information and education have been provided and they have been asked through a personal solicitation.

> ### LIFES Tip
> The number one reason cited by individuals as to why they do not give is that they were not asked. It is imperative that those responsible for raising money for nonprofit organizations remember to ask individuals to help them achieve their mission and vision. The second part of this tip is that face-to-face solicitations for philanthropic support are the most effective and cost efficient to secure a donation.

To educate entrepreneurs, nonprofit organizations must first realize that most entrepreneurs are not very likely to attend a seminar or class to learn more about how to give away their money. They do not have the time. Entrepreneurs tend to rely heavily on their financial advisors, bankers, accountants, and others in their inner circle to provide advice and direction regarding their financial affairs, including their philanthropy. This is because they are working on their business. When entrepreneurs decide to become fully involved in philanthropic work, they suspect they should know how to do this, because after all, they are the experts in everything they do in their own businesses, so how could philanthropy be any different? Many entrepreneurs believe they should be able to figure it out.

Entrepreneurs usually do have good instincts when it comes to philanthropy, but they are not experts. To illustrate this point, one only has to look at the number of entrepreneurial entertainers and high-profile personalities who start private foundations without a clear understanding of the demands. The advice these individuals are receiving is short sighted and not in the best interest of an overall philanthropic strategy. This example can be found repeatedly throughout the entrepreneurial entertainment community. More on this can be found in Chapter 11.

Entrepreneurs want to make a difference. Entrepreneurs want to be charitable and give back to the organizations and communities near and dear to their heart, but often they have difficulty finding the right path to follow. They need help and advice, and this is where nonprofit leaders can play a pivotal role. Entrepreneurs need assistance, and nonprofit organizations and their leaders are some of the best teachers, having the ability to show them the difference between philanthropy and charity and how to achieve their goals.

During their successful business-building years, entrepreneurs have little time to become knowledgeable about issues they care about. They are aware that there are hungry people in the world, aware that students need scholarships or that the elderly have special needs, they know that the country's healthcare system needs help and that arts and culture are important to any community. What they do not necessarily know is where to begin. They do not know how to make a difference, and making a difference is a key motivator for entrepreneurs in becoming involved in a philanthropic effort.

Leaders of nonprofit organizations, both staff and volunteers, must find a way to engage entrepreneurs while realizing the type of individuals with whom they are working. The entrepreneur is an individual who is confident, very knowledgeable about his or her business and their world, but in need of education, information, and a process that makes the entrepreneur feel in charge of his or her philanthropy.

An analogy I often use when working with nonprofit leaders and entrepreneurs is that philanthropic work is similar to a dance. There are many types of dances, including the waltz, foxtrot, tango, cha cha, ballroom dancing, line dancing, and even the hokey pokey. Each dance requires different steps, and each dance requires different skills and steps to lead. Think about it this way: each dancer—in this case, the entrepreneurial donor or the nonprofit leader—will have an opportunity to lead and times when each will have to be the follower. The key is to pay attention and know the dance that is being done in order to be successful.

ENTREPRENEURS DO NOT TALK ABOUT PHILANTHROPY (OR CHARITY FOR THAT MATTER)

When Ted Turner announced his $1 billion pledge to the United Nations, he hoped to encourage other billionaires, most of whom were entrepreneurs like Ted, to join him. When that did not happen, he attempted to shame other billionaires into giving more. Turner challenged *Forbes* magazine to not only list the richest 400 Americans, but also to create a list of the largest donors. Today, *Slate*, *BusinessWeek*, and *The Chronicle of Philanthropy* publish these lists. But still billionaire entrepreneurs were not moved to make what I call transformational gifts at the level Ted Turner envisioned (see Chapter 2 for more definitions and information about transformational gifts).

Part of the problem is that entrepreneurs do not talk about philanthropy. There are many reasons for this, but the three main reasons are as follows:

- Most entrepreneurs are first-generation entrepreneurs. They did not grow up in a privileged family with a legacy of philanthropy, so discussions and knowledge about philanthropy are limited.
- Most entrepreneurs are so busy building their businesses that they do not have time to become involved in their communities; hence, their civic involvement is limited because they are devoting all their time to their business and are not exposed to philanthropic endeavors.
- Entrepreneurs are focused on filling a niche in the marketplace that does not currently exist. They often work alone, being the only one to believe in their dream; hence, when it comes to learning new things, entrepreneurs usually do it by themselves rather than in group settings.

DEFINING A MAJOR GIFT

Before talking about the steps for becoming actively involved with a non-profit organization, it is best to have a common definition of the term *major gift*. What is a major gift? This question, as well as its answer, often brings with it much confusion. The answer I share is that a major gift is defined by both the donor (in this case the entrepreneur) and receiver (the non-profit organization). First, *major gift* is a term used when working with donors to secure a large financial donation. However, there is no standard answer as to what constitutes a major gift because every nonprofit organization has a different definition. Think about it. Someone who is giving $50 a year to a cause would think $250 or $500 is a major gift, but the non-profit organization to which they are donating might view major gifts as starting at the $1,000 level. Most of the time, the numbers chosen are arbitrary and for the purposes of allowing the nonprofit organization to put some structure in its work—in other words, what level the nonprofit organization will consider to be a major gift and what level it will consider to be an annual gift.

This difference between a major gift and an annual gift can be seen most readily in the different levels of giving expectations between a grassroots organization and a well-established, traditional institution. In the case of the grassroots organization, an individual might be considered a major donor at the $1,000 or even $500 level, but at the well-established, traditional institution these might be considered the price for an admission ticket to its annual gala or an annual gift. The important thing to remember is that these are just numbers.

> ### LIFES Tip
>
> I am often asked at what level is a donation considered a major gift and how to determine it. My response almost always brings a quizzical look to the questioner's face. I tell him or her that a major gift varies from charity to charity as well as from individual to individual. It is defined differently depending on who you ask. Most nonprofit organizations define a major gift at the $1,000, $2,500, or $5,000 level. However, an entrepreneur shouldn't be surprised to be asked to make a much larger gift, perhaps at the $25,000 or even $100,000 level, by some of the long-established nonprofit organizations, especially universities, hospitals, and museums. However, a good starting point for nonprofit organizations and individuals for what to consider a major gift is the following formula:
>
> $$5 \times (\text{Average of the last three years of donations from the individual}) = \text{Major gift}$$

> ### LIFES Tip
>
> An annual gift or annual fund gift is usually a donation that provides for the operational support of a nonprofit organization. These funds are raised in any number of ways including direct mail, special events, such as big dinners and golf outings, raffles and so on.

Dietlin's Discussion Directives

1. What is the difference between philanthropy and charity?
2. What are the most common factors among nonprofit organizations?
3. How many nonprofit organizations exist in the United States?
4. Name the types of positions and jobs available at nonprofit organizations.
5. In the United States, from what group do the most donations come?
6. How is a major gift defined? What dollar amount is a major gift to you?
7. How can entrepreneurs be educated about philanthropy?

Chapter 2

Entrepreneurial Spirit

ENTREPRENEURS: WHO OR WHAT ARE THEY?

Who is an entrepreneur? What does having an entrepreneurial spirit mean? Where do you find entrepreneurs who will support nonprofit organizations? What do you do once you find them? These are some of the questions being asked by development officers, executive directors, and board members at nonprofit organizations in the 21st century.

An entrepreneur is an individual who identifies a niche in the marketplace currently not being addressed and designs a business to fill the gap. Entrepreneurs build and expand markets; they are the backbone of the economy of the United States, employing tens of millions of individuals in their small businesses.

> ### *LIFES Tip*
>
> As a point of reference, the Small Business Administration (SBA) defines a small business as a company employing 500 or fewer individuals (100 for a wholesale business). According to the SBA website, a small business is one that is organized for profit; has a place of business in the United States; makes a significant contribution to the U.S. economy by paying taxes or using American products, materials, or labor; and does not exceed the numerical size standard for its industry. The business may be a sole proprietorship, partnership, corporation, or any other legal form. Using that definition, 98% to 99% of entrepreneurial endeavors would be classified as small businesses, employing almost 55% of the workers in the United States. However in many communities, businesses employing more than 250 individuals would be considered big businesses.

Another characteristic of entrepreneurs is that they are always looking to improve a situation, fix a problem, or address a changing situation. They are fearless, and while assessing the many facets of an issue or problem, will more often than not take a risk, thus initiating the change they believe is necessary. This means entrepreneurs will not run when times get tough. In fact, it is usually in tough times that entrepreneurs are at their best, with the creative juices, ideas, and solutions flowing. This can be great for a nonprofit organization.

> ### LIFES *Tip*
> According to a 2004 study by the National Federation of Independent Businesses, small businesses donated an estimated $40 billion in cash, products, services, and volunteer time annually. Additionally, social services organizations are the largest recipient of support from entrepreneurs, according to a survey conducted in August 2008 by Chamberlain Research Consultants.

A nonprofit organization is often best served by engaging entrepreneurs because of their out-of-the-box style of thinking. Entrepreneurs' analytical skills are excellent, and when they are engaged with nonprofit organizations, they serve them well with their time, talents, and ultimately, their treasure.

GREAT PHILANTHROPISTS HAVE FIRST BEEN GREAT ENTREPRENEURS

When reviewing the history of the great philanthropists of this country, one sees a common thread: most have been highly successful entrepreneurs. Individuals such as Henry Ford, Andrew Carnegie, John D. Rockefeller, Joan Kroc, Bill Gates, George Soros, Doris Christopher, and Oprah Winfrey are just a few entrepreneurs who come to mind who have changed and currently are changing the lives of others by sharing their financial resources with nonprofit organizations that are doing good work.

Entrepreneurs better the lives of others in their community and, in some cases, the world. Here are a few examples:

- Henry Ford built an automobile company, Ford Motor Company, and then started building hospitals in the Detroit area in 1915. Additionally, in 1936 he started the Ford Foundation and upon his death in 1947 left the vast majority of his wealth to it.

Reportedly, Henry Ford made this statement: "Capital punishment is as fundamentally wrong as a cure for crime as charity is wrong as a cure for poverty."

- Andrew Carnegie built a steel company and founded free libraries, known as Carnegie libraries, throughout the United States, as well as educational and cultural institutions such as Carnegie Hall. His donations adjusted to today's dollars would total $7 billion.
- John D. Rockefeller, the first U.S. billionaire, founded an oil company, Standard Oil, and then went on to support schools, including founding the University of Chicago, as well as hospitals and medical research through his private foundations. His philanthropic contributions actualized to today's dollars would equal $11 billion.
- Joan Kroc and her husband built the McDonald's fast food restaurant chain; after her husband's death, Ms. Kroc became even more active in philanthropy, turning her full attention to it in 1990. After her death, her bequest left $1.6 billion to the Salvation Army, $225 million for National Public Radio, and $50 million each to the University of San Diego and the University of Notre Dame, as well as $5 million for San Diego's KPBS public radio and television stations.
- Bill Gates founded and grew Microsoft while becoming a global philanthropist with his wife, Melinda, making gifts to various global initiatives, the charter school movement, and HIV/AIDS and educational endeavors. In June 2008, Mr. Gates stepped down from his role at Microsoft in order to devote his full attention to the philanthropic activities of the Bill and Melinda Gates Foundation.
- George Soros started a hedge fund called Soros Fund Management and founded the Open Society Institute and the Soros Foundations, which provide charitable dollars to international endeavors, including many efforts in countries that were formerly part of the Soviet Union.
- Doris Christopher founded Pampered Chef and then went on to support her and her husband Jay's alma maters, the University of Illinois–Urbana Champaign and Valparaiso University, with very generous gifts, as well as supporting Concordia University. Doris is also very supportive of Feeding America (formerly known as America's Second Harvest).

- Oprah Winfrey is undeniably an entrepreneur and philanthropist. Through her O Philanthropy, she has donated more than $40 million to the Oprah Winfrey Leadership Academy for Girls in South Africa, and through Oprah's Angel Network she has raised more than $70 million since 1998. Her list of charitable donations is quite extensive, and it is clear she is not done yet.

It is imperative that nonprofit organizations recognize that the great philanthropists have first been very successful entrepreneurs. Nonprofit leaders, staff, volunteers, and board members need to look around their community to see the entrepreneurs who are building successful companies in their cities and towns. These are the individuals who own fast food franchises, build manufacturing factories, provide key services (e.g., financial, insurance, computer repair), and are open to new ventures. Do not be frightened by their love of business. Once they are educated and aware of the return on investment that philanthropy brings to society and the joy they will receive, they will become committed and great philanthropists for your nonprofit organization. More on the return-on-investment theory can be found in Chapter 5.

ENTREPRENEURS ARE UNTAPPED WEALTH

Most of us in the fundraising business know that the best future prospects for donations are our current donors. However, even given this true statement, it is important to recognize that untapped pockets of wealth exist. In the 1990s, Sondra Shaw and Martha Taylor wrote a book about women being untapped potential donors, entitled *Reinventing Fundraising: Realizing the Potential of Women's Philanthropy*. Today, it is the entrepreneur who is often overlooked as a potential donor.

When I first started my major gifts career, I was much more comfortable meeting and talking with CEOs, vice presidents, directors, or managers of major corporations than with entrepreneurs. I readily skipped over individuals whose company bore their name when reviewing lists of people to call for appointments. I thought corporate officers and leaders were the individuals capable of making major donations to the institution for which I worked. If I had been working at a nonprofit organization that had Michael Dell on its prospect list, my thought process would have been foolish because I might have overlooked Michael's company, Dell Computers, which had revenues in excess of $61 billion last year, simply because his last name was in the company name! Or how about Ted Turner and his company Turner Network Television (TNT)?

This same premise holds true for the "small" business owner in your community. The largest employer in your community, although considered small by the U.S. government, could have an owner capable of making major, if not transformational, gifts to a nonprofit organization.

Many leaders, both staff and volunteers, overlook entrepreneurs all the time. One of the reasons is that there is more information available about corporate officers or employees than about entrepreneurs. For example, if a nonprofit organization is working with the CEO of a *Fortune* 500 company or a publicly traded company, it can find out his or her salary as well as stock options because all of this is public information and published. From this information, it can often be determined what a "major" gift would be to this person. In other words, a nonprofit organization can base its projected "ask" amount on the publicly available information about income and stock options, not necessarily the CEO's assets or wealth. Conversely, when working with an entrepreneur, it is important to recognize that a major gift for them will more often than not be defined by their assets and wealth. I became aware of this difference when a *Fortune* 500 CEO told me I would be better served working with entrepreneurs than working with individuals like him long term (see sidebar).

On a visit to solicit a donation from the president and CEO of a major corporation located in Midland, Michigan, this executive said, "Lisa, you are only getting a gift from my income; work with entrepreneurs and you will secure gifts from their assets and wealth." It took me a while to completely understand what he was saying, but eventually I got it and began working with entrepreneurs in earnest. I did have a few missteps—meaning there were a few "strange" entrepreneurs I encountered along the way who readily agreed to meet with me but who clearly were not major gift candidates. Overall, however, the majority of entrepreneurs I met were thrilled to be contacted by a nonprofit organization from their community and more than willing to meet.

Remember, most entrepreneurs have tremendous assets and wealth as well as an extensive network. Once convinced of the value that the nonprofit organization adds to the community, they are usually willing to become very involved.

Annually, *The Chronicle of Philanthropy* lists the 50 most generous donors in America. In 2007, of the 50 individuals listed, 35 were entrepreneurs. This means that 70% of the individuals on the list had made their own wealth through their business enterprise. This is where nonprofit leaders and staff should be focusing their time and energy on engaging individuals in their philanthropic efforts.

Forbes magazine annually lists the 400 wealthiest Americans. Twenty-eight of the largest donors on the listing from *The Chronicle of Philanthropy* were also on the *Forbes* listing in 2008.

ENTREPRENEURIAL SPIRIT

So what does having an entrepreneurial spirit mean? It means having a spirit willing to risk it all, a spirit that says, "I so believe in this idea, project, program, etc., that I am willing to give everything I have to ensure that it happens." It is a spirit that will not let naysayers and detractors stop the entrepreneur. It is a spirit that believes that when tough times arrive, the fun is just beginning.

I recall in the 1990s hearing that some people who worked inside large corporations were being described as having an entrepreneurial spirit. I even heard a new word being created to describe them: "intra-preneurs." These are not the individuals being discussed here. This book addresses those individuals who have started, purchased, or acquired their own business and are definitely risk takers.

INFORMATION ABOUT ENTREPRENEURIAL BUSINESSES

As noted earlier, the Small Business Administration of the United States defines a small business as a firm with fewer than 500 employees. It further asserts that in the last ten years 60% to 80% of the net new jobs created in the United States have been created by small businesses. The number of entrepreneurs, alternatively known as self-employed individuals, is only expected to grow. In a 2004 Gallup Organization Youth Survey, 57% of teens said they would rather be their own bosses and run their own business than work for corporate America, a finding that replicated a 1994 Gallup Organization poll on the same subject. Given this attitude, young people are more likely to take risks with their careers and start their own businesses in greater numbers than their parents.

Recently, *Forbes* magazine listed the 1,062 billionaires in the world, with the vast majority having made their money through their entrepreneurial businesses and efforts. What is probably not surprising is that 44%, were Americans, the largest group from any country. What *is* surprising is that there were eight American billionaires under the age of 40 on the list.

What does this mean to a nonprofit organization? It means the nonprofit organization has to look everywhere for successful small businesses. There is no traditional model; by using the description provided by the Small Business Administration, one will find successful small businesses in all communities. Remember, these businesses will not look like traditional corporate America. Small business owners sometime operate their businesses out of their garages, basements, and homes. The nonprofit organization able to identify these small businesses in its community early and engage them in the life and work of the nonprofit at the appropriate time will be most successful in laying the groundwork to secure transformational major gifts in the future.

WHERE EXACTLY CAN YOU FIND ENTREPRENEURS?

A comment I often encounter from groups is that although they know individuals, especially entrepreneurs, are where the bulk of charitable donations come from in this country, they don't know how to find them. My response is always the same: "You could look at lists like the ones that are found in *Forbes* and other magazines, but the best places to look are in your own backyard." You need to look in your community, your neighborhood, your circle of friends, and so on. Here are basic steps to follow:

1. Review the nonprofit organization's database for those individuals who have the titles of President, CEO, Founder, or Chairman. Most databases allow sorting on the title field, and this is a good place to begin. Once you have the printout, review the names one by one. You will probably be surprised to find people who you were not even aware existed, let alone lived in your community.

2. Ask your board of directors, advisory board members, community groups, volunteers, and others about people they know who operate successful businesses in your community. It usually helps to provide a listing of industries for them to consider (see Appendix B for industry categories). This usually works better than distributing a blank sheet of paper and asking the board members to complete it by filling in the names of those they know and are willing to speak with about the nonprofit organization.

3. Access your local chamber of commerce. Most cities and towns, even geographic areas, have a chamber of commerce, and their members are normally the local business owners. These individuals usually have a strong commitment to civic and social engagement. Perhaps the nonprofit organization's board members or volunteers are members of the local chamber and can provide a directory. If not, have your nonprofit organization become a member and get the directory of other members. Take it a step further by becoming involved with a chamber committee or activity that allows you to interact with these individuals. You will be amazed at not only who you meet, but also what you learn. Networking opportunities will abound for the nonprofit organization.

4. Read your local newspaper and periodicals for information on business owners. This is an activity I recommend all the time to my clients. On average, the nonprofit organizations my company works with identify three to seven entrepreneurs weekly by reading and reviewing various newspapers and periodicals. Review publications on a daily basis. If this is not feasible, then a review should be done weekly. Translating these prospects into donors depends on the nonprofit organization following up, securing appointments, and beginning the Moves Management cycle (see the following section).

> **LIFES Tip**
>
> One suggestion for what to do once you find individuals in newspapers and periodicals is to send a congratulatory note for appearing in the periodical saying that you will follow up—and then follow up! (See Appendix C for a sample letter.)

5. There are a number of organizations geared toward helping entrepreneurs, such as the Entrepreneurs' Organization, the Young Presidents' Organization, National Association of Women business Owners, and the World Presidents' Organization, which focus attention on leaders of business who happen to also be entrepreneurs. See if there is a chapter in your geographic area. If there is a group, try to become involved either by offering to host the meeting at the nonprofit organization's location if this is feasible or by presenting on the topic of charitable giving to this group.

6. Finally, look for civic clubs, economic organizations, and other groups in your geographic area that serve the community and attract entrepreneurs. Be creative with a way to become involved.

This method works! My company, Lisa M. Dietlin and Associates, Inc. (LMDA), worked with a national scholarship organization that had no database of individuals, let alone a listing of entrepreneurs, when we started the project. Our work consisted of conducting research to secure the contact information as well as creating an initial cultivation strategy for the individuals and entrepreneurs identified. Within two years, the database had over 700 major gift prospects—many of whom were entrepreneurs—identified from reading and reviewing various periodicals.

WHAT DO YOU DO ONCE YOU FIND ENTREPRENEURS?

So now that you have found these entrepreneurs, what do you do with them? You know you are supposed to get them involved with the nonprofit organization, but you also realize they behave differently from traditional donors (Chapters 3 and 4 discuss these differences in more depth). You need to get them involved with the nonprofit organization. This is accomplished by determining ways to approach each entrepreneur individually (entrepreneurs will not respond as readily to "group" activities or calls) to ascertain whether he or she is interested in the nonprofit organization and would like to become involved. This process is known as Moves Management and was designed by G. T. "Buck" Smith as a way to put science into the art of fundraising.

Moves Management (or the Moves Management cycle as it is sometimes called) is a five-step process describing the relationship a nonprofit organization has with a prospective donor—in this case, an entrepreneur. The five steps are as follows.

1. *Identification*: The process of identifying individuals thought to possibly be interested in supporting the efforts, programs, projects, clients, and so on of the nonprofit organization.
2. *Qualification*: The process of actually discovering whether the individual is interested in supporting the nonprofit organization's efforts, programs, projects, clients, and so on; this happens best in a face-to-face meeting. It is also a time for the nonprofit organization to determine whether it wants to engage this potential donor. Although it rarely happens, there are times when a donor is not worth the demands he or she is making.

3. *Cultivation*: Once it has been determined the individual is interested in supporting the mission, vision, programs, projects, clients, and so on, both the nonprofit organization and the individual need to get to know each other better; this means the nonprofit organization will be finding ways to get the individual involved. Some suggested ways include inviting interested individuals to attend special events, participating in board meetings, touring the headquarters or facilities of the nonprofit organization, serving on an advisory board or ad hoc committee, and volunteering. Activities and interactions are designed to bring the potential donor closer to the nonprofit organization and its mission.

4. *Solicitation*: After some time, the nonprofit organization will need to ask the person if he or she would consider making a significant financial contribution. More often than not, if the nonprofit organization has done its work correctly, the individuals themselves will ask what they can do to help, especially entrepreneurs.

> **LIFES Tip**
> On average, 18 months is the length of time it will take to ask for and receive a charitable donation from a new prospective donor who has not been involved with the nonprofit organization previously.

5. *Stewardship*: It is very important to appropriately thank and steward the donor after the gift is made. Too often nonprofit organizations appear to take the money and run. This is the step often missed or overlooked by the development office in most nonprofit organizations. Information on how to do good stewardship can be found in Chapter 9.

> **LIFES Tip**
> Stewardship is the most overlooked step in the Moves Management cycle.

Figure 2–1 graphically depicts the process of moving an individual from the identification to the stewardship stages.

This cycle is how it is "supposed" to work, but with entrepreneurs you never know! The basic challenge is that entrepreneurs move very fast; the process for them may not take 18 months. It can be much shorter.

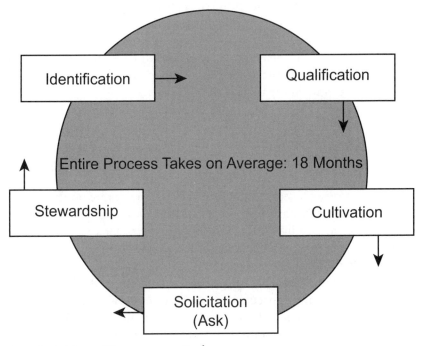

Figure 2-1 Moves Management Cycle

Remember, the overall goal is to get them involved with the nonprofit organization in achieving its mission and vision.

Although each move was described briefly, an analogy for how to think about Moves Management might prove helpful. When I am presenting to groups, I often tell them that Moves Management is like dating, courtship, and marriage, an analogy shared with me by Bud Edwards, a long time fundraising expert. The first step in dating is identifying who you would like to date. I remember sitting in the cafeteria in undergraduate school and scoping out the guys. This is what must be done in the identification stage of the Moves Management cycle: scoping out the entrepreneurs with which the nonprofit organization would like to work.

In dating, the next step is to actually go out with that person and see whether you like them and they like you. In Moves Management, this is called the qualification stage. An entrepreneur will tell you at this meeting whether he or she wants to get involved with the nonprofit organization. This step almost always has to be a face-to-face meeting that is convenient for the entrepreneur to attend, meaning it probably will take place at the entrepreneur's office and on his or her time frame. Just like when you are on a first date, each of the participants will communicate to the other whether a second date is likely, meaning they want to get involved further. Entrepreneurs will tell a nonprofit organization this by sharing that they want to get involved, take a tour, meet some clients, or see a program in action. Entrepreneurs at this stage will also be asking lots of questions. All of these are positive indicators of the entrepreneur's interest in the work being done by the nonprofit organization.

By being willing to become more involved, the entrepreneur moves to the cultivation stage of the relationship. The cultivation stage can take a while and, as mentioned previously, includes activities such as having the donor tour the facilities, interacting with clients, meeting with board members, attending special events, reading materials sent about the nonprofit organization, or serving on a committee. These activities are similar to a couple touring each other's hometown, interacting with their friends, meeting their families, attending work functions together, or looking at pictures of when they were younger. This stage continues until someone asks, "Where are we headed? What is the next step?" On many occasions after proper cultivation is done, especially with entrepreneurs, they will ask, "What can I do to help?" When this occurs you know the donor is engaged. This happens with entrepreneurs who get excited about the possibilities and opportunities that exist within the nonprofit organization and decide they want to get involved and make a difference. The next move after a solicitation or gift has been made is stewardship.

DON'T FORGET DIVERSE COMMUNITIES AND THE ENTREPRENEURS WITHIN THEM

We all tend to congregate with individuals who are like ourselves. I know this is a hard statement to accept, but I have generally found it is true. Think of any recent dinner party you have attended. What usually happens? The men gather together in one part of the house, usually in front of a large television screen on which a sporting event is being played, and the women gather in the kitchen area. This statement also tends to be true when recruiting for board membership and major donor prospects. It seems that when discussing diversity as it relates to nonprofit organizations and their boards, most of us do not realize that although ethnic diversity is very important, there are other types of diversity that are important, too. These other types of diversity include gender, profession, age, lifestyle, disabilities, class year (if an educational organization), and geographic location. The list could and often does go on and on.

As an example of an "other type of diversity," I served on the board of directors of Cabrini Green Legal Aid Clinic (CGLA), which was located in one of the historically worst neighborhoods in Chicago. Of the 17 board members, only 4 were not lawyers. Think of all the missed opportunities to secure major gifts from different sectors and walks of life by having a board composed of "like individuals." Through the actions of the new executive director, Rob Acton, the organization began recognizing the opportunities being missed, and the board began to diversify in ways other than just ethnicity.

Diversity is being outside your comfort zone with either people or situations. We initially only view as viable prospects those with whom we are comfortable or those who are likely to take a meeting with us. I recommend looking beyond these self-imposed borders. Think more globally, even if the issue is focused in your own local community. Think about diverse communities, meaning individuals from different ethnic backgrounds as well as different lifestyles, especially entrepreneurs. Although in the beginning you might be uncomfortable and anxious about offending the prospective donor because of something you do or don't do and the knowledge you may or may not possess, it will generally be all right. Most people are forgiving about mistakes as long as you are honest and candid about it while learning from them.

I once had the privilege of working with a newly formed national nonprofit organization focused in the Asian Pacific Islander (API) community called the Asian and Pacific Islander American Scholarship Fund. I admit there was some trepidation on my part after my company had been hired when I perused the board member directory and found a number of names I could not pronounce, let alone even begin to guess their API heritage.

The one thing I did know, however, was how to work with donors and board members. I will admit some mistakes were made, especially with mispronunciations of names, but over time, things got better. My pronunciation of names became more accurate, and I learned a great deal about communities I had only heard about in discussions or in news broadcasts. Know that if a nonprofit organization is willing to work in diverse communities, however *diverse* is defined, the organization will have success in areas that cannot even be imagined. This includes the entrepreneurial world.

Diverse communities, whether based on ethnicity, lifestyle, disability, or status, are often overlooked by most nonprofit organizations because they do not look the way organizations expect major donors to look. But one group we cannot overlook and who are diverse are entrepreneurs. It is a nonprofit leader's job to make sure to reach out to diverse communities, especially those who are entrepreneurs.

> **LIFES Tip**
>
> There are more than 35 different ethnicities within the API community, including Indian, Korean, Japanese, Chinese, Filipino, Hawaiian, Taiwanese, Vietnamese, Indonesian, and Bhutanese to name a few.

For example, women business owners are often overlooked even though they are prime examples of success. As reported by the *Washington Post*, according to the Center for Women's Business Research, "The face of women entrepreneurship is changing. Today women of color represent 26 percent of all women business owners—up from 20 percent just a few years ago." The article further stated that "[t]here are 2.3 million firms that are 50 percent or more owned by women of color, providing 1.7 million jobs and generating $235 billion in revenues, according to the new data. Between 2002 and 2008, the number of privately-held firms in which women of color had at least a 50 percent stake grew 30 percent while all other business grew 9 percent." The article also noted that Latinas have the highest number of businesses, followed by businesses owned by African American women. Firms owned by Asian American women saw the largest growth in the time frame studied.

> **LIFES Tip**
>
> Once a week, reach out into a community that you have overlooked; make three calls every week to individuals in those communities. Slowly and over time, you will begin to see diversity reflected in your prospect portfolio as well as your donor base. Start with entrepreneurs and see how the nonprofit organization changes and benefits.

TRANSLATING THE ENTREPRENEURIAL SPIRIT TO NONPROFIT ORGANIZATIONS

The entrepreneurial spirit in nonprofit organizations is what most entrepreneurs are looking for. As potential donors, entrepreneurs think about what matters to them. Where do they want to make a difference? I have worked with entrepreneurs who want their names associated with well-known institutions and I have worked with those who want to give to lesser-known entities. There is no right or wrong answer. An entrepreneur simply needs to find a nonprofit organization or organizations that match his or her entrepreneurial spirit. An entrepreneur also has to decide where to effect change within his or her life and community. It is important to remember that an amount of money that seems small to an entrepreneur might be transformational to the nonprofit organization that is receiving it. This again is a value entrepreneurs will consider when making a donation. In other words, entrepreneurs need to decide whether they want to be a big fish in a small pond or a potentially smaller fish in a big pond.

FINDING THE ENTREPRENEURIAL SPIRIT

The First Test

Entrepreneurs have been and continue to be busy, if not consumed with, building their businesses. However, at times and almost simultaneously, entrepreneurs want to become involved with their communities as well. The first question for them is usually when they should start becoming involved; the second is how they should begin.

According to research, it appears that entrepreneurs begin making major gift donations to nonprofit organizations approximately 8.5 years after they start their businesses. While they may have been involved before, but the involvement was generally on a limited basis. The real question for entrepreneurs might not be when to get involved but how. How does an entrepreneur choose a nonprofit organization with which to become involved? An organization that is as entrepreneurial in spirit as the entrepreneur is a prime candidate.

A first test for an entrepreneur to take in order to assess whether a nonprofit organization has the entrepreneurial spirit is to call the organization and ask for someone to call you back. In your voicemail or first message, tell the organization that you are calling because you are interested in getting involved and considering making a financial donation. The test is how long it takes the nonprofit organization to call you back. Think of it this way: If a potential customer for your business called and said he or she wanted to purchase a product or service that the entrepreneur offered, how long would it take you or your sales team to respond? All of us know an entrepreneur's response time would be immediate. This is the entrepreneurial spirit and what most entrepreneurs are looking for in a nonprofit organization.

What I am recommending you do actually happened to me when I was at the University of Illinois at Chicago. A man who, with his wife, later became major donors told me that when he initially called and left the message he was really wondering how long it would take for someone to get back to him. He shared that he was pleasantly surprised when I called back within about three hours. During the first phone conversation, I arranged for his wife and him to be on campus within four days for an initial meeting and a tour. This type of quick response time resulted in a six-figure bequest and an initial gift of $25,000 over five years. They saw the entrepreneurial spirit alive and well, and they responded.

I learned first hand from an entrepreneur about a potentially valuable opportunity missed by a nonprofit organization. This revelation occurred when I had the privilege of accompanying the donor, a very unassuming but successful entrepreneur, to the offices of the nonprofit organization where he had volunteered for over six months right after Hurricane Katrina. Joe (as I will call him) shared with me that he really enjoyed his volunteer experience, which began after hearing a story about displaced individuals on National Public Radio. The next evening he simply walked into the offices of the nonprofit organization and volunteered to staff a phone line helping people who were fleeing the storms and their aftermath in Louisiana and Texas. After one week, the nonprofit organization realized that Joe, who was the CEO of a large company that he and his wife had founded, had high-level skills and could be trusted to be the supervisor of other callers on a certain night of the week. The staff of the nonprofit organization asked him to volunteer to take on this role, and he readily agreed, again sharing with me that he really enjoyed the experience and the responsibility. Joe also let me know that he shared this attitude with those staff members associated with the nonprofit organization. The sad part was that the staff of the nonprofit organization did not realize the potential major, if not transformational, donor they had in their midst. They simply saw Joe as an outstanding volunteer.

One day after Joe and I were finished meeting and about 18 months after his initial volunteer experience, he asked that I accompany him to the offices of this nonprofit organization. During our ride to the location, Joe encouraged me to drop hints that he wanted and was capable of doing more, that he wanted to fund large projects and make a significant, potentially even a seven-figure, donation. During our meeting at the nonprofit organization, I did drop hints—actually some boulder-sized ones. To my astonishment the CEO and the director of development with whom we were meeting did not pick up on the financial capacity of the individual literally sitting in front of them. To date, this nonprofit organization has not asked for a major donation from Joe. He has since moved on, recognizing other ways for his philanthropic work to come to fruition through working with his local community foundation. What a missed opportunity!

To Joe's credit, he did not give up. I encourage entrepreneurs who have had a disappointing, negative, or less than anticipated experience to not give up either. The nonprofit organization detailed in this story did not have the entrepreneurial spirit. However, one can find the entrepreneurial spirit in the nonprofit world. It does exist. The best analogy again is to compare these experiences to an entrepreneur's client and customer base. Some clients work with you very well, and some are just difficult. However, the entrepreneurial spirit keeps motivating entrepreneurs to try to find the best customers for the products available or clients for the services offered. My guess is that most entrepreneurs do not miss an opportunity sitting in front of them!

The Second Test

A second informal way to determine or test whether a nonprofit organization has an entrepreneurial spirit is to see how they respond to first-time donors. Unfortunately, the belief that gift size influences attention does still hold true in much of the nonprofit world. The test involves starting with a small charitable donation to the charity. Pay attention to what happens. Does the donation get noticed? Did the nonprofit organization send a thank-you note? How long after the gift was made was the response received? Did the organization make a thank-you phone call? Who reached out? Was it the CEO? The director of development? A volunteer who is your peer? An intern? This is a simple way to ascertain how the nonprofit organization you are attracted to reacts to donations. The key questions are as follows: Does the nonprofit organization pay attention, and does it have the people and systems in place to react to first-time unsolicited gifts? Does the nonprofit organization have the entrepreneurial spirit?

To illustrate this point, I share a story I read in David Lansdowne's book *Fund Raising Realities Every Board Member Must Face*. The tale is that John D. Rockefeller sent a donation of one dollar to Tuskegee Institute when Booker T. Washington was raising funds for that institution. Now, it is assumed most individuals would have been insulted at the size of this gift because at that time Mr. Rockefeller was one of the richest men in America, if not the world. However, Booker T. Washington was not insulted. He chose instead to steward the gift very, very well. He first sent a kind thank-you note to Mr. Rockefeller for the gift. Then at the end of the year, he sent an accounting of what had been done with that one-dollar gift. I bet all of us can guess the ending to this story. John D. Rockefeller became a strong supporter of Tuskegee Institute because Booker T. Washington responded to his first gift as if it were a million-dollar donation. Booker T. Washington had the entrepreneurial spirit.

> **LIFES Tip**
>
> Every person involved in the nonprofit world should read David Lansdowne's book *Fund Raising Realities Every Board Member Must Face.* It is a perfect educational tool for newcomers to the field and a reminder to those who have been involved in the nonprofit world for a while of what are some tried and true practices.

Another analogy is the new customer who places a small order with a company. How do most entrepreneurs and their employees treat them? My belief and experience is that entrepreneurs treat them each as if they were their largest customers in the hopes that one day they will become a large account for the company. This is how each individual should be treated by a nonprofit organization that has the entrepreneurial spirit.

The Third Test

Entrepreneurs are well known for thinking outside the box. This is a primary reason behind their success. Their willingness to take chances and do things others think are crazy or pointless is what makes their successes, and at times their failures, so spectacular. Although this attitude works well in business, when brought to the nonprofit world it can sometimes wreak havoc. Thus, the third test for entrepreneurs to ascertain whether a nonprofit organization possesses an entrepreneurial spirit is to see how it responds to their ideas. I urge entrepreneurs to use the same skills, instincts, and determination that made their businesses a success in the work they do with nonprofit organizations. However, it is important to note that most nonprofit organizations do not operate in the realm of change and of taking chances. An entrepreneur's assessment will occur when he or she sees how a nonprofit organization reacts to his or her ideas and suggestions. Does the nonprofit organization throw up barriers and walls, telling an entrepreneur it can't be done because of one thing or another, or does the nonprofit organization inform an entrepreneur it can't be done because it has been tried before? Is the nonprofit organization simply unwilling to dream big?

As an example, assume for a moment that feeding hungry children is the entrepreneur's cause and that the entrepreneur finds a nonprofit organization that is doing this well; however, there are still hundreds of children in this community who have no food. If the entrepreneur were to ask the nonprofit organization why it can't feed all the children who are hungry in that community, the reasons might vary from lack of volunteers to lack of food supplies to lack of space, but the only thing the entrepreneur sees is that not all the hungry children are being fed. All of the reasons listed are valid to a point. Being ever the entrepreneur, he or she will have ideas of how to get more volunteers, more food, and additional space; however, the non-profit organization might have policies or programs in place that prohibit the addition of any of the things the entrepreneur brings to the table.

Although this seems outlandish, I have actually seen it happen in real life. In my career, I had the unfortunate luck of seeing this happen at several large universities. In the course of leading the fundraising efforts for one of the colleges on the campus of a large university, it was determined that a new building to house the college was going to be built at a cost of $55 million. An entrepreneur approached us with a gift of $1 million for this project. The only condition was that if the building did not get built, meaning if there never was a shovel of dirt moved for this initiative, the entrepreneur wanted his money back. This seemed to be a straightforward request. So in speaking with the dean of the college, we agreed to accept these terms because we were confident we were going to raise the money for the building project—that in fact the building would be built.

We provided the details to the university's foundation and requested a gift agreement. It was only a matter of minutes before the phone rang in my office with a key member of the university's foundation staff telling me that these terms, or in particular this term, was not acceptable. When I questioned as to why the university's foundation could not accept these terms, there was a lot of hemming and hawing on the other end of the phone line, with phrases such as "We have never done this" and "We don't know how we would give the donor their money back." Finally I was told the reason the university foundation was unwilling to accept these terms was because it would cause undue challenges and potential tax issues to the donor if we were to give the money back. The donor would have to refile his tax return, because it was assumed he would have already taken the charitable deduction or part of it, and the list went on. The institution stated all the "problems" that would occur if we agreed to this.

In actuality, the perceived problems would be more of a nuisance and challenge to the donor than the institution. If the donation were returned, there would be tax implications for both the donor and the institution. Amended tax returns would have to be filed by the donor, and records amended by the institution. These are not insurmountable issues, but to have witnessed the institution's reaction to returning the money, one would have thought the donor was asking for the impossible. Although I recognized the problem was real, I told the university foundation staff person that it would be the donor's problem and that as long as the donor was aware of the potential problem with getting his donation back (and he was), the university should be willing to accept this gift. You can only imagine the tug of war that ensued. The donor, who remember was an entrepreneur, was adamant that this condition needed to be met; it was the only way he was going to make the gift. The university foundation finally agreed, but very reluctantly.

This might have been a premonition or, better yet, a reading of the political wind, because the building project was never started. In consulting with the institution several years later, we discussed how to communicate with the donors that the project was not going to happen. The issue that was avoided was offering to return the donated funds. In reviewing the communication that was going to be sent, I noticed the institution was informing the donors of all the wonderful projects and programs to which their donation could be redirected. There was no mention of returning the money, as had been agreed when the initial gift or pledge had been made. It was astonishing! After many discussions, it was agreed that those donors who had asked to have their money returned if the building project did not happen would be given that opportunity. Out of the many donors, only one insisted that the funds be returned. The other donors did indeed redirect their gifts to other projects in the college and on campus.

An entrepreneur might ask, "What was the problem?" The problem was that the nonprofit organization—in this case, the university foundation—had a certain way of doing things and the entrepreneur was rocking the boat by asking for something different. This might seem like a minor thing to request, but to the university it was huge.

The final test for a nonprofit therefore is to see how they respond to requests for things to change. Remember, philanthropy, and especially transformational philanthropy, can become a complex relationship and transaction. Entrepreneurs will want to work with nonprofit organizations that are willing to think outside the box and challenge their paradigms. It will definitely be a give-and-take relationship, but in the end, when an entrepreneur finds a nonprofit organization that stirs passion and can respond in a manner satisfying to him or her while also achieving the entrepreneur's goals, everyone will be amazed at the transformation that occurs.

WHAT IS TRANSFORMATIONAL PHILANTHROPY?

I am frequently asked to define the phrase *transformational philanthropy*. It is a phrase I use often in my discussions with nonprofit organizations, donors, and others. Transformational philanthropy is charitable work that transforms both the giver and the receiver of the donation. Too often in my career, I have heard sad, if not horror, stories of how philanthropy was done poorly, looking more like a transaction. Philanthropy should be transformational, not transactional. The very act and subsequent good things that happen because of the charitable contribution should be transforming to all involved. This is what individuals, especially entrepreneurs, expect when they become involved with charitable work. Actually, they expect the transformation to happen throughout the organization that is receiving the money, affecting its clients, members, and mission. But what also happens is a transformation to donors, especially entrepreneurs, and the way they view the world and their role in it. Donors, especially entrepreneurs, realize that beyond making money, they can really make a difference in their community, society, and world.

Transformational gifts change a nonprofit organization. They have a life-altering impact on the programs and the future of not only the nonprofit organization but also the clients served or services offered. However, to ensure that a nonprofit organization can attract transformational gifts, it must have an attitude, or culture, that believes wholeheartedly it will happen and takes the necessary steps to get ready. These steps include things such as being results-oriented, including how the nonprofit organization is presented via its communication and marketing messages. It must have strong leadership, both volunteer and paid, in terms of board members, gala chairs, committee chairs, and staff. Although the executive director, president or CEO is often the public face of the nonprofit organization, it is critical to the success of attracting transformational gifts that the volunteer leadership, especially the board of directors, be viewed favorably in the community. Donors who are willing to make these types of donations are looking for opportunities to have a long-lasting impact and involvement.

Most social service organizations do not allow themselves to dream big. It is my dream that one day social services organizations will attract transformational gifts on a regular basis.

THE "NO MORE THAN THREE" RULE

My final recommendation in regard to the entrepreneurial spirit is directed to the entrepreneur. Often entrepreneurs have a tendency to overcommit themselves, thinking they can do more than what is realistically possible. This is where the "No More Than Three" rule applies. Although I give people a pass on being involved with their house of worship and alma mater, individuals, especially entrepreneurs, should identify only three other nonprofit organizations at most with which they become involved. Why three? Because beyond three, one's time and financial donations tend to wane, meaning there will be some nonprofit organizations that are not being transformed by your involvement and donations. As my good friend—and entrepreneur—Stedman Graham reminds me constantly, "We all have one thing in common no matter where we live, work, or to what situation we were born into, and that is we all have 24 hours in a day to live and accomplish things." By being involved with your church and alma mater (I will even give a pass for your children's school) as well as three other nonprofit organizations, you will definitely be engaged with the charitable world and making transformation happen.

We all know that each rule has an exception, and this one occurred when I met Alfredo Molina in 2006. Alfredo was honored in 2005 as one of the most caring Americans and received the National Caring Award from the Caring Institute. This is a nonprofit organization that was founded by Val Halamandaris on Mother Teresa's command. Mother Teresa said to Val that whereas Americans are the richest people in the world in terms of material possessions, they are the poorest in the world in terms of their caring spirit. She commanded he start a program whereby those individuals in America who are rich in a "caring" spirit be recognized.

During the ceremony in which Alfredo was inducted, I learned that he and his wife, Lisa, give millions away annually to 167 nonprofit organizations both locally and nationally. As I sat there, I thought 167 is about 164 too many! I was going to talk to Alfredo and tell him my rule of no more than three. But once I met him, I realized that here was an individual who was totally committed to doing good and who felt that by helping others he was doing his life's work. As he said, "I was put on Earth to do great things, but it's not about doing great things for me. . . . It's about doing great things for others" (*Arizona Republic*, December 7, 2005). In my 27 years in this business, this is one of the few outstanding exceptions to the rule of three where it has been done well (see the section entitled "Entrepreneurial Stories" for more details about Alfredo and his philanthropic endeavors).

Although I do not encourage entrepreneurs to emulate Alfredo and get involved with 167 nonprofit organizations, I do encourage all entrepreneurs to get involved and start making a difference in the charitable world. Your efforts will be transformative.

Dietlin's Discussion Directives

1. Describe some nuances about entrepreneurs.

2. Where can you find entrepreneurs?

3. What is Moves Management and what are its five steps?

4. What is the SBA definition of a small business?

5. What is the first test for finding the entrepreneurial spirit in a nonprofit organization?

6. What is the second test for finding the entrepreneurial spirit in a non-profit organization?

7. What is the third test for finding the entrepreneurial spirit in a nonprofit organization?

8. What is transformational philanthropy?

9. What is the "No More Than Three" rule? Are you applying it in your charitable efforts?

Chapter 3

Factors Affecting Philanthropy

"WHAT ARE THE ISSUES I NEED TO KNOW TO WORK WITH ENTREPRENEURS?"

Entrepreneurs are by nature problem solvers. They are interested in addressing issues and problems, and especially in identifying their root causes. These individuals prefer providing this type of support rather than giving resources for ongoing support to institutions and nonprofit organizations. Entrepreneurs want to make permanent and sustainable changes with their philanthropic activities. They want to alter the direction or course that a nonprofit organization is following. If there is a problem, they want to solve it, and they usually have the resources—whether financial, human, or capital—to support the new direction or change. Entrepreneurs will also insist that the change be fast. They will want the nonprofit organization to respond quickly to both the problem and the solution, similar to their own behavior in the marketplace when they see an opportunity present itself or see that an alteration in the path being taken is needed.

An example of this occurred when a higher education institution with which I was working wanted to improve its MBA program. To accomplish this goal, the dean and his leadership team decided they needed to hire a top-notch executive director to lead the program. Hiring this type of individual would require paying a higher salary than what was allotted in the college's budget. The dean decided to ask for the financial difference in the form of a charitable contribution from the advisory board chairperson, who was also an entrepreneur. The advisory board chairperson enthusiastically agreed and delivered the check immediately. Unfortunately, as many of you who are in academia know, there is a cycle as to when hiring takes place. Those academicians who want to change positions and move to a different university and those higher education institutions who want to hire all begin the process in the fall, usually starting in September, with the actual hiring taking place in the spring, usually April. The person hired usually doesn't start the new job until the following summer or fall. Most entrepreneurs are aghast at the idea of a year-long process and become very frustrated when made aware of this system, asking, "Why can't we change it and hire when we want to instead of following the established process?" The challenge is that if you want to ensure you have the best-qualified pool of candidates, you need to follow the academic time frame. Therefore, we informed the advisory board chairperson providing the financial resources that the process would ensure we could hire a top-notch person. After the explanation, he understood the process completely, and the higher education institution was able to secure a great candidate for the job.

Another issue in working with entrepreneurs is that their attention span is short. Once the challenge or problem is resolved, they will become restless and potentially bored. This can become a challenge for the leadership of nonprofit organizations because they usually need time for the staff, leadership, clients, systems, and procedures to catch up with the changes. Entrepreneurs will not understand this type of thinking, processing, or slow movement. To keep the entrepreneur engaged, a nonprofit organization must stay one step ahead of him or her. A nonprofit organization must always be presenting opportunities and ideas for the entrepreneur's further involvement. By doing so, transformational gifts in all sizes will be made to the nonprofit organization, and the organization will potentially have a lifelong supporter.

The word *potentially* is used as a caution here because most nonprofit organizations fall into the trap of thinking that once they have identified the issue, cause, or problem that excites and stimulates the entrepreneur they are good to go, meaning they have found an entrepreneur who is supportive and will be a lifelong donor. To the nonprofit organization, it appears all is well. The problem is that even the nonprofit organizations that work with entrepreneurs as donors will stumble at this point as they switch to treating the entrepreneur as a traditional donor. This is the surest and sometimes fastest path to losing the entrepreneur as a donor.

I have seen it happen again and again, where a nonprofit leader will share with me that his or her organization had found an entrepreneur willing to provide the resources to solve the problem or issues only to discover that 9,

12, or even 24 months later the entrepreneur had lost interest or was asking and sometimes demanding that the issue be resolved permanently, the project be taken to the next level, or a new strategy be created. It is imperative to remember that entrepreneurs, as well as the entrepreneurs who are donors, are always looking for the next challenge or project. They are never ever satisfied with the status quo. They will continually challenge the nonprofit organization to be better. One of my favorite phrases from an entrepreneur is "Work smarter, not harder." This means we each have the same number of hours in a day and need to utilize them to achieve our desired goals. Entrepreneurs use their 24 hours to the maximum, solving problems and issues, growing their business, and producing new products. In other words, entrepreneurs are continually bettering their world. An entrepreneur will expect the same focus and intensity on problem solving and issue resolution from any nonprofit organization with which he or she works.

To be successful with entrepreneurs, a nonprofit organization must have a strategy of bringing not only new ideas and initiatives but also recent challenges or current issues to the attention of the entrepreneur. The nonprofit organization must not be anxious about frightening the potential donor away. Remember, entrepreneurs love challenges and solving problems. This is why they are successful. They believe and often can solve problems that others view as impossible or insurmountable. A nonprofit organization should work diligently and strategically to engage entrepreneurs in the issues that are new, the problems that seemingly cannot be resolved, and the crisis that won't go away. In doing this, nonprofit organizations will be very successful in engaging and retaining entrepreneurs as lifelong supporters and donors.

DEVELOP A MARKETING PLAN THAT IS SEPARATE AND DISTINCT

Leaders of nonprofit organizations need to recognize that marketing to entrepreneurs is different from the traditional or conventional donor approach. As stated earlier, entrepreneurs are quick decision makers, so targeting a lot of nonrelevant—or, in their minds, useless—information at them will be ineffective. Entrepreneurs want to know the following:

- What is the project?
- Who will be affected (in other words, who will it help)?
- How long will it take to implement?
- How much will it cost to achieve the results you are seeking?

have said probably his usual C. Who would have thought that a C-level economics paper would turn into a company with revenues of $36 billion in 2007? And who would have believed that the actor Paul Newman would be more well known by the Gen Xers, Ys, and Millennials for his food and philanthropic efforts than his movies? Fifteen or twenty or even thirty years ago, would any of us have believed any of these businesses were possible? If we had been told this was going to happen, would we have thought these individuals had realistic expectations? Would we have supported them? The likely answer is no.

As the country music entertainer Buddy Jewell, the first winner from the television talent show named *Nashville Star*, writes in one of his songs, "I want to thank everyone whoever told me no; pack it up and get back home. It kept me going, knowing I would prove them wrong, yeah I knew it all along." This is probably the mantra of most entrepreneurs. Someone somewhere along the way said "no" to them, and that "no" spurred them to start their business and succeed.

The expectations of success entrepreneurs have regarding their businesses or even business ideas are the same expectations they will bring to a nonprofit organization. Whatever project you present to them or challenge they hear about, no matter how insurmountable it might seem to the nonprofit organization, will be very realistic to the entrepreneur.

Not only do entrepreneurs possess somewhat unrealistic expectations about what can be accomplished, but also they often possess unrealistic expectations about timelines, staffing, deadlines, turnaround times, and other aspects of the nonprofit world. This can also be called *impatience*. They simply do not understand the way in which many nonprofit organizations are often forced to operate, either because of circumstances, tradition, or need. I am not advocating for the status quo. In fact, I urge nonprofit leaders to continually evaluate what is being done and why, as well as to explore the possibilities that change would bring. But as a leader of a nonprofit organization, it is imperative to plan on continually educating entrepreneurs about the process and nuances associated with working with the nonprofit sector.

Equally important is the need for nonprofit organizations to ratchet up their own expectations and turnaround times. In order to fully engage entrepreneurs, both the nonprofit organization and the entrepreneur need to have candid discussions regarding realistic expectations, with both being willing and able to change their paradigms. If they do this, it will definitely be a win-win situation for both, with the ultimate beneficiary being the clients, causes, or issues the nonprofit organization serves.

FOCUS DEVELOPMENT EFFORTS ON ENTREPRENEURS

I believe and strongly recommend that the majority of all nonprofit development efforts be focused on attracting entrepreneurs to the nonprofit organization. The majority of wealth in this country is held by entrepreneurs, and as we all know, approximately 82% to 85% of all gifts made in this country come from individuals. This is the area to mine for donations, and entrepreneurs are potential mother lodes.

Although having corporate and foundation financial support is important, the real action and, quite frankly, fun is working with individuals, especially those who are entrepreneurs. Financial support from corporations and foundations adds cachet to your organization, serving as one type of seal of approval for the community. Through corporate and foundation involvement, others in the community will recognize the good work of the nonprofit organization. It is thus important to seek and secure corporate and foundation financial support. However, individuals make the overwhelming majority of financial contributions in this country, and entrepreneurs are the group most likely to make the transformational gifts that will ultimately alter the path of the nonprofit organization, lifting it to the next level. Avidly seek out individuals, and especially entrepreneurs, as the nonprofit organization's future donors.

WHERE TO BEGIN

When organizing or, in most cases, reorganizing development office activities at a nonprofit organization, the first thing to do is conduct an audit on the engagement of entrepreneurs with an eye toward reviewing who is in the nonprofit organization's prospect and suspect pool. The following are some important questions for the nonprofit organization to ask itself.

- How many entrepreneurs are currently donors? What are their names? What do we know about them? What do we know about their businesses? When was the last time someone from the nonprofit organization met with them?
- How many entrepreneurs are on the prospect list? What are their names? What do we know about them? What do we know about their businesses? Have we scheduled or attempted to schedule an appointment to meet them?

- How many entrepreneurs are on the suspect list (meaning individuals you think could be involved with the nonprofit organization)? Does the nonprofit organization have a next-step strategy? How do entrepreneurs move from the suspect pool to the prospect pool and eventually to being a donor? Do we have a strategy?
- How many entrepreneurs serve on the nonprofit organization's board of directors? Is there a concentrated effort to ensure they stay involved? Is there a required number of entrepreneurs to serve on the board of directors?
- How many entrepreneurs serve on the nonprofit organization's advisory board? Are all types of industries and sectors represented by entrepreneurs serving?
- How many entrepreneurs are engaged with the nonprofit organizations in some other manner (e.g., committee work, gala, gifts-in-kind donations)? Does the nonprofit organization have a strategy to move them into the inner circle of activity?
- At what stage in the Moves Management cycle is each entrepreneur?
- What is the strategy for each entrepreneur?
- Is the strategy written down?

> ### LIFES Tip
> If it isn't in writing, it doesn't exist. It is imperative that all cultivation strategies especially those for your entrepreneur prospects, be in writing, preferably in a shared database system.

After this assessment, the nonprofit organization needs to develop strategies to engage or further engage these individuals. Procrastination on the part of the nonprofit organization's leadership and staff can cause the loss of a potential gift. Remember, entrepreneurs are always looking for the "next" deal, and whether that ends up being in business or philanthropy is in some cases dependent on the nonprofit organization's efforts. To be considered, you have to get in the game! A nonprofit organization should focus attention on the entrepreneurs in its community.

WHAT FACTORS AN ENTREPRENEUR SHOULD CONSIDER

So, as an entrepreneur you want to jump into the world of philanthropy. You have decided you want to give back and are wondering where to begin. Should you give a small amount to a lot of nonprofit organizations, or should you give a large amount to one or two? How much is considered enough? Can you be anonymous? Who do you call to start the process? Entrepreneurs need to know that they are not alone. These are questions tens of thousands of entrepreneurs have asked themselves over the years once they have decided to become active or more active in the philanthropic world.

First, the world of philanthropy can be very confusing. As mentioned in Chapter 1, even the terminology can be confusing, with terms being interchangeably used. However, there is a way to navigate these seemingly murky waters that will result in outcomes of which the entrepreneur can be proud.

> ### LIFES Tip
> Individuals who are new to the world of philanthropy comment that it often seems as if a foreign language is being spoken. It is important for all involved in philanthropy to learn and understand the terminology.

The process I developed and recommend to all entrepreneurs who want to become involved in the philanthropic world is to take an Individual Philanthropic Audit (IPA). It is a process created after I had an initial and then subsequent discussions with singer/songwriter Beth Nielsen Chapman, who lives in Nashville, Tennessee. Beth and I met when we were both attending a board lunch meeting of the nonprofit organization Attachment Parenting International. Beth was providing the entertainment and I was presenting to the board about how to be effective at raising money. Beth and I were seated next to each other and began talking by introducing ourselves. Beth told me she was a singer and songwriter; I later found out she had written songs that had been recorded by Faith Hill, Michael McDonald, Suzy Boggus, Elton John, Trisha Yearwood, and many others. She is a prolific songwriter with an ability to convey thoughts and words in beautiful songs that many performers seek to record.

When Beth learned that I was involved in the philanthropic world, she anxiously asked, "Can you help me? I am involved with charity work and I can't tell a good charity from a bad charity. I have three requirements when saying yes to perform at a charitable event. The three things are for the charity to raise money, my band to be paid, and to have some PR and marketing around my music and records." She then went on to tell me, "I can perform at an event and have my three goals met and go seventy miles down the road to a similar organization and have it fail." Beth was especially bothered when nonprofit organizations did not raise the amount of money they anticipated they would when bringing her in for that specific purpose. She shared with me that while she believed she clearly articulated these goals to the nonprofit organization, there were times they were still not met. Then she would feel bad and wonder what she could have done to make it work. Beth asked me to help her figure out how to be consistently successful.

I initially encouraged her to be more strategic with her philanthropic work. I suggested that we conduct an assessment of what she was currently doing philanthropically, then review what she valued, and finally determine what she was passionate about to create a Strategic Philanthropic Plan of Action, this process resulted in the IPA being created.

Assessment + Values + Passion = Strategic Philanthropic Plan of Action

By conducting an IPA, entrepreneurs will be able to cause transformation in the philanthropic world just as they have done in the business world in which they operate, because they will have a strategic philanthropic plan of action.

CHOOSING A NONPROFIT ORGANIZATION TO SUPPORT

To begin, an entrepreneur should review and contemplate what he or she really cares about in terms of being willing to provide charitable support. Think about what causes you feel most passionate about. Most of us, entrepreneurs included, default to those entities we know, such as our house of worship, our alma maters, or our children's schools. These types of organizations are very worthwhile nonprofit organizations to support, but, with more than 1.5 million nonprofits in this country, there are a lot more choices available.

I recommend a three-step process that leads to a strategic philanthropic plan of action with outcome-oriented results.

Step 1: Assessment

It is very important to assess the nonprofit organizations you are currently involved with and indicate those for which you are providing financial support. Make a list. Review the list. Are there any organizations that you are involved with where you have lost interest?

> **LIFES Tip**
> See David Weinberg's story in the section entitled "Entrepreneurial Stories" for his Passion-O-Meter, which helps in conducting annual assessments.

Step 2: Valuation

It is equally important to determine what you really value. Generally, there are two categories to think about. Do you want to lift people, things, or projects up? Nonprofit organizations in this category would include museums, art institutes, theater groups, and educational institutions. Alternatively, do you want to eradicate some thing, disease, or situation? Examples of nonprofit organizations in this category include associations dedicated to particular diseases (e.g., muscular dystrophy or cystic fibrosis), organizations battling hunger or famine, domestic violence shelters, and so on. Most individuals usually lean toward one of these categories; in rare situations are there individuals who want to do both. There isn't a right or wrong answer. It is what resonates with each person.

Step 3: Passion

What are you passionate about? What stirs your soul? When I posed this question to some of my country music entertainer clients in Nashville, who are truly entrepreneurs, the responses were varied. Some were all about the music and wanted to incorporate their philanthropic work into their business model. Others wanted to have a separate strategy to practice their philanthropy that aligned with their other interests, such as painting, public speaking, or their child's activities. The common denominator was that each individual I worked with knew what he or she was passionate about and somehow wanted to incorporate that passion into his or her philanthropy.

NEXT STEPS

Once you complete these three steps, you are ready to begin building your strategic philanthropic plan of action. A great place to begin gathering information about nonprofit organizations or researching them as a first step toward potential involvement is the Internet. Two websites I recommend are GuideStar (www.guidestar.org) and Charity Navigator (www.charity navigator.org). Both exist for the sole purpose of providing information regarding nonprofit organizations. Each one offers a different view into philanthropic nonprofit organizations.

GuideStar's mission is "to revolutionize philanthropy and nonprofit practice by providing information that advances transparency, enables users to make better decisions, and encourages charitable giving." The website further states that, "If you care about nonprofits and the work they do, then you're affected by what GuideStar does—even if this is your first visit to www.guidestar.org. You see, we gather and publicize information about nonprofit organizations. Our reach is far and wide. Our database is broad and deep."

Charity Navigator's mission is to guide intelligent giving. The website states, "We help charitable givers make intelligent giving decisions by providing information on over five thousand charities and by evaluating the financial health of each of these charities. We ensure our evaluations are widely used by making them easy to understand and available to the public free of charge. By guiding intelligent giving, we aim to advance a more efficient and responsive philanthropic marketplace, in which givers and the charities they support work in tandem to overcome our nation's most persistent challenges." Charity Navigator states that it is America's premier independent charity evaluator, working to advance a more efficient and responsive philanthropic marketplace by evaluating the financial health of over 5,300 of America's largest charities.

Both GuideStar and Charity Navigator are nonprofit organizations themselves. They both offer search capability, meaning that if you want to give to a hunger program in Montana, you can type in these words and see whether there are any nonprofit organizations doing that type of work. Although this is good information to have, the best way to make your final decision regarding who is going to receive your financial philanthropic support is to meet the leadership of the nonprofit organization and to actually visit the office, site, clinic, facility, hospital, school, museum, or so on. There is nothing like a site visit.

INDIVIDUAL PHILANTHROPIC AUDIT

The Individual Philanthropic Audit (IPA) can easily be conducted by entrepreneurs on their own. It is a series of questions that an individual needs to answer based on the activities currently taking place in his or her life. The purpose of the IPA is to help individuals become aware of what they really care about and what they do not. Although philanthropic activities are not always clear cut, it is important to do this first step in order to begin the process.

The IPA (see Appendix F) consists of series of questions about what you are currently doing, what moves your heart, and finally, what excites you.

It takes into account the professional and personal and builds toward developing a philanthropic strategy that to you will be transforming.

The Basis of the Individual Philanthropic Audit

As discussed earlier, I have found that philanthropic desire falls into two primary categories.

- The first is the desire and commitment of individuals to lift up and improve things in their world. This would include individuals who want to support educational institutions, libraries, art and culture institutions, health clinics, empowerment organizations (e.g., Women Employed, located in Chicago, Illinois, which tackles issues affecting women in the workplace), and the environment (e.g., Earth Share, The Nature Conservancy), to name a few.
- The second category is the desire and commitment of individuals who want to mitigate if not eradicate situations or things in their world. This would include people who support getting rid of a particular disease (e.g., Jerry Lewis and his desire to get rid of muscular dystrophy), or eliminating a condition such as domestic violence, poverty, child pornography, war, slave trafficking, or drugs, or situations such as hunger and homelessness, animal cruelty, and land mines—again, to name a few.

As an entrepreneur, think about what appeals to your heart. Think back to what has motivated you in the past. For example, if you recall that every time you saw an advertisement about a child being hungry you were moved to do something, or at least told yourself that you should do something, then perhaps hunger is your cause. If hunger is your cause, I highly recommend you find a food bank or pantry dealing with feeding people in your area. Or, if you recall that every time you drive by the museum in your community you thought you should do something to support it, then perhaps you support lifting others up. If you don't have any idea of what you want to support, that is just fine. The IPA will help you define what moves your heart and drives your passion!

Most of us, when we think of philanthropy—or even when we call it charity—will make donations to a house of worship or an alma mater. But beyond that, we often don't know where to begin. The IPA is a place to begin your journey into a wonderful world of making a difference and causing transformation to happen to both the nonprofit organization you are helping and to yourself.

> **LIFES Tip**
> Establish a philanthropic budget annually, with a little extra budgeted for those unexpected requests.

WHY GET INVOLVED WITH PHILANTHROPIC WORK?

I am often asked why I think entrepreneurs get involved with philanthropic work or, as we have sometimes been referring to it, charity. I think it goes back to that old saying, "To those that much has been given, much is expected." As noted in Chapter 1, entrepreneurs are repayers. They are individuals who want to give back to those individuals and organizations that have helped them along the way to their success. Entrepreneurs also want to make a difference. For example, I was working with an alumnus from the Midwest. He and his wife had built an extremely successful business initially in the manufacturing industry. The company grew and diversified and was very successful. However, in meeting with him, he unassumingly responded to my congratulations on all of his success that he felt he had not done his life's work yet. Although he acknowledged that he had built a very successful company, he pondered on whose life he really had affected, changed, or transformed. I am happy to report that he is one of the most generous and philanthropic individuals I know; he just needed to be pointed toward the area that moved his heart and stirred his passion. In his mind, he is repaying society for his success by his involvement in the philanthropic world.

> **LIFES Tip**
> Don't let guilt and pressure drive your philanthropic decisions! In order for the support you give to be sustainable, it has to come from the heart.

Another entrepreneur I had the privilege of meeting was Sue Ling Gin. Sue is a very successful caterer in the Chicago area. Her company, Flying Food Fare, provided the food on airlines (when the airlines served food). I asked her how she came to the idea of providing food to the airlines, since after all, her business was a local catering company in Chicago and it ended up providing food to tens of thousands of individuals on planes throughout the country. She smiled and told me that she had always been involved with charitable work, even when she didn't have money. At a charitable function she was attending she was seated next to the CEO of a major airline, and voilà, a new business was born. Through her success as an entrepreneur, Sue is now paying back the community through her continued philanthropic activities.

Dietlin's Discussion Directives

1. What nonprofit organizations are you currently supporting?

2. What do you value? Start by questioning yourself about whether you want to lift things or people up or whether you want to get rid of something.

3. What are you passionate about?

4. Can you identify and list three causes that you want to support today?

5. Can you determine annually how much you donate financially to nonprofit organizations?

6. What issues affect entrepreneurs and their philanthropic donations?

7. Why should nonprofit organizations focus efforts on entrepreneurs who are individual donors?

8. How can a nonprofit organization begin working with entrepreneurs?

9. What type of marketing plan should a nonprofit organization create to attract and work with entrepreneurs?

10. What is one of the reasons entrepreneurs would appear to have unrealistic expectations?

Chapter 4

Qualities

THE QUALITIES OF ENTREPRENEURS

Entrepreneurs have five unique qualities: intuition, will, joy, strength, and compassion. Here is a brief description of each.

- *Intuition* is the ability to tell by one's gut or a feeling whether something is going to work.
- *Will* is the sheer ability to stick with something until it comes to fruition.
- *Joy* is the ability and view to see things as a pleasure instead of a challenge—to see that problems faced are opportunities to seize.
- *Strength* is the innate ability to see things through no matter what the challenges.
- *Compassion* is the ability to see other's pain or discomfort and share it.

Entrepreneurs also possess great courage, a sense of adventure, and a willingness to take risks, as well as a pioneering spirit. Although their businesses are varied, all entrepreneurs have these same qualities. Remember, entrepreneurs are individuals who are able to quickly identify the missing pieces of a marketplace and create an appropriate response, usually a new company. I have yet to hear from an entrepreneur that he or she started or is in business to make money; rather, I hear entrepreneurs say time and again that they are in business to solve a problem. They usually will share this story with anyone who asks how the idea for the business came about. Each entrepreneur has a unique story.

When entrepreneurs become involved with a nonprofit organization, they bring these same entrepreneurial qualities to the table. Above all else, entrepreneurs are risk takers. In their businesses, they love to take chances and explore opportunities that have the potential of solving larger problems. When engaged with a nonprofit organization, entrepreneurs will want and insist on doing and acting this same way. Given this type of spirit, entrepreneurs will become incredibly frustrated with the bureaucratic processes of the typical nonprofit organization. Entrepreneurs will want to be actively involved in the nonprofit organization, not simply attend board meetings a few times a year or be called occasionally for advice and counsel. Entrepreneurs will want to roll their sleeves up and get involved to ensure the work gets done, problems are solved, and things are accomplished.

As shared in the beginning of Chapter 3, entrepreneurs are most interested in addressing issues and causes, not in providing overall support to existing institutions in the form of unrestricted gifts. They are very interested in using market-based approaches to solving today's societal problems. Entrepreneurs are attracted to addressing the root of the problem or issue and ensuring that the changes made possible through their involvement are sustainable, if not permanent. Entrepreneurs also expect a return on their investment. They are usually hands-on and want to guarantee that their donations are leveraged to the maximum possible (more on this topic can be found in Chapter 5).

Entrepreneurs tend to have little patience or tolerance with paperwork and bureaucracies. Thus, holding a two-hour meeting to discuss an issue and not resolving it will not work. Entrepreneurs expect and will demand a quick response and turnaround time to their ideas and potential solutions. They will not expect or tolerate a multiyear plan of action to simply explore the possibility and outcomes of the resolutions proposed.

New philanthropists who are entrepreneurs want to solve today's problems in a specific way, not simply earmark their donation for some vague albeit benevolent purpose. They expect and will demand results or movement toward an outcome that has been identified. At a minimum, entrepreneurs will need to know that the nonprofit organization is responding to their involvement in a way that moves toward resolution of the issue.

DON'T COUNT ON PATIENCE FROM ENTREPRENEURS

Entrepreneurs do not fit the nonprofit organization's traditional perception of a donor. They are different, and the sooner a nonprofit organization realizes this fact, the further ahead it will be in the cycle of cultivating and soliciting a major gift or gifts from them. As stated previously, entrepreneurs have little patience or tolerance with paperwork, bureaucracies, and long decision-making processes. The typical "three-year academic study" that usually occurs in higher education institutions to make a decision will drive entrepreneurs away quicker than any bad investment they might have made. Entrepreneurs are used to receiving quick responses to their ideas and succinct answers to their questions. They do not want to be foolhardy in their endeavors, and they expect a quick turnaround time to secure decisions about and ultimately implementation of their suggestions. They do not necessarily want "yes" people around them, but they do want individuals who think outside the box and are able and willing to offer up their opinions, even far-reaching ideas and proposals. You never know where a "crazy" idea might lead entrepreneurs in their business or in their philanthropic work.

Entrepreneurs need nonprofit organizations to keep up with them and their ideas. They love to be challenged, especially if the questions and ideas being tossed around in the discussion further the initiative first offered by the entrepreneur. However, at the end of all the debates, after all the ideas have been discussed and either approved or discarded, entrepreneurs expect a decision to be made. Entrepreneurs will not tolerate more discussion and debate for the sake of discussion or debate or for fear of hurting someone's feelings who has not been heard. They want to see action on how an idea or decision can be implemented or executed rather than to debate and hold philosophical discussions about why something cannot happen. One only has to recall Senator Ed Kennedy quoting Irish playwright George Bernard Shaw at his brother Robert Kennedy's funeral, stating, "There are those who look at things the way they are, and ask why. . . . I dream of things that never were and ask why not." Although this saying became famous as a statement about Bobby Kennedy and his dream, it also epitomizes the mantra of entrepreneurs.

It should be noted that, once a decision is made, especially if it is to execute or implement the idea suggested by the entrepreneur, it has to be carried out sooner rather than later. Entrepreneurs need to be informed of and understand the time frame in which the proposed change will occur. If a delay is necessary, they need to be educated about that too—again, sooner rather than later. For example, a former university client of mine had the dean of the business school announce his resignation in March, depart the institution in June, and take a July appointment at another university. The entrepreneurs serving on the advisory board were incredulous that a search would not begin until September, with the new appointment taking place

13 to 15 months later, meaning that more than an entire year would pass before the new dean would be appointed and assume the reins of leadership in the college. The entrepreneurs associated with the college could not understand why the university would wait so long to begin the process of replacing this dean. Immediate and serious education needed to take place, for in the academic world there are cycles to hiring, especially leadership positions. The entrepreneurs, as well as other business leaders, needed to be informed that in the fall of every year academicians make decisions regarding whether they wish to seek a new position. If the search for the new dean had begun in the spring, the quality of candidates would have been poor because the university would have been off cycle from the rest of the academic environment. Once educated, however, the entrepreneurs understood the process, although admittedly they still remained a bit incredulous about it.

ADVISORS AND DECISION MAKING

Entrepreneurs have numerous advisors surrounding them. They trust these advisors and will turn to them to bounce ideas around and ask their opinions about anything new, especially about charitable donations. The reason is that entrepreneurs, as noted earlier, know very little about philanthropy, nonprofit organizations, and their work. This will be a new experience for them because, as stated previously, entrepreneurs are used to being the expert or take-charge person in most situations. In areas where entrepreneurs recognize they might not have all the information or knowledge needed, they will turn to their trusted advisors.

> ### LIFES Tip
>
> The old saying "Don't judge a book by its cover" is true when working with entrepreneurs. They can be eccentric individuals, but if a nonprofit organization listens carefully, great ideas and partnership opportunities can often be developed. One of the largest donations received by a particular nonprofit organization in 1998, which totaled more than $3 million, came from an elderly couple who lived in a double-wide trailer house with its original shag carpet. Many of us on the staff were incredulous regarding their wealth, but upon their deaths, the nonprofit organization did indeed receive more than $3 million from their estate.

"TELL ME ABOUT NONPROFIT ORGANIZATIONS; I MEAN, WHY DO THEY DO X?"

I have been asked this question hundreds of times by entrepreneurs during my career working in the nonprofit world. Business owners are often befuddled by the seemingly normal and accepted chaos found in the charitable arena. Entrepreneurs I consult often ask me to help them navigate this seemingly unorganized field. Although entrepreneurs are accustomed at times to working in ambiguity and without all the facts, they do have their eyes always on the prize—at least, the successful ones do. In their view, this is not what they see happening in the nonprofit arena. They see lack of focus, lack of mission, and deployment of limited resources, meaning money, people, and time, in a haphazard way.

To begin, it is important for entrepreneurs to recognize that there are very few rules governing nonprofit organizations. Nonprofit organizations, more commonly known as charities, are often started by well-meaning individuals who want to fix something. It might be that an afterschool program is needed, a river in the town needs to be cleaned up, the library needs more books, senior citizens need nourishing meals, a new disease is affecting a particular population, or the animal shelter is being closed and a new one is needed. The list goes on and on of the needs that can be found in most communities. This is evident by the doubling of the number of nonprofit organizations, in the last 10 years, to 1.5 million. This means there are 1.5 million nonprofit organizations working, or attempting to work, for the greater good. These organizations were founded by individuals who wanted to change, improve, start, alter, or shift something in their community, society at large, or the world.

What qualities do nonprofit organizations possess that might align with an entrepreneur and his or her way of doing things and which qualities and practices will not work with the entrepreneur who is attempting to engage in philanthropic work? Nonprofit organizations possess the ability to respond to societal needs on a rapid basis. One only has to think of American's response to the 9/11 attacks to view mobilization in action. The nonprofit sector was among the first responders providing medical care, organizing Americans to donate blood, and establishing funds such as the Twin Towers Fund. The nonprofit sector provided assistance in whatever way was needed, and individuals responded, raising an estimated $2.5 billion.

Another example is the response by Americans to the disasters in the wake of Hurricanes Katrina and Wilma. Although we witnessed some dysfunction in terms of how the American Red Cross and the federal government responded, we witnessed a huge outpouring of support, both in terms of financial contributions and volunteer time, by many of us in this country. Americans respond when there is a crisis situation, with more than $2 billion being raised just by the American Red Cross for these disasters. This number does not include funds raised by Feeding America, the Salvation Army, and others involved in disaster response and relief efforts for the hurricanes aftermath, which brought the overall total to more than $3 billion.

Entrepreneurs should recognize that the nonprofit sector needs their involvement. I often say that only by engaging entrepreneurs in the life of the nonprofit organization will the organizations survive the challenges of the 21st century. Entrepreneurs bring a cachet of intrepidness and enthusiasm to the projects they undertake, and these qualities will be of immense value to the nonprofit organizations with which they choose to become involved.

"WHY DON'T YOU . . . ?"

When an entrepreneur becomes involved with a nonprofit organization, he or she brings a unique and different set of problem-solving skills to the issues that must be addressed. It is truly a "thinking outside the box" mentality that usually has never been seen, let alone practiced, within philanthropic entities. This type of approach can cause either a great deal of excitement or a great deal of frustration and exasperation for the leaders of the nonprofit organization. But once you are aware of this quality, as a nonprofit leader you learn to value it greatly.

In their businesses, entrepreneurs are rarely detracted from achieving a goal or resolving a problem, because they use all the resources available to them, including both clearly or ill-defined market-based approaches. Entrepreneurs drive through to the end, ensuring that all resources are brought to bear on the challenge. This is the approach they will bring to helping the nonprofit organizations with which they become involved. However, this approach is often misunderstood, and entrepreneurs are often thought of as making waves and even appearing to turn a nonprofit organization upside down.

Because entrepreneurs are at ease using market-based approaches to solving problems that will help nonprofit organizations in the 21st century, they think they know best and believe they have the "best" solution for the organization. Leaders of nonprofit organizations must know that entrepreneurs always mean well but will have to, at times, be educated about how best to use their vast and varied resources to assist a nonprofit organization.

Conversely, a nonprofit organization must be willing to listen to an entrepreneur's ideas and advice. Often strategies and alternative solutions that would never have occurred to the staff and leaders of the nonprofit organization emerge to both benefit and enhance the mission and ultimately assist in achieving the vision.

Most entrepreneurs have good ideas and a track record of success. I strongly recommend that nonprofit organizations listen to the ideas of entrepreneurs and not summarily dismiss their suggestions as crazy or not practical.

"WHAT'S THE PROBLEM AND HOW CAN I FIX IT?"

Entrepreneurs are change agents. The question "What's the problem and how can I fix it?" is a common mantra for most entrepreneurs. Entrepreneurs are attracted to resolving problems by addressing the root of the problem and ensuring that the changes made are sustainable, if not permanent. This reality must be accepted by nonprofit organizations and their leaders when working with entrepreneurs. Things will begin to rock 'n roll when entrepreneurs walk through the door and become engaged with the mission of the nonprofit organization. When a nonprofit organization begins working with entrepreneurs, it needs to have a strategy to keep their attention and keep them engaged, usually on a weekly but sometimes on a daily basis. Remember entrepreneurs have limited time and often a limited attention span.

One of the ways in which to keep them engaged is by detailing a problem or issue the nonprofit organization is facing and asking entrepreneurs for not only their advice but also their help in solving or resolving it. Entrepreneurs will take on this challenge willingly and gladly. More than likely, they will also have innovative ideas and suggestions to solve whatever is the challenge or problem.

Entrepreneurs will not bemoan the fact that the problem has long existed and will not tolerate the excuse that just because it has always been done a particular way, the problem or issue cannot be solved. They will search to discover the root cause of the problem. By knowing how a problem came into existence, entrepreneurs can begin offering suggestions and changes that will be permanent and adjust the direction the nonprofit organization needs in order to work more effectively as well as efficiently. This might include highlighting an ineffective system, procedure, or even a staff member or department. The leaders of the nonprofit organization must be prepared to deal with fixing whatever is identified by the entrepreneur as the root cause of the problem. It is necessary to be mindful that the proposed solution or identified problem might not be easy to deal with. In other words, a nonprofit organization could be forced to deal with a system that does not work but will be expensive to fix, or a long-term employee who is not producing and needs to be terminated or reassigned, or an idea proposed by a major donor that cannot be implemented without long-term financial exposure for the nonprofit organization. In each of these situations, an entrepreneur working with you will discover and tell the truth about the situation no matter how difficult or even painful the information will be to hear. They will then expect you to take the necessary steps to affect the change that needs to occur on a permanent basis. Excuses or reasons why the problem cannot be fixed will not resonate with entrepreneurs. They expect change to occur!

ENTREPRENEURS ARE HANDS-ON AND DEMANDING

Meddling, interfering, demanding, and *domineering* are just a few of the words often used to describe an entrepreneur's involvement with a nonprofit organization. Entrepreneurs can be and are often perceived this way. As previously noted, entrepreneurs are usually hands-on and want to guarantee that their donations are leveraged to the maximum possible. Once I had an entrepreneur tell me that if he was not doing something every day for the nonprofit organization of which he now was a board member, he was not doing his job. Imagine the challenge facing me every day in trying to create a strategy for his daily engagement in the organization's mission without driving everyone else crazy. This is a typical example of working with entrepreneurs. They can show up unannounced in your offices with some great idea they just learned of from a news program or another organization and expect it to be implemented, maybe by day's end, in your nonprofit organization. They view this as an effective way of being involved and hands-on. It is also a way for them to check in and ensure their financial donations are being used effectively.

Entrepreneurs are successful in their businesses, they use all available resources to ensure their overall goals are achieved, and they are often very hands-on, knowing every aspect of the work being done. They will expect no less from nonprofit organizations with which they are involved. At times it will seem like too much work to have them involved, too much effort, too much trouble. They will continually challenge you to think outside the box and test new ideas.

As staff, when working with entrepreneurs, it might seem as if you have another boss or that this effort has become a full-time job. These are real and valid responses. However, the possible outcomes from an entrepreneur's involvement and investment in your organization can be and often are transformational.

Find a way to work with entrepreneurs, allowing those who want to feel involved or familiar with the day-to-day activities access so that through this activity they have assurances their donations are being utilized fully. Nonprofit organizations need to think creatively about using challenge grants, matching grants, publicity, and marketing to engage entrepreneurs. All of these areas should be familiar to a nonprofit organization and possibly exciting to an entrepreneur because often for success to be ensured the entrepreneur will have to employ strategies from his or her areas of expertise to the initiative. In building a successful business, entrepreneurs are always thinking about leveraging dollars and getting increased financial support, as well as publicity and marketing for awareness of their product or service. Although a nonprofit organization needs to be mindful of these expectations, it also needs to see the possibilities. Have fun working with entrepreneurs! They can and will change your organization.

DON'T WASTE THEIR TIME

"Don't waste my time!" is probably the most often-heard phrase from an entrepreneur. These are busy individuals, as stated earlier, and when they decide to give up some of their time, they want it to be spent on efforts that are worthwhile. For nonprofit organizations, this means being prepared, making the interaction informative, and above all else, ensuring that the investment of the entrepreneur's time has worthwhile results. For the nonprofit organization, it also means moving the entrepreneur closer to committing the financial resources being sought.

Entrepreneurs are used to driving efforts and using their time wisely to ensure there is a return on investment. Although usually the phrase *return on investment* refers to a financial investment, for entrepreneurs it also includes their time. Entrepreneurs take their days and the way they spend their 24 hours very seriously. If an entrepreneur commits to participating in a meeting with the nonprofit organization or touring a facility, it is imperative that you make it worthwhile for him or her by being prepared. This means having the staff, leaders, and volunteers who will also be participating ready before the entrepreneur arrives.

BODY LANGUAGE AND OTHER SIGNS

We all know that body language is very telling. With an entrepreneur this is very true. Leaders of nonprofit organizations should be able to read body language. Entrepreneurs are often very expressive people, showing their emotions and feelings more often than not. While looking for a positive reaction to what you are presenting, it is imperative to also be looking at entrepreneurs for any signs of frustration via their body language. Paying attention to what entrepreneurs are feeling or communicating, often without saying a word, is one of the keys to successfully cultivating these individuals. If a nonprofit organization is following a prescribed script and not allowing for flexibility, it will probably not be successful.

It is also important to recognize that entrepreneurs make things up as they go along. Not one entrepreneur I have met or interviewed had his or her business plan fully thought through and developed when he or she started the business. Most had a direction but were also always looking to the market for other opportunities to expand what they had started. Most are astonished at their success but realize it was in some ways achieved because they were willing to go with the flow and to seize the moment and the opportunity presented. In other words, entrepreneurs value flexibility and will want flexibility in their interactions with nonprofit organizations. For more on this idea, read about Stephan Pyles in "Entrepreneurial Stories."

At a university I once worked for, a very wealthy entrepreneur and his wife were invited to a meeting on campus with a specific college. The spouse was an alumna of the institution, whereas her husband did not attend college but had started and was still running a very successful telemarketing business. After following a much prescribed script, the meeting was not moving forward and the funding opportunity being offered was not capturing the attention of the entrepreneur. This was because he had already done what was being proposed at another higher education institution and was somewhat frustrated with the lack of imagination in the project being presented.

Although not paying attention to the body language of the entrepreneur, the vice president in the meeting excused himself, saying he needed to attend another meeting regarding a new building that was to be constructed on campus. Hearing this, the entrepreneur perked up and became very interested in the new building project in the other college, much to the chagrin of the dean of the wife's college. What I learned from this situation is to always pay attention to the entrepreneur's body language, recognizing that what you think is important might feel like a waste of time to them. Also, what to you is a casual comment might result in a large charitable contribution; in this example, it provided an eight-figure verbal commitment to a new building.

Pay attention to the cues being given during any interaction. Although entrepreneurs can multitask very well, it is also very easy to recognize when they are becoming disengaged with a conversation or a project. Don't let this happen to you by not paying attention and wasting their time.

> **LIFES Tip**
> Entrepreneurs can often be late to appointments; be patient and budget extra time. I have often waited an hour or more to meet with an entrepreneur I was cultivating to be a donor, but in the end, it was usually worth it.

ENTREPRENEURS LOVE TO GIVE ADVICE (AND CASH)

Entrepreneurs love to be asked for their opinion and advice. This is actually true of most individuals, but especially entrepreneurs. They like to talk about their successes and to share their wisdom. I found this true with entrepreneurs who were either trying to prove something or were trying to repay a community or group of people for their successes. But they also like to make financial contributions to ensure that the advice they are giving or the direction they are suggesting comes to fruition.

PROVING SOMETHING

Entrepreneurs by definition operate outside the norm. They are individuals who generally are not part of the establishment, let alone corporate America. Entrepreneurs can and often do feel like outsiders, aware of what is going on but clearly not feeling part of it. Think of it in terms of a person who is not invited to the party or event of the season, but is able to look through the windows at what is taking place inside. Often they want to be included but do not know how to ask for an invitation.

Entrepreneurs know what others in society are doing in terms of providing support to community and charitable endeavors. They read newspapers, watch the television news, and listen to the radio, all of which are now more and more highlighting the work being done in the philanthropic sector by many people, especially corporate America.

In addition to entrepreneurs wanting to participate and contribute, they also have a need to prove themselves. Many of today's successful entrepreneurs have taken the path least traveled, meaning they have often not followed traditional methods for achieving success, including attending college. In my conversations with many entrepreneurs who do not have a college degree or have never taken college classes, they have often expressed the feeling that those with these type of credentials are somehow more interesting to nonprofit organizations as potential donors. What they are recognizing is that such individuals are often highlighted for their charitable work. They feel that somehow these individuals, the ones who attended college or work in corporate America, must know something they do not know or be more attractive to nonprofit organizations. In other words, entrepreneurs have something to prove. They want to prove that they as entrepreneurs, whether running a successful food franchise or operating a service consulting company, have value to contribute. Once you get entrepreneurs involved, they will at some point begin giving more than just advice, but cash as well.

> ### LIFES Tip
> We in the nonprofit world are somewhat to blame for the situation of entrepreneurs feeling less valued than corporate donors. As noted in Chapter 2, although we can easily find information about those individuals working as leaders in corporate America or those with inherited wealth, entrepreneurs and their assets are more difficult to find. Note that I said *difficult*, not *impossible*. A number of websites and search engines exist that can help you ascertain the giving capacity of these donors. Some are free and some you need a subscription to access.

THE NEED FOR IMMEDIATE DECISIONS

Entrepreneurs are decision makers. A lot of the time, after getting counsel, they make decisions immediately, independently, and alone—after all, they usually own the company and the buck stops with them, meaning the decision is made by them. Although they seek advice and counsel, they generally are the experts on the issue facing the company and are in the best position to make the final decision. A word of strong caution to the leaders of nonprofit organizations: placing entrepreneurs in a committee decision-making situation will frustrate them. Entrepreneurs are action-oriented people. They need to see progress sooner rather than later. Although entrepreneurs will sometimes agree to serve on committees, such as the gala committee, the golf tournament committee, or even the dreaded food committee for a conference, they want decisions to be made in a short amount of time. After all, in their minds, it should not take half a dozen meetings to decide on the color theme for the gala, the golf course for the tournament, or the food to be served for the conference.

Food committees are notorious for taking much longer than necessary to make a decision. I once served on a committee for a conference targeting development professionals in higher education. It took us months, and many tastings, to decide the menu. It was a frustrating experience, and I was with individuals who were used to serving on committees. Imagine how an entrepreneur would view this use of his or her time.

WHAT QUALITIES SHOULD AN ENTREPRENEUR LOOK FOR IN A NONPROFIT ORGANIZATION?

Entrepreneurs are experts within their field. As discussed earlier, an entrepreneur is someone who recognizes an opportunity in the marketplace that is not currently being addressed and builds a business to respond. These are the qualities entrepreneurs will naturally look for in the nonprofit organization with which they engage. But the question always arises from entrepreneurs as to what they should look for either when being asked to become involved with a nonprofit organization or when considering actively supporting a nonprofit organization. Here are some basic items to consider:

- Does the nonprofit organization have a vision statement in writing?
- Does the nonprofit organization have a mission statement that is in writing?
- Does the nonprofit organization have a strategic plan in writing?
- Does the nonprofit organization have an active board of directors?
- Does the board of directors have both financial and time expectations?
- Does the nonprofit organization serve a cause, population, clients, or area that moves your heart?
- Does the nonprofit organization have an annual financial audit?
- Does the nonprofit organization have a prioritized list of projects?
- Does the nonprofit organization have a website?
- Is the website up-to-date, meaning, is the information on it current?

If the answers to all of these questions are not "yes," then as an entrepreneur and potential supporter of the nonprofit organization, you need to think about your involvement. It is important for nonprofit organizations to have their ducks in a row, so to speak. I am not saying don't get involved if the answers are negative, but I am recommending that you proceed with caution, knowing full well what you are getting into.

If a vision statement, mission statement, and strategic plan are in writing, an entrepreneur can be assured that the nonprofit organization and its leaders know which direction it is pursuing. The documents are of the utmost importance and must be in place.

THE THREE STAGES OF DEVELOPMENT FOR NONPROFIT ORGANIZATIONS

Most entrepreneurs entering the nonprofit world do not have the knowledge to understand that nonprofit organizations go through three stages: forming, coalescing, and mature. The information in this section is based on Valerie Ingram's graduate work in this area.

Valerie serves as the director of development for the Santa Fe Community Foundation, and her research in this area was groundbreaking at the time it was conducted in 1999.

The parameters of each stage are as follows.

FORMING STAGE

Age: Usually under 10 years of age, sometimes even under 7
Staff: Usually no professional or paid staff, but rather a volunteer, who is usually the founder, fulfills all roles (i.e., executive director, director of development, chief financial officer, and, yes, even janitor)
Budget: Usually under $100,000 and secured from very few sources
Location: Usually in the founder's home or office; occasionally located in the office of a friend or colleague of the founder
Characterizations: Emotional and intense energy by the founder; lack of written policies and procedures; no distinction between the staff and board roles; small and informal; founder/leader dislikes management activities; little to no formal planning; personal sacrifice is the mantra; very loose

COALESCING STAGE

Age: Sometimes begins at 7 years but usually around 10 years and lasts for anywhere from 5 to 10 years
Staff: Paid staff; a nonprofit organization usually transitions to this stage when someone other than the founder is brought into the nonprofit organization and is paid, thus beginning the professionalizing of the organization
Budget: Usually over $100,000 and from several funding sources, including corporations, foundations, and, if applicable, government grants
Location: An office location outside the founder's home or office; generally there are multiple moves during these years
Characterizations: Policies and job descriptions are formalized and in writing; organizational infrastructure is more complex; board and staff share power, with the board setting policy and the staff (primarily the executive director) responsible for day-to-day operations and activities; board plays a larger role in fundraising, with members expected to contribute; very controlled

MATURE STAGE

Age: Always beyond 15 years in existence
Staff: Multiple paid staff members; the founder is usually not involved in the day-to-day operations

Budget: Usually over $500,000

Location: Office; stability in location, meaning a long-term lease or the purchase of an office

Characterizations: Board of directors is large, with upward of 35 members; most board work is now done in committees; board members have the capacity to give and ask others to donate; board membership is seen as prestigious; fundraising is viewed as a board responsibility and becomes a primary focus; sometimes direction is lost because there are other nonprofit organizations in the community providing similar services; a balance between the looseness of the forming stage and the control of the coalescing stage

LIFES *Tip*

Founder-itis can be identified, at times running rampant, throughout the philanthropic world. Founder-itis means that the original founder or one of the original founders will not leave the nonprofit organization he or she started, even though the focus and growth of the organization is beyond anything the individual dreamed of or has the skill set to handle. It is at these times that it is important to have strong members on the board of directors who can work with the founder on a graceful exit.

Entrepreneurs like to make a difference, and the stage where they can most affect change is the coalescing stage. Most entrepreneurs respond to the coalescing stage first, then the forming stage, and finally the mature stage. This is because they can easily make things happen in the coalescing stage. In the forming stage, there could be and are great frustrations because the entrepreneur will be moving faster than the nonprofit organization and there might be confrontation with the founder on a continual basis. In the mature stage, entrepreneurs will find frustrations unless there is a leader who is willing to think outside the box. Most mature nonprofit organizations have policies, processes, and procedures in place, and veering from them can cause great consternation for the nonprofit organization. Change is a delicate balancing act that has to be understood by both the nonprofit organization and the entrepreneur in order for success to be the end result.

> **LIFES Tip**
> Find the stage of organizational development you work well with and then choose to become involved with nonprofit organizations that are in that stage. This advice also holds true for nonprofit staff and board members.

AN ENTREPRENEUR'S GUIDE TO NONPROFIT ORGANIZATIONS

Here is a personal guide to the qualities you need to look for in a nonprofit organization and yourself before you become involved.

- What stage is the nonprofit organization in (forming, coalescing, or mature), and does it align with your values?
- Does the nonprofit organization respond in a timely matter to your phone calls, emails, or other contact?
- Is this a cause or nonprofit organization that moves your heart?
- Is this a cause or nonprofit organization that stirs your passion?
- Is this a cause or nonprofit organization that excites you?

Dietlin's Discussion Directives

1. Name some qualities of an entrepreneur.
2. Name qualities an entrepreneur should look for in a nonprofit organization.
3. Name the three stages of a nonprofit organization's development and evolution.
4. Which stage usually best fits an entrepreneur?
5. What stage best fits your personality?

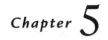

Expectations and the Return-on-Investment Theory

ONE BIG GIFT, NO SMALL GIFTS

So your nonprofit organization is engaging entrepreneurs. You are securing gifts from them. You are even securing large gifts from them. You think this is going to continue. Wrong!

Because entrepreneurs are consummate deal makers, the growth of their businesses can be erratic, which leads to their charitable donations being erratic. One year, an entrepreneur may be able and willing to contribute a major gift (however that is defined by both the nonprofit organization and the donor); but the nonprofit organization shouldn't necessarily count on that size gift for the next year. Entrepreneurs will not behave like traditional annual fund donors or even traditional major gift donors, meaning individuals with inherited wealth or corporate officers. Their gifts will be specific to a project or program and timed to their business cycle. The old adage that a donor gives on his or her timeline, not an institution or agency's timeline, is very true with entrepreneurs. Nonprofit organizations that understand this will be very successful in courting and securing donations from entrepreneurs.

Often entrepreneurs will give a major gift without ever making an annual fund gift. Again, they will focus on the new building, program, or project, not necessarily the overall sustainability of the nonprofit organization. Although this can cause frustration to the nonprofit organization, leaders who are able to work with the unpredictability of these types of donations will, in the end, be very successful in receiving generous donations from entrepreneurs.

I once worked with an entrepreneur who intended to make his first gift to a particular institution an eight-figure gift. When I suggested during the time of negotiation that he consider making a gift of $25,000 or $50,000 to support a scholarship, he rejected the idea. He was not interested in that size of gift, nor did he feel a need to dip a toe in the shallow end of the pool when he was already swimming in the deep end. This is a typical example of entrepreneurial behavior. My best advice for nonprofit leadership, both staff and boards, is to get used to it!

TRANSFORMATIONAL GIFTS: WHAT ARE THEY AND HOW CAN I GET ONE OR TWO?

Entrepreneurs consistently make transformational gifts to nonprofit organizations. An individual only has to read the annual listing of major donors in *The Chronicle of Philanthropy* to confirm this fact. But what is a transformational gift? And how does a nonprofit organization secure one of them, let alone many on a consistent basis?

A transformational gift is one in which either the donor or the recipient nonprofit organization—preferably both—is changed because of the contribution. It is a donation that changes the way a donor views the charitable work he or she is involved with and that changes the actual work a nonprofit organization can accomplish. In other words, it alters the course and ultimately the future of the nonprofit organization. Examples of this would include Warren Buffet's donation of more than $30 billion to the Bill and Melinda Gates Foundation. By making this transformational gift to a well-established nonprofit organization, Mr. Buffet changed the scope of work the Gates Foundation is able to tackle and accomplish. He also was changed by having the courage to not create another nonprofit organization. His gift changed the way he and others view charitable donations and, it is hoped, the way other high-net-worth individuals will think about their philanthropic decisions. In other words, he encouraged individuals to find nonprofit organizations that exist and are doing the work they want to support instead of creating yet another new nonprofit organization.

Entrepreneurs want to make differences in their communities and sometimes internationally. However, most are not interested in creating new nonprofit organizations or foundations to achieve this goal. They would rather make transformational gifts. Remember, entrepreneurs are successful because they identified a niche in the marketplace that was not being addressed and created a response through their business. They will do the same to nonprofit organizations. However, the leadership of the nonprofit organization needs to share with the entrepreneur the challenge or problem (in other words, the niche that is not being addressed by the nonprofit organization) and allow the entrepreneur to make the transformational gift to address it.

An example is how a small nonprofit organization in Chicago, Illinois, Cabrini Green Legal Aid (CGLA), motivated existing donors to make transformational gifts. The executive director, Rob Acton, accomplished this by sharing with existing donors the need for them to increase their donations. He did this by offering them an opportunity to serve on the newly revised advisory board to provide him with advice and counsel on a regular basis. He also asked them to increase their donation from their current level of giving to a $5,000 unrestricted gift to the CGLA. He was successful, and these individuals, many of whom were attorneys as well as entrepreneurs, provided an annual and consistent stream of income to the clinic of over $60,000 annually. Although providing recurring gifts on an annual basis is not the normal pattern for entrepreneurs, it does occassionally happen. Through the donations of these entrepreneurs, a difference was made, more clients were served, programs sustained, and transformation began for this nonprofit organization.

THE RETURN-ON-INVESTMENT THEORY

Entrepreneurs love to leverage their business investments and will view their charitable donations as an investment of a different type, but still an investment. They therefore will have very similar expectations. They will expect a return on their investment that will benefit the nonprofit organization. When working with entrepreneurs, nonprofit organizations should position charitable monetary requests as an investment toward solving a societal ill, one that will reap a large return on investment to the nonprofit, its mission, and the community being served.

Entrepreneurs love to try new things; therefore, pitching a new project, idea, or program will excite them. Although their enthusiasm will often cause the leadership of the nonprofit organization to believe the gift is a done deal, it must be realized that entrepreneurs will expect goals and objectives to be met. They will have difficulty if, after their investment, the status quo remains in place. The nonprofit organization will encounter real challenges from the entrepreneur if the reason the status quo is unchanged is because of inactivity or a reluctance to try to achieve the goal or vision. It is very important to entrepreneurs that progress be made or at least attempted.

Although the terminology *return on investment* is for-profit language, it is making its way into the nonprofit world via entrepreneurs and their expectations as well as their demands. Nonprofit organizations that recognize this opportunity and capitalize on it will be making great strides toward achieving their mission and vision. Return-on-investment strategies in nonprofit organizations might seem daunting, but those philanthropic organizations that embrace and actualize the philosophy will be better able to engage entrepreneurs in the life of the nonprofit organization.

Entrepreneurs are often thought to have more courage, or guts, than logic and strategy. In truth, they have both. They are willing to take a leap when most other individuals stand on the side valuing a position of safety and security. A leap means that entrepreneurs are willing to try new things in their business world, often at great calculated risks, because they expect a significant return on their investment. This is their expectation in working with nonprofit organizations as well. Entrepreneurs expect a return on their investment. They are the new and emerging group of philanthropists. Leaders in nonprofit organizations must begin to recognize this and develop strategies to attract them to the mission, vision, and work being done. And given their beliefs, values, and the way they approach problem solving, entrepreneurs are transforming the way philanthropy is done and viewed in this country. Just as in business, in their philanthropic work entrepreneurs will expect a return on their investments. However, the return in the latter case is not one of personal gain or profit; rather, it is the fulfillment of the nonprofit organization's mission. Whether an entrepreneur has invested time, energy, or finances, he or she will be dedicated to getting the results needed to affect the desired change.

In other words, accountability is a huge factor in a nonprofit organization's success when working with entrepreneurs. Leaders of nonprofit organizations need to view an entrepreneur as an investor of the very best kind. Entrepreneurs need to be seen as individuals who have the best interests of the organization's work at heart in solving whatever current issue is facing the nonprofit organization. This means that as a leader of the nonprofit organization, you may need to educate an entrepreneur about the do's and don'ts in the philanthropic world, especially regarding establishing realistic expectations on the return-on-investment theory held so dearly by them. It is up to both the entrepreneur and the leaders of nonprofits to work toward common goals and realistic expectations while advancing the work of the nonprofit organization.

"SO, LET ME TELL YOU HOW WE NEED TO SOLVE THIS PROBLEM

Entrepreneurs want to solve today's societal problems in a specific way—usually their way, using techniques they have used to build their businesses. Today's new philanthropists who are entrepreneurs do not want to simply earmark their donation for some vague and benevolent purpose. They want to make sure the specifications and criteria attached to their gift are followed.

To be successful, nonprofit organizations must understand this completely. When an entrepreneur says, "If this program/project does not happen, I want my donation back" you must realize this is a real condition of the gift. They do not mean "if the program does not succeed" or "if it does not get completed." They truly mean if the program or project does not even get started. As stated in Chapter 2, if you state you are going to build a new facility in order to achieve your vision, an entrepreneur who is supportive might require, as a condition of his or her donation, the reassurance that the money will be returned if the construction process never starts. Rest assured, entrepreneurs will not bail on you if the campaign becomes stalled or if the fundraising efforts take longer than originally anticipated. These are not the conditions they are referencing when dictating the terms of their gift.

Again, most nonprofit leaders think it will be too complicated to give the money back and usually argue against this condition. This is usually futile if one hopes to secure a large transformational gift from the entrepreneur. You need to recognize the fact that, yes, it will be complicated and a nuisance to give the money back. Yes, it might even be messy, requiring direction and expert advice from your legal counsel and accountant. As you know, not only will the nonprofit organization be required to file amended returns, but so will the donor. But by agreeing to this condition of using the money only for what it was intended for, the nonprofit organization will gain a life-long friend and unequivocal supporter.

I have witnessed many nonprofit organizational leaders resist agreeing to the conditions that most entrepreneurs demand. In doing so they often pass up an outstanding opportunity to make transformational changes in the work they do. These conditions are not something to be afraid of, but rather something to be embraced. It means that an entrepreneur believes in your vision, not just your mission. It also means he or she is willing to commit up front the financial resources for you to take the nonprofit organization to the next level. Whatever your vision, through the entrepreneur's charitable donation, he or she is saying to the community that this is a worthwhile goal.

VENTURE PHILANTHROPY

Entrepreneurs by their very nature are risk takers, so they will take chances in business and life that others might not. This includes their choice of charitable and philanthropic projects. A term has been coined in recent years to describe the process of entrepreneurs making philanthropic gifts that come with a "guarantee" of sorts: *venture philanthropy*. Venture philanthropists want to ensure that the donations they make will bring to reality what they have been told by the nonprofit leadership and staff will occur, so they will often negotiate to have their money returned if the project or program does not happen. In the realm of philanthropy, entrepreneurs will use their ability to make transformational gifts to hold nonprofit organizations accountable for what they say they are going to do.

TRUE PHILANTROPISTS OR INVESTOR DONORS

When working with entrepreneurs, you might often find yourself questioning their motives. In other words, what is driving them to become involved with a nonprofit organization? Are they truly being philanthropic, or is this charitable act viewed as another investment opportunity? The answer is "A little of both." Entrepreneurs are always looking for the next deal that can be made. This is how they are wired; this is what has made them successful. There is debate in the nonprofit community about the intention of donors at times. Are they a true philanthropist in the traditional sense of the word or are they an investor donor expecting a "return," meaning a social change, because of their involvement?

Fortunately for nonprofit organizations, entrepreneurs have an ability to learn new things quickly and will readily realize that the contribution they are making is an investment, but an investment of a different type: not one that will create a huge return in profit for them personally, but one that will create long-lasting effects in the community. It is an opportunity to make change in a way that is both familiar and foreign to entrepreneurial individuals. It is familiar to them because they make changes every day in their business world. They are constantly looking at the situations that exist in their world and viewing them with an eye toward improvement. This same technique will be used when entrepreneurs become first aware of, and then involved and committed to, a nonprofit organization.

Dietlin Discussion Directives

1. What is the return-on-investment theory?

2. Do entrepreneurs make major or transformational gifts without making other smaller gifts first?

3. Discuss the change Warren Buffet brought to the philanthropic world.

4. What are the signs of an investor donor?

Chapter 6

Common Misconceptions and Frustrations

MISCONCEPTIONS

I Know What It Means to Become Involved with a Nonprofit

When deciding to give back, many entrepreneurs hold misconceptions about the nonprofit world, including how nonprofit organizations operate. These misconceptions can and often do lead to frustration. One of the most common misconceptions is what becoming involved with a nonprofit organization will mean. For example, I recently presented to approximately 40 women who were clients of Merrill Lynch. Many of these women were entrepreneurs, and all were successful. When I asked them how many had served on a board of directors for a nonprofit organization, about 80% of the participants raised their hands (approximately 32 or 33 women). When I asked how many had had such a positive experience they would do it again, I was astonished because only three hands were raised. This means that fewer than 10% of the women attending this presentation felt their nonprofit board experience had been worthwhile enough that they would do it again. How sad!

When I asked why they did not enjoy their experience, the answers were multifold, including the following:

- I was not aware of the fundraising expectations.
- I was not aware of the requirements to serve (i.e., number of meetings, requirements to attend, etc.).

- There was never a quorum of board members attending meetings, so nothing could be accomplished.
- There were only so many of us willing to work; the rest of the board members just wanted their names associated with the nonprofit organization.
- I did not have an opportunity to network with individuals in business as I was promised.

This is just one example. The example highlights the need for entrepreneurs to become well versed in the ways and processes of nonprofit organizations.

> ### LIFES Tip
>
> Garth Fundis became the president of the National Academy of Recording Arts and Sciences (NARAS), commonly referred to as the Grammys. When Garth began his involvement in the nonprofit world, his wife, Ann, helped educate him on how to be a leader in the nonprofit world. Garth took the time to learn about this new arena he was entering. For his entire story, read the section entitled "Entrepreneurial Stories."

If the Entrepreneur Supports a Nonprofit Organization, All His or Her Friends and Colleagues Will Too

A second common misconception among entrepreneurs is that if they support a nonprofit organization (i.e., a charity) then all their friends and colleagues will too. This type of thinking is incorrect because most entrepreneurs want to do something that is unique and different with their charitable activities. For example, consider Ted Turner and his $1 billion commitment to the United Nations and its programs that he announced on September 18, 1997, when he was honored with the Global Leadership Award. By all accounts Ted Turner is an entrepreneur extraordinaire. He started in 1970 with a single UHF television station located in Atlanta, Georgia. He grew his company to a point at which it now includes an assortment of cable channels, movie studios, and professional sports teams. Ted Turner began the TBS satellite superstation in 1976 and CNN in 1980 and in his spare time, Ted won the America's Cup in 1977. He is an all-around entrepreneur.

According to an article on CNN's website about his generous commitment to the United Nations, Turner said, "This is not going to go for administration. This is only going to go for programs, programs like refugees, cleaning up land mines, peacekeeping, UNICEF for the children, for diseases, and we're going to have a committee that will work with a committee of the U.N. The money can only go to U.N. causes." As announced, the donation was to be made over 10 years using Time Warner stock in donations of $100 million annually. As a side note, Ted Turner had wanted to donate the money directly to the United Nations, but was informed by his legal counsel that would be illegal. Legally, the United Nations cannot accept money from any individuals. Mr. Turner had to establish a separate foundation, which is named the United Nations Foundation, to receive funds and administer the programs. The donations are expected to focus on programs in the areas of jobs, land mines, education, and global warming. At that time, Ted Turner said he intended to become a fundraiser for United Nations causes, stating "[E]verybody who is rich can expect a call." However, no one else gave at or even near the level at which Ted Turner donated. At the time of this announcement, Ted was listed as one of the 25 richest Americans and was chastising fellow billionaires Warren Buffet and Bill Gates for not contributing more to charity.

At the end of nine years, in 2006, the goal of securing $1 billion for the United Nations Foundation and the programs it funds was reached. Mr. Turner had contributed $600 million himself, with the remaining $400 million being received from government entities, corporations, and some individuals, but no big-league entrepreneurs. Although the individuals Turner wanted to get involved with this cause did not, he still was very successful and made a difference. The fairy tale ending to this story is that Ted Turner has committed another $1 billion to the United Nations Foundation. He is continuing to make a difference, even though the others he hoped would join him did not.

This story is important because it illustrates a common misconception held by many entrepreneurs that once they get excited about a cause or organization, all of their colleagues and friends will too. What should be remembered is that entrepreneurs want to do their own thing, even in the philanthropic world.

FRUSTRATIONS

A Long Decision-Making Time Is the Norm for Nonprofit Organizations

One of the most common frustrations for entrepreneurs is the long decision-making time of nonprofit organizations. It is hard for individuals who are always quick to make decisions to understand the long process and why it is necessary. Entrepreneurs need to take the time to become aware of this practice in the nonprofit community. Group buy-in and shared governance are often key steps used by nonprofit organizations, because most nonprofit organizations seek support from the public in the form of charitable donations. Remember, nonprofit organizations exist to serve the public. It is therefore imperative they take the time to secure agreement from the community. Although this may frustrate an entrepreneur, especially if he or she is offering the financial resources that will seemingly resolve the situation or problem, it is important to the overall success of the nonprofit organization and the philanthropic world to be inclusive.

Why Does Everything Take So Long?

Another common frustration among entrepreneurs is that everything in the nonprofit world seems to take a long time to implement, execute, and change. I have lost count of the number of times entrepreneurs have asked me this question as they express their exasperation at the snail's-pace movement of charities. An entrepreneur can readily see the solutions to problems that exist in society, such as the increase in hungry people in America. As they do in their businesses, once faced with a challenge, they begin to seek opportunities to resolve it. This is especially true when entrepreneurs become involved with large nonprofit organizations such as higher education institutions or hospitals. Often these entities find themselves enmeshed in restrictions and obligations because of their governing bodies or the government, especially those nonprofit organizations that are state supported or receiving corporate and foundation contracts that prohibit them from implementing what seems like an easy solution to an entrepreneur.

The converse of this is working with small nonprofit organizations. Entrepreneurs can and do become frustrated because these charities are so small they are often unable to rise to the level that the entrepreneur believes is possible. Limited resources, in terms of contributions, staffing, leadership, facilities, or physical plant, can inhibit or even prohibit a smaller nonprofit organization from moving forward to the level thought possible by the entrepreneur.

Entrepreneurs should not stop pushing nonprofit organizations to the next level. They must continue to share their ideas and even their vision while providing or garnering the resources necessary to achieve that level. Frustrations will occur, but with a better understanding of why the nonprofit organization is being held back, they will be easier to handle. Entrepreneurs need to take the time to ask questions and listen carefully to the answers about why something can or cannot be done. Once an entrepreneur has gathered all the background information, then he or she can take the next steps to move the suggestion, idea, or recommendation forward, working with the nonprofit organization while it adjusts and moves its boundaries.

Why Don't Nonprofit Organizations Operate Like Businesses?

If I had a nickel for every time I heard an entrepreneur say this, I would be a rich woman! Entrepreneurs are quite frequently exasperated by the way nonprofit organizations run their offices, which are, in fact, businesses if you ask an entrepreneur. In regard to this frustration, I think entrepreneurs might be right most of the time. Let's look at how nonprofit organizations are established.

To start a nonprofit organization, one must first file paperwork to establish a corporation within the state in which it will operate. Once the corporation is established, it applies for tax-exempt status from the federal government. This is part of the IRS tax code that allows entities to be tax exempt. Specifically, according to the IRS website:

> To be tax-exempt under section 501(c) (3) of the Internal Revenue Code, an organization must be organized and operated exclusively for exempt purposes set forth in section 501(c) (3), and none of its earnings may inure to any private shareholder or individual. In addition, it may not be an action organization i.e., it may not attempt to influence legislation as a substantial part of its activities and it may not participate in any campaign activity for or against political candidates.

> Organizations described in section 501(c) (3) are commonly referred to as charitable organizations. Organizations described in section 501(c) (3), other than testing for public safety organizations, are eligible to receive tax-deductible contributions in accordance with Code section 170.

> The organization must not be organized or operated for the benefit of private interests, and no part of a section 501(c) (3) organization's net earnings may inure to the benefit of any private shareholder or individual. If the organization engages in an excess benefit transaction with a person having substantial influence over the organization, an excise tax may be imposed on the person and any organization managers agreeing to the transaction.

What does this all mean? It means nonprofit organizations can and should use practices that make businesses successful, but they operate as entities that are not focused on making money. Nonprofit organizations, or charities as we often call them, are focused on doing good in their community locally, their society nationally, or their world globally.

If you are a business owner wanting to effect change, my recommendation is to begin your involvement with an existing nonprofit organization.

LIFES Tip

Do not start your own nonprofit organization or foundation unless you want to run another business. Often when entrepreneurs sell their businesses they start a nonprofit organization or a private foundation, not realizing the amount of work that will be needed in order to be successful. In addition, some of their advisors do not give the best advice. Here are my top three items to consider when evaluating whether to start a new nonprofit organization or foundation:

1. Do you want to run another business?
2. If you are starting a private foundation, are you willing to contribute at least $10 million?
3. If you are starting a new nonprofit organization, are you willing to ask anybody and everybody (this means people, not corporations and foundations) for charitable financial contributions?

If you answered "yes" to either questions 1 and 2 or questions 1 and 3, then you are ready to take the first steps in starting your own foundation or nonprofit organization. But, a word of caution: Warren Buffet, one of the richest men in the world, planned to donate more than 80% of his fortune to the Bill and Melinda Gates Foundation in 2006. He revealed as his reason that he did not want to start yet another nonprofit organization or foundation. You might want to consider following his example. After all, Warren Buffet has often been cited as one of the world's greatest stock market investors, with an estimated net worth of more than $60 billion.

Why Aren't Nonprofit Organizations Quick to Respond to Market Conditions and Opportunities?

The last frustration to be discussed is one often cited by entrepreneurs when working with nonprofit organizations: Why don't nonprofit organizations respond more quickly to market conditions and opportunities? This is a complicated question. There are many examples of nonprofit organizations actually responding to market conditions—specifically, those times in history when disaster strikes, such as the 9/11 tragedy in 2001, the Indonesian tsunami in 2004, Hurricanes Katrina, Rita, and Wilma in 2005, and the earthquake in China in 2008. Nonprofit organizations responded to these disasters primarily by raising large sums of money as well as providing on-the-ground resources such as staffing, food, clothing, and shelter. A scan of some of their efforts shows the following:

AMERICAN RED CROSS

- 9/11 tragedy: $1.1 billion
- Tsunami: $581 million
- Hurricanes Katrina, Rita, and Wilma: $2.56 billion
- Earthquake in China: $50 million (approximated)

SALVATION ARMY

- 9/11 tragedy: $92 million
- Tsunami: $25 million
- Hurricanes Katrina, Rita, and Wilma: $394 million
- Earthquake in China: $167,000 (with an ongoing effort)

FEEDING AMERICA

- Hurricanes Katrina, Rita, and Wilma: $36 million

All told, more than $4.8 billion was raised in these instances. This sampling of nonprofit organizations shows that they do respond to market conditions and seize opportunities, at least in times of disaster.

I believe the frustration from entrepreneurs stems not from nonprofit organizations' response to disasters but from their response to everyday opportunities, such as an entrepreneur calling or walking into the office of a nonprofit organization and offering an idea with funding behind it. What would most nonprofit organizations do? My experience is that the first reaction is disbelief, and then the automatic next step is to default to established policies and procedures, basically indicating that a discussion with the board of directors needs to take place. While this is true, the timing is often what is frustrating to an entrepreneur.

Entrepreneurs need to continue to push nonprofit organizations out of their comfort zone and into the areas where they can respond more quickly and efficiently to market conditions and opportunities. Entrepreneurs also need to work with nonprofit organizations, providing expertise and their company's knowledge as resources for improvement. For example, if the nonprofit organization the entrepreneur is involved with does not have good checks and balances in its finance office and is unable to respond in a timely manner to an increase in the charitable donations it is receiving, the entrepreneur can bring his or her business experience as well as the business's tried and true processes and policies to this situation to provide assistance to the nonprofit. Expertise at responding in a timely and appropriate manner to market conditions is one of many things entrepreneurs bring to nonprofit organizations.

Dietlin's Discussion Directives

1. Name two common misconceptions regarding working with nonprofit organizations.
2. Name four common frustrations experienced by entrepreneurs when working with nonprofit organizations.
3. What is the recommended amount of money for starting a private foundation?
4. What example in the philanthropic world did Warren Buffet set in 2006?
5. How does a nonprofit organization come into existence?

Chapter 7

Accountability/Dependability

"BUT I SENT THEM THE ANNUAL REPORT . . ."

Accountability means more than sending donors the nonprofit organization's annual report. It is not just sharing the audited financial statements either, although both of these documents are helpful in the overall process of accountability. Accountability means that nonprofit organizations are being good stewards of the resources entrusted to them by all donors, including entrepreneurs. It means being responsible for the assets of the nonprofit organization, especially the financial donations made by contributors. This is known as *stewardship* and is the one step of the Moves Management cycle that is most often overlooked and neglected. It is curious that more attention is not paid to this step in the cycle, because the nonprofit organization has already secured the financial donation and all it needs to do now is to thank the donor in a meaningful way. More on stewardship can be found in Chapter 9

> **LIFES Tip**
>
> Remember that your best future donors are your past donors. To ensure this happens, steward your current donors well by not only thanking them but also holding the organization accountable for their donations and any restrictions appended to them.

Accountability and being a good steward of resources are very important in the philanthropic world, but perhaps a better example is thinking of how we handle accountability and stewardship in our personal lives. Imagine you give someone a birthday gift that you know the person wants because he or she asked for it. You spent the time and energy to secure the gift, purchase it, and then present it in a timely manner so that it could be part of the birthday celebration. Assume that after the gift is presented, you never hear a word. Depending on what the gift is, you never see the person wearing it or displaying it, nor does he or she mention it. More important, you never receive an acknowledgment beyond the cursory nod or quick thank-you when you actually gave the gift to the birthday person. How would you feel? What would you do?

Now translate those thoughts and feelings into how you would react if you made a charitable donation to a nonprofit organization and did not hear anything about how the donation was used beyond the standard acknowledgment receipt and thank-you letter. What would you do? How would you feel?

Unfortunately, this scenario is how donors are sometimes, if not often, treated. Whether their gift is large or small, nonprofit leaders and staff like to take the money and run, so to speak. I used to be like this—afraid to speak to the donor after the financial gift was received for fear I would mess up the gift somehow by saying or doing the wrong thing. Sometimes nonprofit organization leaders and staff are so busy securing the next donation they forget to be mindful and truly grateful for the gift they have just received.

Entrepreneurs are especially sensitive to accountability because of how they are wired. As repeatedly stated throughout this book, entrepreneurs know everything about the niche in the marketplace they identified and filled by developing a business. Most entrepreneurs know a great deal about every single aspect of their business. Their businesses usually start small, with the entrepreneur doing every job in his or her own company, including bookkeeping, selling, shipping, distribution, and even the cleaning—you name it, they did it or are currently doing it.

As the company grows, entrepreneurs are able to parlay this experience and knowledge into every aspect of their company. In essence, they are able to hold employees working in their company in the various departments and areas accountable. Accountability is of great importance to entrepreneurs in part because they attribute the success they have found in their business to it.

When working with entrepreneurs, accountability is the key to having a successful and continuing relationship. Accountability and stewardship go hand in hand in furthering the relationship with an entrepreneur. Whereas small-gift donors, corporate donors, and even inherited-wealth donors might be a bit more forgiving in this area, entrepreneurs will not. They will expect and demand accountability for their charitable donations.

"CAN I COUNT ON YOU?"

Entrepreneurs want dependability among the individuals, vendors, businesses, and even the nonprofit organizations with which they work and are involved. This is important to them because again they are viewing things through their own experiences. To be successful, entrepreneurs have had to be dependable. Even though they have identified a niche in the marketplace not being addressed and filled it, there are usually other individuals who have seen the same unaddressed niche and are also trying to fill it. For example, during the end of the 19th century and into the first half of the 20th century, the horseless carriage (as the automobile was referred to by Thomas Edison) was well on its way to becoming a standard mode of transportation. However, it was not just the Big Three automobile companies that we know today in America (i.e., Ford Motor Company, General Motors, and Chrysler) plus the half dozen or so foreign companies that had identified this missing niche in the marketplace. There were many, many more, including R. E. Olds, Dodge, Tucker, Pontiac, Winton, Oakland, Benz, and Daimler, which are just a few names familiar to us. It is estimated that over 100,000 patents contributed toward the creation of the modern automobile, meaning that lots of individuals were involved in the development and creation of the automobile. Why did only three companies survive in the United States? My guess is that it is because their original founders were dependable to their customers, much like the successful entrepreneurs of today. It is imperative that nonprofit organizations operate in the same manner.

So what does dependability mean to the nonprofit organization with which an entrepreneur is working? It means honoring and fulfilling all obligations associated with the charitable donations made. This should be the standard practice of the nonprofit organization with all donations, of course, especially if they are designated for a specific cause, program, or project. However, with entrepreneurs it is even more critical that they know they can depend on the nonprofit organization to fulfill all its obligations.

WHAT IF THE NONPROFIT ORGANIZATION CANNOT MEET THE AGREED UPON TERMS?

But what about reality? What if the nonprofit organization truly cannot meet the terms agreed to when it accepted the money from the donor, especially if the donor is an entrepreneur? Will the donor demand his or her money back? Will the donor never interact with the nonprofit organization again?

Things do happen that are out of our control. Changes occur that have nothing to do with a nonprofit organization's goals and objectives. Budgets get cut, leadership changes, staff members leave, and program priorities shift. When this happens, many nonprofit organization leaders and staff panic and decide to avoid donors, especially when they cannot meet the terms as outlined in a gift agreement. This is the absolutely worst thing a nonprofit organization can do. To leave the donor uninformed, unaware, and essentially in the dark is a great detriment to the nonprofit organization. The best recommendation to nonprofit leaders and staff is to be honest and candid with donors—all donors, and especially entrepreneurs—when plans, projects, and programs go awry or don't come to fruition. By doing this you will have a higher likelihood of keeping these individuals as donors.

Regarding entrepreneurs, I know you will be pleasantly surprised by their response. Entrepreneurs will understand because in their businesses, and, with their business plans, change happens often. This surprises most nonprofit leaders and staff because they expect the donor, especially if he or she is an entrepreneur, to ask for the money back and run. But what entrepreneurs do best is solve problems! They are able to readjust their plans to meet the changes or challenges that have evolved during the life of the project, or even at its beginning, if circumstances have changed. This is what they do on a monthly, weekly, or even a daily basis in their own businesses. They can help, and usually will when asked to do just that. After all, they have already made an investment in the nonprofit organization and will want to see their investment succeed.

What does one do when a $15 million gift goes away? I had the opportunity to witness this first hand when in 2003 I was working at the University of Illinois at Chicago (UIC). I was serving as the assistant dean of development, and my role was to raise money for the College of Business Administration (CBA). It had been decided that the CBA needed a new building that was going to cost $55 million. Because UIC is a state-supported institution, it was anticipated that the state of Illinois would provide half the funds and that the CBA needed to raise the rest. The state of Illinois expected the college to raise $27.5 million. As luck would have it, an entrepreneur self identified, stating that he would like to provide a gift of $15 million to support the project and have some naming rights. To keep the momentum going, the dean and the leadership team announced the $15 million verbal commitment (even though there was nothing in writing) to the faculty, staff, advisory board members, university community, and anyone else who would listen.

Unfortunately, the gift never materialized. The stock of the donor's company fell precipitously, and suddenly what had appeared to be a sure thing was not going to happen. The college's dean and I called three advisory board members into a meeting to tell them the news, and what happened was amazing. First, I need to share that two of the three individuals were entrepreneurs, with the third running a large division of a public company. All three of them said, "No problem. We will simply start again." The dean and I were dumbfounded. This was the last thing we expected to hear from them, but was a very valuable lesson to me. Entrepreneurs are willing to take risks, and when the risks don't produce the desired results, they try again!

IS THE PHILANTHROPIC WORLD ACCOUNTABLE?

In a word, yes. The philanthropic world takes accountability very seriously. Most nonprofit organizations assure donors they will follow through on what they agree to do. Unfortunately, it seems that the only stories that get published in newspapers and aired on the television or radio are ones about the wishes of donors not being honored. I can assure you that these stories are primarily the anomalies, not the everyday practice of nonprofit organizations. Most charities work hard to ensure accountability exists.

There are organizations, some of them nonprofit organizations, serving as watchdogs for the philanthropic world. If you are a potential donor, I encourage you to check them out for information on the charity you wish to support. A couple are described here.

According to its website, the Better Business Bureau Wise Giving Alliance (www.bbb.org/charity)

> [H]elps donors make informed giving decisions and advances high standards of conduct among organizations that solicit contributions from the public. The Alliance was formed in 2001 through the merger of the National Charities Information Bureau with the Council of Better Business Bureaus' Foundation (which housed the Philanthropic Advisory Service). The merger partners offer over a century of combined experience in charity evaluation. The Alliance produces in-depth evaluative reports on national charities based on comprehensive Standards for Charity Accountability and publishes a quarterly

magazine, the *Wise Giving Guide*. National charities that meet the standards can apply to participate in the Alliance's National Charity Seal program.

The BBB Wise Giving Alliance produces reports on nationally soliciting charitable organizations. Approximately one-third of the BBBs in the United States report on the regionally soliciting nonprofit organizations in their area.

The Alliance does not rank charities but rather seeks to assist donors in making informed judgments about charities soliciting their support.

Perla Ni started her nonprofit organization and website, GreatNonprofits (www.greatnonprofits.org), in 2007 to give prospective donors an opportunity to see how others have reviewed the charities they are interested in supporting. The website states:

GreatNonprofits is a place to find, review, and talk about great—and perhaps not yet great—nonprofits. You already know that reviews by other people who have gone to a restaurant or tried out a doctor are the best way to find out about the quality of those services. If you have direct experience with a nonprofit, GreatNonprofits makes it easier for you to share your knowledge so that other people can discover the great nonprofits that are out there.

We don't review nonprofits ourselves. Much like Amazon book reviews or consumer reviews site (Epinions, Zagats, TripAdvisor, Yelp, etc.), the reviews and ratings are posted by people who have been touched by a nonprofit and want to share their story about it. You'll see on our site stories of people who have volunteered for or donated to nonprofits and stories of people who have received services. GreatNonprofits is a nonprofit 501(c) (3) organization itself, which is funded by the Kellogg Foundation, Forbes Funds and individuals who believe that we provide a needed information source for nonprofits, volunteers and donors.

There is a disclaimer on this website stating it is still in the beta test phase and asking for feedback on any bugs or challenges discovered throughout the website. While it currently operates only in three areas—San Francisco, Philadelphia, and Washington, DC—it has plans to be a national resource.

As you can see, there are a number of entities (including those listed in Chapter 3) working to make information more easily accessible to individuals who are looking for independent verification and evaluation of the charities to which they are considering providing financial support.

"HOW DO I HOLD NONPROFIT ORGANIZATIONS ACCOUNTABLE?"

I hear this question frequently from donors or prospective donors, especially after a story about a nonprofit organization airs in which something appears to have not been done properly. Donors and prospective donors begin to wonder whether existing nonprofit organizations are dependable or if they should start their own nonprofit organization instead. The answer is that the majority of the time nonprofit organizations are accountable and able to fulfill their end of the agreement they have made with you.

To be assured that accountability exists with the nonprofit organization you are interested in financially supporting, I recommend the following steps:

1. Call and meet with the nonprofit organization leadership and staff; begin having discussions about what you want to do.
2. Ask if the nonprofit organization utilizes gift agreements; if they do this, you will be able to ascertain whether they are at a level of sophistication that is comfortable for you.
3. Over time, ask to be introduced to other donors so you can speak with them about their experiences, especially their expectations when they have made a financial contribution.
4. Check out the nonprofit organization through one or all of the following websites to see how they are rated:

   - Better Business Bureau Wise Giving Alliance: www.bbb.org (click on For Charities and Donors)
   - Charity Navigator: www.charitynavigator.org
   - GuideStar: www.guidestar.org
   - GreatNonprofits: www.greatnonprofits.org

"CAN I TELL THEM EXACTLY HOW TO SPEND THE MONEY I DONATE?"

In a 2006 survey by the polling firm Zogby International, nearly 60% of Americans stated that a nonprofit organization should return a contributor's money if the organization intentionally ignores what the donor wants done with it. It further found that 97% of Americans say that they would consider charities' spending donations on unauthorized projects to be a "serious" matter. Nearly, 80% of those polled said they would stop giving to a charity that accepted contributions for one purpose and used the money for something else. Finally, those surveyed went even further, saying that the managers of a nonprofit organization should be held legally or criminally liable if the money is not used for the purpose for which it was intended.

So, can you tell a nonprofit organization exactly how to spend the money you donate? The answer is no. No, you cannot tell a nonprofit organization exactly how to spend the dollars you contribute; however, you can articulate your intentions and wishes. Most nonprofit organizations will work to honor your request by fulfilling the details of any gift agreement. Usually, with a donation that has restrictions (meaning directions regarding the areas in which the funds are to be used), there is a gift agreement. Some would-be donors might ask what a gift agreement is and how it differs from a pledge agreement.

A *gift agreement* is a legal document that is enforceable, although most nonprofit organizations are reluctant to sue a donor. The gift agreement outlines how the donation will be used—what is expected or the responsibilities of each party, as well as alternative uses of the funds in the event the program or project fails to exist in the future or is changed. See Appendix D for an example of a gift agreement.

A *pledge agreement* is a promise to make a donation in the future. It provides the details of the money that is being donated and usually includes the date the pledge is being made and the details of how the gift will be made, in what amounts, over what period of time, and on what dates, as well as signatures of the donor and representatives from the nonprofit organizations. Depending on the size of the gift, witnesses and a notary might also be recommended. See Appendix E for an example of a pledge agreement.

By using gift and pledge agreements, minimal misunderstandings will occur regarding donations and pledges. But always remember, the nonprofit organization's leadership has ultimate responsibility to administer all gifts, both restricted and unrestricted. It is important to also realize that nonprofit organizations are always evolving and changing, just as entrepreneurial businesses do. While restricting your gift or making requests for the money to be allocated in a certain way seems appealing, you must realize that no one can see the future. Remember, those individuals who made restricted donations to support the Hurricane Katrina recovery efforts could not have their gifts used for recovery efforts related to Hurricane Rita. Now, my best guess is that the majority of individuals making these donations simply wanted to help people who had been adversely affected by a natural disaster. They were not thinking when the gifts were restricted to a specific disaster (Hurricane Katrina) that those funds would not be able to be used for a disaster that followed within weeks (Hurricane Rita), even though in some cases the same people were affected. Donors must be careful in outlining details and expectations. Things do change.

In 1961, Charles S. and Marie H. Robertson established the Robertson Foundation as a supporting organization to benefit Princeton University's Woodrow Wilson School of Public and International Affairs. After their deaths, family members sued Princeton University in 2003, alleging the university was not spending money from the foundation for the purposes originally outlined by Charles and Marie. The Robertson Foundation had grown from the initial donation of $35 million to more than $800 million. Obviously, the heirs of the Robertsons believed that the intentions for which the Robertson Foundation was established—to provide financial resources for graduate programs at the Woodrow Wilson School and in particular to help prepare students for international jobs in the federal government—were not being fulfilled.

In March 2007, Princeton University reimbursed the Robertson Foundation $782,375, stating that the university had provided "inadequate disclosure" to the board because the money supported graduate students in economics, politics, and sociology, which are academic departments not in the Woodrow Wilson School. Although Princeton argues that these departments are closely associated with the school, they acknowledged they are not located within the school.

The legal battle continued and in late 2008, a settlement required Princeton University to pay $50 million, and $40 million in legal fees to the foundations controlled by the Robertson's heirs. The endowment, valued now at more than $700 million, will be dissolved with Princeton retaining most of the money in a new fund that the University will control totally. According to an article in *The Chronicle of Philanthropy*, Martin Morse Wooster, a historian and author of the book, *The Greatest Philanthropists and the Problem of "Donor Intent"* stated, "If Princeton had consulted the Robertson family more between 1995 and 2002 this might not have happened."

SOME SOUND ADVICE FOR ENTREPRENEURS

After determining where you want to make your charitable donations, meaning what causes and areas you want to support, you need to find nonprofit organizations that do what you want very well. Although it is somewhat hard for entrepreneurs to comprehend, nonprofit organizations will at times shift their mission to accommodate a potential financial opportunity they believe is available to them. When this occurs, the results are usually not good. Whereas most entrepreneurs will capitalize on opportunities that align with their business plan, with nonprofit organizations it is almost always an alignment in a new direction.

To illustrate the point, consider the example of a nonprofit organization whose mission is to feed hungry people. It would seem natural for this organization to reject an opportunity in the cancer research area, right? Although it seems apparent that the answer should be "yes," imagine what might happen if a funder approached the leadership with an offer of $10 million if the nonprofit organization would begin conducting research in the area of cancer and pesticides, stating he believes pesticides in foods cause cancer and hungry people should not be given food with pesticides. What should the leaders of the nonprofit organization do? Most of us would say reject the opportunity, but you would be amazed how many leaders and staffs of nonprofit organizations would actually consider this opportunity. While it appears to most of us that this offer takes the nonprofit organization off mission, people can make themselves believe anything. A situation of this type actually happened after Hurricane Katrina, when many nonprofit organizations decided they could and should solicit donations and help out in the disaster recovery efforts even though they had no experience or expertise in disaster recovery efforts.

> ### LIFES Tip
>
> According to *The Chronicle of Philanthropy*, a California animal-rescue charity raised $8.4 million to care for animals left behind following Hurricane Katrina, and then subsequently spent more than 33% of the money raised expanding its operations. This is a prime example of a nonprofit organization thinking it should be in the business of raising money for a certain situation when perhaps it should not.

My strong advice to donors, especially to entrepreneurs, is to make sure the nonprofit organization you are supporting has as one of its core missions the cause or area you want to support. Again, think of Warren Buffet's philanthropic work when he donated more than $30 billion to the Bill and

Melinda Gates Foundation. He did not start his own foundation in this area. What he did was identify a nonprofit organization that could accomplish what he wanted to do, one that was in alignment with his goals. With 1.5 million nonprofit organizations in existence, you should be able to find one that does the work you want to support. By choosing wisely, you will eliminate the frustration, disillusionment, and angst that occurs when trying to make something work that is not in alignment. Basically, you will be avoiding the square-peg-into-a-round-hole syndrome.

Dietlin's Discussion Directives

1. What does an entrepreneur expect from a nonprofit organization?
2. Name some dependable nonprofit organizations.
3. Can you direct what your charitable donation funds?
4. What details are in a gift agreement?
5. What details are in a pledge agreement?
6. Name two of the four places where you can check out nonprofit organizations.

Chapter 8

Strategies and Evaluations

LONG-TERM ADVENTURE: CULTIVATION STRATEGIES FOR ENTREPRENEURS

A nonprofit organization should be prepared for cultivation strategies to perhaps be long-term adventures when dealing with entrepreneurs. This might appear to go against earlier chapters, which indicated that entrepreneurs are quick decision makers. They are, but the process of getting them involved with the nonprofit organization, getting them to think of something other than business, can be lengthy. Hence, entrepreneurs can take a long time to cultivate.

Consider entrepreneurs to be like wine. Some wines you can drink immediately or relatively soon after purchasing them. Other types of wine need aging and take a longer time to come to fruition. Entrepreneurs can be like wine in the length of time needed to cultivate them. Some are eager to get fully involved early in the development of the relationship with the nonprofit organization, especially if there is a pressing need or issue to be resolved and they believe they have a solution. Other entrepreneurs will take a longer time for their involvement and commitment to the nonprofit organization to become full-fledged. No matter the length of time required for their cultivation, I can guarantee it will always be an adventure when working with an entrepreneur.

I think back to an entrepreneur I was privileged to work with in securing an eight-figure financial commitment. The initial cultivation strategy time was 22 months—22 months of developing and executing unique ways to keep this person involved, engaged, and, most important, interested in the nonprofit organization. During those 22 months, there were many doubters and naysayers. Many people told me to give up, that the commitment was never going to happen. I knew it would not happen if we did not have a cultivation strategy to engage the entrepreneur in the life of the nonprofit organization. I also recognized that the cultivation strategy needed to be unique. This was an individual who, at least on paper, was a billionaire. It was important that the nonprofit organization find ways to keep him constantly and consistently engaged and interested. There was nothing we could buy or give him that he could not purchase himself. Our goal was to create experiences and opportunities, even adventures that would keep him involved and, upon reflection, remind him of his affection and commitment to the nonprofit organization.

RESEARCH THE PROSPECT'S FAMILY AND/OR BUSINESS

Research is an essential component to the overall operations of a nonprofit organization, especially if it has a development office. In today's age of access to just about everything, almost anything can be discovered. With the advance of the Internet and tools such as Wealth Engine, Lexis-Nexis, corporate annual reports, and other materials, information is relatively easy to obtain. While overall I think that all of the available information is a very good thing, I urge caution. Researching entrepreneurs, and especially their business if it is still privately held, as well as their families, can prove challenging. Often, these entrepreneurs do not come from a family dynasty that has conducted interviews or had numerous articles or books written about them. One only has to think of well-known families in the United States to realize how easy it would be to learn about them simply by reading an article or book. With most entrepreneurs, this will not be the case. Research is still a vital part of developing a cultivation strategy for the prospective donor, however. You will often find that entrepreneurs have not received numerous accolades or been honored with awards, so much of their personal information is not easily available.

Although research is necessary when cultivating and engaging entrepreneurs, one of the most effective and truly easiest ways to obtain the information is often overlooked. Time has often been wasted searching for some piece of information that, had this other methodology I am proposing been used, would have been gathered almost instantly. I have also heard fundraisers, especially those in small or grassroots organizations, say that they cannot afford the research aspect of development. However, there is a type of research that is readily available and affordable to any nonprofit organization, regardless of staff size or budget I often find reluctance from the non-profit organization's staff to commit to using it. The research I am alluding to is to actually meet on a fairly regular basis with the entrepreneur who is the prospective donor. It is amazing what a development officer can be learned by simply talking with the entrepreneur and, if possible, his or her family members. I would go so far as to state that talking directly to the prospective donor is the best research method available.

> ### LIFES Tip
>
> During a feasibility study, an LMDA associate met with a very prominent entrepreneur who proceeded to share many, many details about his life, beliefs, and family without any prompting from the associate. The associate reported that it was difficult to keep the interviewee focused and to actually get through all the questions in the study. This is a prime example of the kind of information a nonprofit organization staff member or volunteer can obtain by simply meeting and having a conversation with a potential donor.

The second-best way to obtain information is to work in collaboration with others in your nonprofit organization who might have knowledge about the entrepreneur; the research department in particular will be very helpful, if it exists. When the nonprofit leadership, development officers and research staff work together, the results are often transformational to the cultivation and solicitation strategies being developed.

A third way to conduct research about entrepreneurs, their businesses, and their families is to talk to others in your community, individuals who might know or be connected with the entrepreneur in question. You will be surprised what people are willing to share, especially if someone is successful.

A final suggestion regarding how to conduct research is to read about the person via what you find on the Internet or in periodicals such as newspapers, trade journals, and weekly business journals.

To summarize, the four methods to obtain information are as follows:

- Meet face to face and converse with the entrepreneur and if possible his/her family
- Work with others in the nonprofit organization to ascertain what they might know about the potential donor who is an entrepreneur
- Talk to other community members about what they know about the entrepreneur
- Conduct research via the Internet, newspapers, trade journals, periodicals, and other printed and electronic media

> ### LIFES *Tip*
>
> When it is discovered that a donor, prospective donor, volunteer, or community leader has done something and it is appropriate for you to send a note of congratulations or make a phone call, do it. Have the nonprofit organization's executive director, director of development, board chair, or volunteer write a note or call to offer the nonprofit organization's best wishes! (See Appendix C for an example.)

SO, NOW WHAT?

Once you obtain this information, you must incorporate it into your cultivation strategy for the entrepreneur. Be sure you keep your strategy—and database—fresh. For example, I once had the opportunity to work with an entrepreneur named Kevin. When I called to ask if he and his wife, Susan, were going to attend the gala later that month, he responded that he would be attending with his wife, Wendy. He shared with me that he and Susan were divorced. After I apologized for the error and we laughed a bit, I realized that all the research I had done in creating the list of invitees had not yielded the information I needed to know—primarily, that Kevin's wife was named Wendy. After I hung up the phone, I double-checked the database and spoke to other staff members who knew him. None of it yielded the information Kevin had just shared with me. Of course, there was an immediately apparent response in this scenario, but it was also important that I be sure to incorporate this new information into my strategy for engaging Kevin and Wendy in the life of the nonprofit organization in the future.

On another occasion, I was meeting with a donor who was an entrepreneur at a restaurant in Florida. He was sharing details about his wealth that the nonprofit organization was not aware of, including a home he had on Ussepa Island. When I reported this back to the director of research, she was thrilled. Later she came to my office telling me she could not find the island. She wanted to know where it was located, what city it was near, and whether I had the home's address. Of course, my answers to all of these questions was "no." As I told her, I had a conversation with the donor; it had not been an interview in which he completed a questionnaire. The end of the story is that we worked together, with me having additional discussions with the donor;

through those discussions we discovered the location of the island and his home. Again, I incorporated the information I was learning through having interactions and conversations into the overall cultivation, solicitation, and stewardship strategies.

TELL ENTREPRENEURS EXACTLY WHAT IS GOING TO BE DONE WITH THEIR FINANCIAL SUPPORT

Like other major gift donors, entrepreneurs will usually need to review a proposal and will probably require a gift or pledge agreement before committing their financial resources to a nonprofit organization. The goal of both documents is to articulate to the entrepreneur and his or her advisors exactly what is going to be done with the charitable donation being provided. Often, the proposals need to be tightly edited, with clearly presented options outlining the expected outcomes and benefits to each party. The nonprofit organization should recognize that an entrepreneur who is about to become a donor will ask a lot of questions, especially if this is the first time he or she has made a charitable gift of a significant size. The nonprofit organization needs to be patient.

Most entrepreneurs are first-generation business people, meaning they did not come from wealth and still believe they can lose their wealth any moment (and many have!). One simply has to speak with successful women entrepreneurs who often feel they are only one step away from being a "bag lady" or homeless to know the truth of this statement. Therefore, it is difficult for many entrepreneurs to freely give their financial resources to a nonprofit organization or to make a significant gift for the first time. However, if the interaction is positive and the entrepreneur clearly understands how his or her financial support is going to be used, then it is likely the entrepreneur will make the donation and that he or she will continue to be a charitable individual. Conversely, if an entrepreneur is confused and not certain what his or her gift is for or whether it will be used for its intended purpose, then the possibility of the entrepreneur's further involvement with the nonprofit community will be limited, if not ended. Every person involved in the charitable world has a responsibility to ensure that interactions with donors, and especially entrepreneurs, are positive.

> **LIFES Tip**
>
> I have had the privilege of working with some entrepreneurs who believe that from those to whom much has been given, much is expected. This is the philosophy by which they live their lives. Find these entrepreneurs and get them engaged in your nonprofit organization.

TIME YOUR REQUEST FOR DONATIONS TO BUSINESS CYCLES

Entrepreneurs are consumed by their business. It is their life and their focus. However, once they become successful—meaning once the company starts turning a profit—they often want to give back and begin venturing into the philanthropic world to make charitable donations. But be advised, the business is never far from their minds. The business, with its successes and troubles, budgets and staffing, growth and decline, is always there. Leaders of nonprofit organizations need to be cognizant of the business cycles entrepreneurs deal with and time their requests for charitable donations to the right business cycle.

One might ask, what are the right business cycles? The right business cycles are the profitable ones when the entrepreneur feels successful, the business is making money, or the business has just been sold; they could also be when the business receives a large financial investment that allows it to grow to the next level or has a big sale or lands a large contract. These are the positive business cycles.

Recently, I had the opportunity to accompany one of my clients, a priest from a local church celebrating its 100th anniversary, to a meeting. We went to meet with the owner of a company, who happened to be the son of the founder. What the priest and I expected was a meeting and perhaps lunch. We waited for a while for the owner to come into the conference room to meet with us. Shortly after he arrived in the conference room and we began our discussion, his father, the founder, arrived. The priest was delighted to see him because he had recently blessed the founder's marriage of 50 years. Then, two high school friends of the priest showed up, along with the sister of the owner. In the end it was a festive, familial, and fun atmosphere, with many of us going to lunch. The priest and I rolled with the situation, hoping to make the best out of it as we had not envisioned, strategized, or planned all the people joining us. On the particular day we met with this entrepreneur we were beginning to cultivate him for a donation. It should be noted that this entrepreneur was not a member of the parish, nor had he ever attended a mass at this particular church. However, on the day we selected to meet him, he shared with us that his company just received notice of a large contract from Honda, the automobile company, and the entrepreneur made a $7,000 donation to the church's restoration/renovation campaign that day. Entrepreneurs definitely work in their own way and according to their own timetable and it was definitely the right business cycle in which to ask for a gift!

The negative or challenging business cycles are when business owners are strapped for cash, sharing with you during conversations that their largest customer has stopped using the company's services, or telling you they have just purchased their competitor's company and leveraged all their assets to make this happen. In these situations an entrepreneur will be asset rich but most likely cash poor and not likely to make a major cash donation. A nonprofit organization will have to be very creative to keep entrepreneurs engaged during these particular business cycles. If the entrepreneur has been engaged and financially supportive, the nonprofit organization will have to be patient for the business cycle to turn back to the positive. Entrepreneurs will most likely want to continue their involvement but may need to scale back their financial contributions. Good nonprofit leadership will recognize this and work with the entrepreneur during these times of tight cash flow. In turn, entrepreneurs will remember you and be even more supportive when they are in a position that affords them the opportunity to fully reengage.

Remember, entrepreneurs are repayers, a term coined by Russ Alan Prince and Karen Maru File in their book *The Seven Faces of Philanthropy*. Repayers tend to be donors second, after first having benefited from the nonprofit organization as a constituent, meaning that somehow or in some way a nonprofit organization provided services to them or someone they knew. Services can mean many things, including direct aid, a place to serve as a board member, or a place to make a difference. Repayers, according to Prince and File, are by a 2-to-1 margin predominantly business owners. Repayers are an excellent demonstration of social exchange or reciprocity: they give because they have received.

The nonprofit leadership that learns how to create a strategy and work with entrepreneurs during both the positive and the negative challenging business cycles that they face will be very successful in securing large, major, and even transformational gifts from these individuals.

ENTREPRENEURS ARE CREATIVE WITH THEIR GIFTS

Entrepreneurs are creative individuals, and this creativity extends to how they make their philanthropic gifts. Let this serve as fair warning for any nonprofit organization preparing to work with and engage entrepreneurs in their work: the level of creativity entrepreneurs bring with them is at times unbelievable. Patience is a required skill set when working with them. Patience is needed when listening to entrepreneurs regarding how the "deal" can be done. Patience is needed in ascertaining their ideas for getting the project or program up and running in a short amount of time even though they do not know the history or have complete knowledge of the situation. Patience is again needed in moving the entrepreneur to an understanding of all the challenges of the project or program.

In addition to this type of creativity, entrepreneurs will be creative with how they want to make their charitable donation. They are often hard pressed to part with a cash contribution on any sort of regular basis, so be prepared to accept private stock, negotiable securities, real estate, and other noncash gifts. Entrepreneurs will quite frequently make their pledges or write their gift agreements based on the value of their company's stock, both stock that is publicly traded and privately held. The pledge agreement can often be based on the value of a certain number of shares of stock. If the stock value increases during the payment period or time the gift is to be made, then the overall contribution could be increased. Conversely, if the stock value decreases during the time of the gift payment period or pledge period, then the total amount of the gift pledged will be decreased, which I have seen happen on more than one occasion.

Nonprofit organizations must be very astute when negotiating any gift or pledge agreements based on the value of the stock, especially those gift or pledge agreements that are intended for a bricks-and-mortar project (sometimes known as a capital project). I have witnessed and learned of many instances in which the construction of buildings has begun only to be stopped midway because the anticipated gift has been greatly reduced as a result of a fall in the value of the stock shares donated via the gift or pledge agreement. In other words, the nonprofit organization was depending, in fact relying, on the gift to meet the construction costs of whatever structure was being built or renovated. This is a very dangerous position in which to put a nonprofit organization. Caution is necessary when negotiating any gift or pledge agreement, especially those based on the value of a particular number of shares: it is imperative that the nonprofit organization be aware and mindful of the precarious situation it is potentially putting itself in if it proceeds with a brick-and-mortar project. It is better to wait until all the funds are raised and in the bank before turning a shovelful of dirt!

RESPECT AN ENTREPRENEUR'S TIME

Entrepreneurs are busy people. One might respond that everyone is busy, but this is particularly true for entrepreneurs. I know of one successful female entrepreneur named Marsha whose business generates annual sales of more than $8 million. She stated in an interview recently that except for when she is taking a boxing lesson or going to church, she is always thinking about and doing things for her business. In other words, she is extremely busy, and finding time for her to tackle something that is not related to her business goals will be challenging if not downright difficult. Engaging her will be a challenge even though she has expressed interest numerous times in being involved philanthropically.

If a nonprofit organization is going to attract entrepreneurs, it needs to be respectful of their time. That means starting and ending meetings on time, but allowing for more time if the entrepreneur decides he or she wants to stay to continue a discussion or take a tour of the offices or facilities. The bottom line is that a nonprofit organization must recognize that an entrepreneur will always take care of business first. On one visit to secure a multimillion dollar verbal gift commitment from a prospective donor who was a very successful entrepreneur, the leader of the nonprofit organization and I were kept waiting for over an hour as the potential donor traversed the lobby going from meeting to meeting, acknowledging us with a very friendly hello, but still keeping us waiting. Then, instead of a meeting in his office as was planned, this entrepreneur took us to lunch at his country club in his private dining room. Thank goodness the leader of the nonprofit organization and I had not planned any afternoon meetings that we would have had to cancel.

It is important to remember that entrepreneurs operate on their own time frame. The best way to ensure that a meeting with an entrepreneur happens is to go to him or her. Going to the entrepreneur's business location is usually a great way to guarantee the meeting will occur because the entrepreneur is almost always there. You should plan on touring the company, meeting some of the key people, and being made aware of developments that have changed the business. These are all things the entrepreneur will want you to be aware of—milestones and steps that brought him or her to the success they are enjoying today.

Remember to keep to the time frame you set. If you said you needed a half hour of the entrepreneur's time, then plan on spending a half hour, not one or two hours. Entrepreneurs are more likely to work with you if they know you keep your word, and one simple, and often early test, is the time issue. As discussed in Chapter 4, it is important to pay attention to body language. There will be times when an entrepreneur cannot meet or would like the meeting to be cut short, but could be caught with you waiting in the lobby and a crisis going on in the back room. If this occurs, you should offer to come back at another time, realizing you will gain much more than you are losing if the appointment is canceled. Be gracious and understanding. If the meeting is going well, acknowledge that you have spent your thirty minutes and ask whether the entrepreneur would like to continue. By following these simple rules, the nonprofit organization will reap tremendous results, including additional meetings and most likely a financial investment by the entrepreneur.

MAKE NO SMALL PLANS

Entrepreneurs are big-idea people. When working to engage them in the life of your nonprofit organization, thinking big will be to your advantage. Many entrepreneurs want to change the world like they have changed something via their businesses. Entrepreneurs want nonprofit organizations to think big, to dream big, and with their financial help, to act big. Most of us have read or heard of James Collins's book, *Good to Great*. We have also heard of his challenge for us to have a "Big, Hairy, Audacious Goal" (BHAG, pronounced BEE-hag). The phrase was introduced by James Collins and Jerry Porras in their 1996 article entitled "Building Your Company's Vision." A BHAG is a sort of vision statement: "an audacious 10-to-30-year goal to progress towards an envisioned future. A true BHAG is clear and compelling, serves as a unifying focal point of effort, and acts as a clear catalyst for team spirit. It has a clear finish line, so the organization can know when it has achieved the goal; people like to shoot for finish lines."

This is what most entrepreneurs are looking for: an audacious goal and a way to make a huge impact. Daniel Burnham, the famous Chicago architect who helped rebuild the city after the great fire of the late 1800s, said, "Make no small plans." He was an entrepreneur, and his BHAG resulted in rebuilding Chicago into one of the best cities in the world.

Think big and outside of the box. What is your nonprofit organization's audacious goal? What do you wish you could accomplish? How many more children could you feed if . . . ? How many more senior citizens could you serve if . . . ? How many more patients could you see if . . . ? How many more animals would be saved if . . . ?

NONPROFIT ORGANIZATIONS' STRATEGIES FOR ENGAGEMENT WITH ENTREPRENEURS

So what should a strategy to engage an entrepreneur look like for a non-profit organization? There should be a distinct plan of action for each entrepreneur; do not take a cookie-cutter approach. Remember, entrepreneurs are unique, and the nonprofit organization will want to be sure their philanthropic experiences are tailor made for them. However, there are some basic questions to consider when developing a plan for each entrepreneur:

- Does the entrepreneur want to be involved on a regular basis? Daily? Weekly? Monthly? Annually?
- Does the entrepreneur want his or her spouse and family members to be engaged with the nonprofit?
- Does the entrepreneur desire to serve in a leadership role, such as on the board of directors? Or does he or she prefer to serve in an advisory capacity, such as on an advisory board? Remember that for most entrepreneurs, board service is highly unlikely unless their involvement is related to the bottom line of their business.
- Does the entrepreneur want to be known for his or her involvement or does the entrepreneur prefer to remain anonymous? Either desire will have an affect on your strategy.
- Does the entrepreneur have the ability to have his or her employees engaged in the nonprofit organization serving in various volunteer roles?
- Does the entrepreneur understand the philanthropic world? If the answer is "no," then educational information might be the place to begin.
- Does the entrepreneur need to be honored for his or her past work in the community or area in which the nonprofit organization provides services?
- Does the entrepreneur want to leave a legacy with his or her involvement?
- Is it important to the entrepreneur to be recognized for the his or her work, contributions, or involvement?

> **LIFES Tip**
>
> Do this exercise for your nonprofit organization: How many more _____ could be _____ if _____?
> For example, how many more children could be fed if we had $100,000 more in the budget? By conducting this exercise, you might discover opportunities that will appeal to entrepreneurs.

A recent study in 2008 by Bank of America of high net-worth philanthropy revealed that nearly 60% of wealthy households had stopped making charitable donations. According to the press release they, ". . . . attributed their change in philanthropic behavior to 'no longer feeling connected to the organization.'" The study further revealed the following themes for individuals with annual household incomes of $200,000 or more and/or a net-worth of at least one million dollars:

- A desire to "give back to the community" was the leading reason for giving
- "Public recognition" appears to be of little importance if not a non-factor
- Donors believed their charitable donations have a larger impact on their personal fulfillment than on the nonprofit organization(s) for which they provide financial support
- Families use involvement in philanthropic activities as a way to pass on their philanthropic values to the next generation
- Protection of privacy, accountability, and transparency are expectations that are key from donors of nonprofit organizations

ENTREPRENEURS' STRATEGIES FOR ENGAGEMENT WITH A NONPROFIT ORGANIZATION

Nonprofit organizations are looking for involvement from entrepreneurs. I have often said that in order to survive the challenges of the 21st century, nonprofit organizations will need to engage entrepreneurs. No longer will some of the tried and true methods of dealing with constituents, clients, and even donors be as effective as they used to be. One only has to think of how things have changed during the past 15 years, with the powerful rise of the Internet and the fact that most people now view the world in a global manner; change was rapid and will continue. Challenges that are currently recognized by the leadership of nonprofit organizations and those that will emerge will require out-of-the-box thinking, which is where the natural skills of an entrepreneur will be of immense value. Right now, nonprofit leaders are wrestling with the importance of having both high touch and high tech in their operations. Although they recognize the need for both, the path to achieving this goal is often fraught with politics, red tape, bureaucracy, and the ever-famous line that every entrepreneur cringes upon hearing—"because we have always done it that way."

Do not get pulled into the high technology trap using only email, Facebook, Twitter, and so on to communicate and reach out to entrepreneurs. Nonprofit organization staff and leaders need to meet face to face with entrepreneurs. Be high touch, not just high tech.

The question is, what strategies should an entrepreneur employ when considering engagement with a nonprofit organization? First realize that, similar to an entrepreneur's business, every nonprofit organization, no matter what its worthwhile cause, has the same challenges and issues. This means that in terms of personnel, budgeting, space, operations, and programming, all will not be smooth sailing. Many entrepreneurs make the mistake of thinking that all philanthropic and charitable efforts will be noble because of their causes and that the nonprofit organizations working to address these issues will be well equipped, if not perfect. Entrepreneurs may assume that the same issues that face them in their businesses do not exist in the nonprofit world. This assumption is incorrect.

As stated in Chapter 6, every nonprofit organization begins by filing for registration in a state as a corporation. Once it receives corporate status, the organization then applies to the federal government to become a tax-exempt organization, which in the language of the nonprofit world is known as a 501(c) (3), because this is the part of the IRS code that allows for tax exemption of charitable groups. But a funny thing happens: it appears that once you slap a nonprofit label on the organization—which, remember, started out as a corporation—somehow the best practices of the business world often fail to materialize. Entrepreneurs can bring a lot of business sense to the table in terms of providing guidance and help to nonprofit organizations.

Four Strategies to Employ

Find Nonprofit Organizations

The first strategy for an entrepreneur to employ when considering involvement with a nonprofit organization is to find and interview groups, agencies, and institutions that align with your areas of focus. As discussed in

Chapter 3, you should assess what you are currently doing, discover your values, and align these with your passion to create a plan for your philanthropic activities. It is important to find the right nonprofit organizations, ones that align with what you believe is important and where you want to spend your time and energy. Then make the call or send the email to begin your involvement.

Ask Questions

After determining the causes and nonprofit organizations you want to help, you must ask the questions that are important to you. For each entrepreneur this will be different. Some entrepreneurs will be interested in numbers and outcomes, some will be interested in timelines and overall objectives, and still others will be interested in who is serving on the board and who are the other donors. It is imperative for an entrepreneur to ask those questions even if it is difficult to begin the conversation. Most entrepreneurs I know want to be involved with a nonprofit organization that is able to answer these questions.

> ### LIFES Tip
> A word of caution to entrepreneurs: be careful of those nonprofit organizations that dodge answering questions. If they cannot or will not answer your questions at the beginning of the relationship when things are good, they will not answers questions when times get tough—and there are always tough times with nonprofit organizations.

Conduct Mini-Tests

Some entrepreneurs jump into working with nonprofit organizations head first and become fully immersed immediately. And sometimes this works. But because of the nuances of the philanthropic world, most entrepreneurs want to begin slowly, gathering information as they become more and more involved and knowledgeable about this new area in which they are investing their time and money. My recommendation, as shared in Chapter 2, is to begin by conducting what I call mini-tests with the nonprofit organizations you are considering.

The first test most entrepreneurs make is to contact the nonprofit organization either via phone or by email to see if anyone calls them back. If they do not, then the nonprofit organization has failed the test, and my advice is to move on and find another organization with which to become involved. A second test might be to make a modest donation to see how the money is spent and how you are treated as a donor. Again, this third test is to see how the nonprofit organization responds to ideas and suggestions. In other words, it is wedded to the status quo or willing to explore opportunities. You should compare these mini-tests to the way in which you interact with your business partners and vendors. My guess is that in most cases you moved slowly when first engaging them in your business. Most of the time you do not jump headfirst into a full-blown working relationship, but rather proceed with caution, checking references and work products. By conducting these mini-tests, you will begin to develop a sense of whether this is the right nonprofit organization for you to be working with on your charitable efforts.

Become Involved

After determining the areas with which you want to be involved, asking the questions, and conducting the mini-tests, you are ready to become involved—so become involved. Do more than just write a check: get to know the nonprofit organization and find ways to become involved. This might mean visiting the facilities and volunteering or serving on a committee or the board of directors. To fully appreciate the work that is being done through your financial support, however, you should get involved in other ways. As my mother often says, "In for a penny, in for a pound!" This old adage definitely holds true for entrepreneurs wanting to become involved in the nonprofit world, especially when their focus is to help others. You also need to decide how much time and money you want to spend in your philanthropic activities. Depending on your life's activities, there will be times when you have more to give both in terms of volunteering and donations than at other times. This is all right, because life and your philanthropic role will ebb and flow.

Evaluating a Nonprofit Organization Annually

Evaluating a nonprofit organization is a key strategy often overlooked by donors. It is important to evaluate on some sort of regular basis the efforts and resources directed toward nonprofit activities. I recommend a three-step process.

1. Evaluate how the nonprofit organization responds to the questions you ask. Does it provide answers? Are the answers received on a timely basis? Do you feel comfortable with the answers you are receiving?
2. Did you see the results you were expecting? In other words, did your donation cause the change to occur? Were more children fed? Was the facility built? Did the additional staff get hired? Was the program expanded to the next level? Whatever you were expecting to occur with your involvement and financial donation, did it occur?

3. Were you excited about your involvement? For example, did you get excited about what you were doing? Think back to how you felt when your business landed a big contract or when you hired a new person who was outstanding. That same type of feeling should be translated into your philanthropic activities. Again, I encourage both entrepreneurs and leaders of nonprofit organizations to read the interview with David Weinberg and learn about his way of assessing his continuing interests in various nonprofit organizations through the use of his Passion-O-Meter (see the section "Entrepreneurial Stories"). His system is truly fascinating but simple, and best of all, it works!

Education

Once you decide to become involved in the nonprofit world or with a particular organization, it is imperative that you become educated: do research and learn about the organization and philanthropy. Appendix H lists several outstanding books recommended to further the education of those wishing to be involved.

Also, use the Internet for locating information. While there are classes and conferences you can attend, I urge you to talk to others involved in philanthropic activities. Ask to be assigned a mentor from the nonprofit organization who will provide guidance and support as you learn about the intricacies and nuances of philanthropy.

> **LIFES Tip**
> If you choose to serve in a volunteer leadership role in a nonprofit organization, become educated by reading books, talking to others, and learning more.

MAKING A DIFFERENCE

The first thing one learns when working with entrepreneurs is that they are focused on making a difference. It begins with the work they do in their businesses and extends to their activities in the philanthropic world. They will begin to fill a niche in the philanthropic arena that is not being met. Entrepreneurs will find great success and comfort in their lives by becoming involved strategically in the nonprofit world.

> **LIFES Tip**
> It should be noted that in this post–9/11 world, most individuals want to make a difference, recognizing that it is not how much money, houses, or cars one has that is important, but how many lives one has affected.

Dietlin's Discussion Directives

1. Name the four research methods a nonprofit organization can use when trying to obtain information about an entrepreneur.

2. Which is recommended as the best and most reliable research method?

3. What strategies should nonprofit organizations use to engage entrepreneurs?

4. How can you keep an entrepreneur involved with the nonprofit organization?

5. Name the successful business cycles in which an entrepreneur will be more likely to respond to a request for a financial donation.

6. Name the four strategies entrepreneurs should follow when beginning to consider involvement in the philanthropic world.

7. Name the three evaluation steps that an entrepreneur should follow annually to ensure that a good nonprofit experience continues to exist.

8. Discuss with the nonprofit organization you select how you want to make a difference.

9. Discuss with your family how you want to make a difference, and work to possibly involve them in your plans.

Chapter 9

Honor, Recognition, and Some Networking

HONORING AND RECOGNIZING ENTREPRENEURIAL DONORS

One of the most common mistakes made by nonprofit organizations and their leadership lies in how they honor and recognize entrepreneurs. The most overlooked step of interacting with donors is thanking them. It is necessary to find a way to be grateful, sincere, and—most of all—genuine in appreciation of a donation. I counsel my clients to embrace this step and find meaningful ways to be thankful for donations. Again, I often suggest they think of how they feel when they give a present to a friend. If the friend asks whether he or she can open the gift right away, most of us feel pretty good. However, if the friend takes the gift, politely says thank you, and disappears with it, we often do not know what to make of the situation.

This problem needs to be remembered when thinking about how to recognize and honor all donors to nonprofit organizations, but especially entrepreneurs. The reason I am suggesting it could be more important with entrepreneurs is that they are not as familiar with the philanthropic world. As noted in Chapter 8, they often feel only one step away from losing it all. Thanking them will help ensure they remain lifelong donors.

BEING CREATIVE

As shared, entrepreneurs are creative, and nonprofit organizations must to be able to deal with their creativity and respond appropriately. It is imperative to remember that the entrepreneurs who make donations to nonprofit organizations are generally very successful individuals who usually can purchase or get anything they need or want. As I have been heard to say frequently, "No one needs another walnut plaque." What donors need, especially entrepreneurs, is meaningful stewardship and sincere gratefulness. In my opinion, this is not accomplished by a standard walnut plaque or typical donor wall listing.

Creativity comes in many forms and can be achieved by nonprofit organizations of any size, regardless of budget. Some of the best thank-you gifts I have learned about did not cost exorbitant amounts of money but were very thoughtful. Take the university in the Midwest that, when working with a donor couple who had met, dated, and fell in love during their days on campus, heard them share a story about putting their names in wet cement on a sidewalk that was being poured. The couple wondered aloud during a conversation with the university staff whether the sidewalk cement with their names was still there. The staff of the university listened closely and then cleverly decided to find the sidewalk. They found it, did a rubbing, framed and presented it as a thank-you gift to the donor couple. Imagine their surprise when they received this gift. Imagine how special this type of gift was to them. This is the type of creativity that is needed when working with donors, especially entrepreneurs. Remember, entrepreneurs are business people who found a niche in the marketplace that was not being filled and filled it. They are unique and different. The stewardship of these individuals needs to be unique and different as well.

For some entrepreneurs, attaining the status of being recognized as philanthropists brings them to a new level of acceptance within their communities—or at least this is what they believe. Entrepreneurs take many routes to being successful, with a number of them forgoing a formal postsecondary education in order to bring their ideas to the marketplace. In other words, some entrepreneurs may feel as if they have to prove themselves worthy of the success they have attained, and one way to do this is to give back to the community via philanthropic donations.

> ### LIFES Tip
>
> Most donors say they don't want the standard premiums that accompany donations of a certain size. They do not want the nonprofit organization to spend its resources on a trinket such as a coffee cup, pen, t-shirt, or mailing labels. However, in my experience there are three things most donors appreciate and will not toss: books, music CDs, and framed photos. In our society, we do not throw away books, we are apt to listen to a music CD, and we are likely to display a framed photo from an event.

CREATIVITY, PART TWO

Jack Wilson is a very successful entrepreneur and President and Founder of JWA Videos, one of the country's leading producers in business to business videos as well as training videos and television specials. He recently told me that when times get tough, as they can in the entrepreneurial world, he purposely gives more to nonprofit organizations. Jack and I met as he serves on the board of directors for Easter Seals Metropolitan Chicago, one of my company's clients. Jack shared with me that he cringes every time he hears others, especially entrepreneurs saying that because business has slowed down they are not going to give to the nonprofits they have supported in the past. Jack believes just the opposite. When business is slowing down, that is the perfect time for increasing your philanthropic engagements. He has found that every time he does this, his business improves. As Jack says, "The more you put out there, the more it returns to you." This is important to know because nonprofit organizations are often not very creative about keeping individuals, especially entrepreneurs, engaged when they state they need to lessen their activities or leave the nonprofit organization because of their business demands.

When I served as the assistant dean of development at the University of Illinois' College of Business Administration, I strived to be very creative with the business advisory council members when they would indicate they needed to resign from the council. I focused on keeping them engaged if the reason they gave was that they were too busy with their businesses, especially if it was because the business was slowing down or they had hit the proverbial bump in the road. One example is when Scott Gordon, who was then the chairman of the Chicago Mercantile Exchange, informed me that he was going to have to step down from the business advisory council. Scott was very important to us because he was the link the College of Business Administration had to the four financial exchanges that operate in Chicago. Scott shared with me that the reason he needed to resign was that he was flying every week to Washington, DC, and testifying before Congress trying to secure approval to take the Chicago Mercantile Exchange public. Scott was feeling guilty that he was not able to attend business advisory council meetings or committee meetings.

I asked Scott whether he would consider taking a sabbatical from council service, meaning he did not have to attend the meetings, but he would have to take on a special project. The special project was hosting a breakfast or lunch with all the chairmen and presidents of the four financial exchanges for the college's dean and Finance Department head. My reasoning was that the College of Business Administration at the University of Illinois at Chicago is an outstanding business school, but is often overlooked due to having Northwestern University and the University of Chicago in the same town. Scott readily agreed, and within four months (primarily because of scheduling conflicts), the dean, department head, and I had breakfast with the leaders from the four financial exchanges in Chicago. The best outcome was achieved because the four financial exchanges agreed to work together to teach a graduate-level class, collaborate with the college's researchers, and attend a function with the students. This would not have occurred if Scott and I had not been creative about ways he could stay involved while he was pursuing an opportunity that would transform the Chicago Mercantile Exchange. By being creative, the final outcome was a win-win situation. Scott was recognized and honored at the advisory council meeting and in the college's magazine for his outstanding efforts to further develop the relationship and to position the college well in the eyes of the financial exchanges.

COMMON MISTAKES AND ASSUMPTIONS

Nonprofit organizations make a number of assumptions and hence mistakes when trying to recognize and honor entrepreneurs. Knowing what these are and taking the necessary steps to avoid common mistakes and assumptions can only benefit the nonprofit organization.

1. Mistake/Assumption: The bigger the gift, the bigger the recognition. Truth: This is not necessarily true. As a matter of fact, there are a number of entrepreneurs who make large financial donations anonymously with little fanfare or public acknowledgement. Discussions must take place between the donor and the nonprofit organization's leadership regarding expectations.

2. Mistake/Assumption: All donors, especially entrepreneurs, want to be recognized.

   Truth: Not all donors want to be recognized. One simply has to look at the annual reports of nonprofit organizations to view the number of anonymous donations. Some donors, and this includes entrepreneurs, prefer that others not know how wealthy they are or what they are doing.

3. Mistake/Assumption: Once you honor the entrepreneur, it is done.

   Truth: This is not true. The old adage is to thank a donor seven times. This does not mean sending seven thank-you letters or making seven phone calls in one day to the donor, but rather finding ways to be sincerely grateful for the donor, especially if the individual is an entrepreneur who is making his or her first philanthropic donation.

4. Mistake/Assumption: Not listening or paying attention.

   Truth: Although we are often applauded for multitasking in our society, it is very important when working with entrepreneurs that a nonprofit organization listen and pay attention to what they are saying. Nonprofit organization leaders will often hear something unique or telling about the entrepreneur's future thoughts regarding possible increased involvement through what he or she says.

5. Mistake/Assumption: Entrepreneurs trying to outdo each other.

   Truth: Entrepreneurs do not often try to outdo each other. Remember, entrepreneurs by definition are unique individuals and often loners. They did not go to work in corporate America—or if they did they have left—and usually do not follow the paths of others. The same is true in the philanthropic world. Entrepreneurs will want to do their own thing and not try to outdo one another.

6. Mistake/Assumption: Give an expensive thank-you gift to show appreciation.

   Truth: Entrepreneurs who are successful can usually buy anything they want or need. It is not prudent for a nonprofit organization to try to think of an expensive gift to give them. I have found two things that always seem to work well: providing them an experience they could not otherwise have and sending flowers. Although entrepreneurs can usually buy anything they desire, they cannot buy sitting with the Big Ten football coach during a game, decorating a holiday tree with foster children, touring behind the stage of the ballet, and so on. Find a unique experience. And remember, flowers do say it all. As Christian Slater's character, Lewis Farrell says in the movie *Bed of Roses*, everyone smiles when they receive flowers. This is true!

> *LIFES Tip*
>
> I recently was invited through a friend to attend a private concert given by Brooks and Dunn at the home of Ronnie Dunn. The concert was a fundraiser for the school that Ronnie's daughter attended. The event was incredible because it took place in his backyard and everything was top notch. My host, Sylvia, was a very successful entrepreneur with access to anything she wants. My dilemma was what to send her as a thank-you gift for the ticket, backstage passes, a photo with Ronnie and Kix, and an afterparty at her home. My answer was flowers, which she greatly appreciated. Remember, flowers really do express appreciation!

NETWORKING DONE RIGHT

Another way to honor entrepreneurs is to help them and their businesses by providing networking opportunities. I have often had entrepreneurs thank me for providing opportunities that allowed them to expand and grow their business. These were opportunities I did not know I was providing, because, in my mind, I was simply doing my job. But through paying attention, listening, and acting upon best instincts, things happened that allowed entrepreneurs who served in various volunteer capacities to have their businesses flourish and grow.

I have witnessed many times the "getting it back 10 times over" theory that most entrepreneurs hold about their involvement in philanthropic work. The first time I saw it happen was when I was working at Michigan Technological University. An alumnus that I will call Bob, who was an entrepreneur, was back on campus for the Homecoming activities as well as being interviewed for a board position. While in meetings with the staff, Bob began talking about a problem he was having with an item his company manufactured. One of the staff members suggested he speak to the CEO of a *Fortune* 500 company, who I will call Don, who happened to serve on the board for which Bob was being recruited as well as being a fellow alumnus. To make matters even better, at the time this discussion was taking place, Don was standing a mere 10 feet away. As you can imagine, great things happened for both Bob and Don on many levels. And it all began because Bob, an entrepreneur, was willing to give of his time to his alma mater. Both Bob and Don believed in giving back and making a difference and, in doing so, made a difference in both of their businesses.

Another story involves my work with a university on the east coast. The associate vice president for institutional advancement had met with an alumnus who worked for the federal government and was able to provide loans to farmers but needed financial institutions to participate. The associate vice president identified banks that were owned and operated by alumni of the university and facilitated the introductions of the individuals and the federal program. Again, it was a win-win situation: because these individuals chose to begin giving their time, they ended up having a business opportunity that might not have been realized if not for their involvement with a nonprofit organization, in this case, their alma mater. Another win for this story is that the farmers, who are entrepreneurs, also benefitted.

CONNECTING AND RECONNECTING ENTREPRENEURS

When working in the philanthropic arena, there are opportunities to connect and reconnect entrepreneurs with the nonprofit organization on a daily basis. You have to be mindful of the potential connections. Whether it is programs or people, there are always introductions and relationships to be made that will create winning scenarios for all involved. These connections and introductions will also deepen the relationship and commitment to the nonprofit organization. The relationship will grow organically, and there will be opportunities for all.

> **LIFES Tip**
>
> I believe that working in and with nonprofit organizations is similar to putting together a giant jigsaw puzzle. All the pieces are there—you simply have to locate them and, in a systemic or organized way, put them together so they fit nicely.

Here is another illustration of how connections and networking can work when done right. Al Johnson is an entrepreneur who was the first African American to have a GM dealership for cars (see the section "Entrepreneurial Stories" for his complete story). When I began working at the University of Illinois at Chicago (UIC) for the College of Business Administration, Al served as a member on the Business Advisory Council, which was a group providing advice and counsel to the dean of the college. Al and I became acquainted during my first day on the job. About nine months later, Al came into my office carrying a book entitled *You Can Make It Happen*, written by Stedman Graham. Al gave me the book and suggested I read it. I immediately began thinking about what message Al was sending me. Did he think I was not doing my job, not making it happen? Is this why he gave me the book? Al could see my puzzlement and shared that he knew Stedman and wanted to get him involved with the College of Business Administration at UIC.

It took me a few months to find time to read the book, but once I did, I realized that Stedman, an entrepreneur, would be a perfect fit with the college's Institute of Entrepreneurial Studies (IES), which was housed in the Department of Managerial Studies. I arranged for the dean, the director of the IES program, and me to meet with Stedman to ask him if he would consider teaching at the College of Business Administration. To our great delight, Stedman said yes, and again another win-win situation was created whereby an entrepreneur who was constantly giving back to nonprofit organizations was receiving something in return. Stedman was being given the opportunity to expose students to his knowledge and experience as an entrepreneur and successful businessperson. The students learned much, and Stedman became a friend and supporter of the College of Business Administration at UIC.

This is how networking is done right. It is easy, not forced, and creates the best outcomes.

When I worked at Michigan Technological University (MTU) in Houghton, Michigan, which is located in the Upper Peninsula, I had the privilege of meeting Suzanne Jurva. Suzanne is an alumnus of the Scientific and Technical Communication (STC) program and worked for Steven Spielberg at Dreamworks. To my great surprise, a number of development officers at MTU were anxious about meeting her. The result was that no one had traveled to California to meet with her. So, in January 1994, when there was about 15 feet of snow on the ground, I boarded a plane to Los Angeles to meet with Suzanne. I went to the offices of the Dreamworks Studios in Hollywood and was in awe of who Suzanne was. Her entrepreneurial spirit was clear to see. It should be noted that Suzanne currently works as an independent film producer, having just completed the film *Changing Keys* about Billy McLaughlin and his battle with focal dystonia (see the section "Entrepreneurial Stories" for her story).

When I met her, my first question was, how did she come to work for Steven Spielberg? Her reply was that he had read her script, "The Prince of Egypt," and while buying it offered her a job as head of research for his new studio. Suzanne was his first hire for a new collaboration with Jeffrey Katzenberg and David Geffen; these two men plus Spielberg are entrepreneurs. Suzanne and I had a few meetings over the next few years, both in Hollywood and her college town of Houghton. After three or four meetings, Suzanne asked me what I wanted, to which I replied that I wanted to have the world premier of her film, The *Prince of Egypt*, in Houghton. She incredulously asked me why. I said it was because she had written it. She readily told me that was not possible because the film was being handled by Jeffrey Katzenberg and was going to premier at the White House. Suzanne continued her questioning, asking me why I didn't want the first film out of the Dreamworks Studios. I asked her what that movie was, to which she replied *The Peacemaker*, starring Nicole Kidman and George Clooney. She said it was about science and technology and would be perfect for the MTU environment, which educates primarily engineers and scientists. I said yes and she made a call. To the great surprise of both of us, the Dreamworks Studios said yes. In the end a small community with a population of approximately 7,000 people had the world premier of Steven Spielberg's first film from his new studios, beating New York City's premier by 20 minutes! This was a very entrepreneurial endeavor by all who were involved.

LIFES Tip

If networking, connecting, and reconnecting is done right, entrepreneurs will usually ask you what they can do to provide assistance to your program. In other words, you do not have to ask for donations or assistance for the nonprofit organization; these individuals will ask what they can do to help and offer opportunities, such as premiering a major studio film—things you perhaps would not think possible.

THE KEVIN BACON GAME, OR SIX DEGREES OF SEPARATION

I assume most people have heard of the two games mentioned in the section head, which, when played, identify how many degrees of separation there are between individuals. The Kevin Bacon Game focuses on how many degrees of separation there are between other actors and Kevin Bacon. For example, you could ask about the relationship or degrees of separation between Elvis Presley and Kevin Bacon, given that the two never starred in a movie together. The following solution is from Wikipedia:

- Elvis Presley was in *Change of Habit* (1969) with Edward Asner
- Edward Asner was in *JFK* (1991) with Kevin Bacon

Therefore Ed Asner has a Bacon number of 1 while Elvis Presley (who never appeared in a film with Bacon himself) has a Bacon number of 2.

The game Six Degrees of Separation works in the same way, with individuals when they meet declaring they probably somehow know someone in common. By playing this game, individuals become acquainted in a risk-free manner.

The reason I mention the details of these two games is that in working with entrepreneurs I have seen this type of game played over and over again. It is important to entrepreneurs and the growth of their businesses to be connected to others. It is through doing this that they are successful.

I witnessed this first hand when working with David Weinberg (see the section "Entrepreneurial Stories" for more details), who chaired the Business Advisory Council for the College of Business Administration at UIC. David, a very successful entrepreneur, often played a leadership and pivotal role in courting high-profile and high-net-worth individuals to become involved with the College of Business Administration. After one particular meeting, David and I met with the potential donor to have a drink. I was amazed by David and the other entrepreneur's gamesmanship in playing this game. As David later said, "Oh, that was just Jewish geography." In other words, David and the entrepreneur, who both happen to be Jewish, were figuring out who they knew in common. It was amazing. So whether you call it the Kevin Bacon Game, Six Degrees of Separation, or Jewish Geography, it is a way that individuals use to get to know each other better. What is more important is that by becoming involved with nonprofit organizations, entrepreneurs are likely to reap even greater benefits. Nonprofit organizations need to find ways for these types of games to be played by entrepreneurs with which they want to become involved.

HONOR AND RECOGNITION OF THE WORK BEING DONE BY NONPROFIT ORGANIZATIONS

Entrepreneurs should recognize the work being done by nonprofit organizations. Too often, entrepreneurs only see the work that is not being done and where they can help. This is natural given that this is what they do every day in their businesses. They seize upon opportunities that are not currently being met by others in the same arena and fill it. This allows them to start a business or grow the one they have to the next level. However, in the nonprofit arena, there could be any number of reasons why certain things, such as programs, projects, classes, treatments, and so on, are not being implemented. My best recommendation to entrepreneurs is to honor and recognize the work that is being done by the more than 1.5 million nonprofit organizations. Most are doing a really good job. Most are trying to address the ills, challenges, and problems that exist in their world as well as capitalize on the opportunities being presented. Rushing to judgment is never a prudent thing to do, and this holds true for the philanthropic arena as well.

When entrepreneurs begin to become involved with nonprofit organizations, they should realize they are not the experts. They are outsiders attempting to learn about the challenges and opportunities that exist in this area. Sometimes, a well-known success or a well-publicized failure has brought them to the nonprofit organization.

Entrepreneurs likely become aware of a situation in the charitable world that needs addressing and with which they would like to become involved through individuals they know, a personal experience or through media coverage, which today is available all the time. There are many opportunities and ways to help nonprofit organizations, but the first step, as previously stated, is to recognize and honor the good work they have done to date, or at minimum to try to understand the overall nonprofit organization. Do not just focus on the problem. To bring about a sustainable solution, it will be necessary to have all the information at hand, reviewed, and understood.

KEY UNDERSTANDINGS FOR ENTREPRENEURS

When becoming involved and working with nonprofit organizations, entrepreneurs should have some key understandings. These understandings will help an entrepreneur recognize and honor the good work of nonprofit organizations.

1. Understanding: Traditions in nonprofit organizations are important. Rationale: It is important to recognize there are traditions within each nonprofit organization. As a potential supporter, you should ask about the history and why the gala, golf outing, walk, program, or other project takes place. How did it start? How long has it been taking place? Do annual evaluations take place? By asking these types of questions you will learn about the traditions and be able to affect change when and where necessary.

2. Understanding: You can't save everyone.
   Rationale: When individuals, particularly entrepreneurs, become involved in the charitable world, they hope to save everyone. There is a desire that every hungry child will be fed, every homeless person will have a place to live, that cancer will be cured, and that scholarships will be available to all who want to attend school—and the list goes on. This is not realistic. By becoming involved, you will make a difference, but there will most likely always be needs beyond what the nonprofit organization can provide in services.

3. Understanding: Sometimes "no" is really the right answer.
   Rationale: "No" is a hard word for entrepreneurs to hear, let alone accept. It is essential however, in the nonprofit world for the word "no" to be heard. To be successful in causing the change most entrepreneurs seek, there will likely be times when choices have to be made because of the limited resources of nonprofit organizations. This is true regardless of the size of the nonprofit organization: even the Bill and Melinda Gates Foundation has to make choices.

4. Understanding: Your way may not be the right way.
   Rationale: Again, this is a very difficult idea for some entrepreneurs to accept. But those entrepreneurs who are accustomed to and comfortable with having individuals around them who are smarter than they are will understand this concept. Again, each nonprofit organization has a history, traditions, and policies; some even have regulations and laws to follow. The reason your way may not be the right way could be because of one of these considerations.

5. Understanding: You cannot make demands.
   Rationale: Entrepreneurs are used to making demands. That is not a negative statement. Making demands is one of the ways in which entrepreneurs have been successful in achieving their desired goals. They know what the company needs to do in order to be the expert

in the marketplace. Entrepreneurs need to realize that they cannot make demands on the nonprofit organization, however. There are many factors that affect why a nonprofit organization operates the way it does. Simply swooping in and making demands that will "fix" the perceived situation is not the answer. It is vital for an entrepreneur to recognize that making demands will not necessarily fix or even alter the situation. Entrepreneurs need to work with nonprofit organizations, bringing their ideas to the table in a collaborative manner.

6. Understanding: You can really make a difference.
   Rationale: Most entrepreneurs know this in their businesses, but it holds true in the nonprofit world as well. An entrepreneur's involvement, both in terms of time, knowledge, and financial resources, really can make a difference.

The most important thing to remember is that there usually is a reason or a situation that has caused a nonprofit organization to have certain traditions, policies, and procedures. In working with nonprofit organizations, the goal is to understand the evolution to this point, honor it, and then try to take the organization to the next level. In some instances, this might be possible. In other situations, an entrepreneur might have to work within the confines that exist.

Dietlin's Discussion Directives

1. Name three of the six mistakes made when recognizing and honoring entrepreneurs.
2. Name three of the six understandings that are necessary when interacting with nonprofit organizations.
3. What are the three things donors are likely never to throw away and maybe will even treasure?
4. What factors affect the traditions that often exist in a nonprofit organization?
5. Describe a creative way in which a nonprofit organization can honor and recognize entrepreneurs.
6. How often should a donor be thanked?

Chapter 10

Social Entrepreneurs

WHAT IS A SOCIAL ENTREPRENEUR?

Social entrepreneur is a confusing term and a relatively new one, but it is gaining a lot of traction these days in the business as well as the nonprofit world. Social entrepreneurs, by whatever name they have been called, have been around for centuries, however. They are individuals with big ideas whose influence results in the reconstruction of whole social and economic systems. They identify and solve social problems on a large scale. They are change agents for society, forcing us to think differently about a problem or situation. Through their efforts, social entrepreneurs allow us to view things with a different lens. They work to transform a situation, people, or society.

HISTORICAL SOCIAL ENTREPRENEURS

Although we tend to think social entrepreneurship is a relatively new phenomenon, if you do a simple Internet search you will find people from the 19th and 20th centuries such as Florence Nightingale, John Muir, Dr. Maria Montessori, Susan B. Anthony, and Frederick Law Olmstead listed and viewed as social entrepreneurs. These were individuals who made a difference both short and long term. Here is a short synopsis of the efforts of each.

- Florence Nightingale became a nurse, much to the chagrin of her family, and fought to improve hospital conditions during the Crimean War, which in the short term affected the care and recovery of wounded soldiers. Long term, Florence eventually established the first school for nurses, thus affecting the treatment of injured people for perpetuity.

- John Muir worked with President Theodore Roosevelt to establish the national park system in the United States, including the first federal set aside of land for protection as an inalienable public trust: the Yosemite Valley and the Mariposa Grove of Giant Sequoias to the state of California, which in 1890 became Yosemite National Park. It is thought that this act which took place in 1864 lead to Yellowstone National Park being established in 1872 as the first national park in the United States. John Muir helped immediately to protect beautiful lands in the United States, and in the long term allowed them to be enjoyed for years to come by many generations.
- Most of us have heard of the Montessori Schools. It is because of the efforts of Dr. Maria Montessori that they exist. She believed children should teach themselves. In 1906 she founded Casa dei Bambini, or the Children's House, in Rome, where her beliefs and theories about children doing things by themselves became a reality in action. She changed children's lives immediately, and her work changed the way we think about children and how to instruct them; her Montessori method is now used throughout the entire world.
- Susan B. Anthony and her work with the women's suffrage movement in the United States is something with which many individuals are familiar. Through her efforts and intense energy, the 19th Amendment, which guarantees a woman's right to vote, was adopted. Her work led to change in a society where women were asking and demanding to be treated equally. In the short term, her contemporaries achieved something none of their mothers, grandmothers, or any women in their families had obtained—the right to vote. Long term, Susan B. Anthony transformed the way we think about and treat women.
- Frederick Law Olmstead and his work transformed cities, especially urban centers. He is recognized as the founder of American landscape architecture as well as the nation's foremost park maker. He is the architect who created New York City's Central Park, which won a design competition in its day. He also created the Rock Creek Park in Washington, DC, and Boston's Emerald Necklace, which stretches from the Boston Common downtown to the Arnold Arboretum and Franklin Park in Roslindale and Roxbury and is one of the oldest series of public parks and parkways in the United States. During his life, Frederick Law Olmstead transformed the urban landscape of several cities, but long term, he and his work changed the way society thinks about landscape architecture.

DOING BUSINESS FOR SOCIAL REASONS EQUALS SOCIAL ENTREPRENEURSHIP

So, specifically, what is social entrepreneurship? Social entrepreneurship is described in various publications and research literature as applying business models to solving social problems. The social entrepreneurship movement has primarily focused on issues such as disease, homelessness, hunger, poverty, unemployment, and pollution, trying to align their solutions with the business enterprise model.

There is a distinct difference between business entrepreneurs and social entrepreneurs, and even the nonprofit sector. The first difference between business entrepreneurs and social entrepreneurs is the profit component. A business entrepreneur focuses on seeking the greatest possible profit for the product or service provided, whereas a social entrepreneur focuses on seeking or increasing a social value in return for products or services offered. Second, although the social entrepreneur might sound like a nonprofit organization enterprise, there are differences. Primarily, social entrepreneurs are looking for both immediate and maybe even incremental changes while still seeing the broader, long-term, and -lasting changes possible, and they might make a profit. A nonprofit organization exists to serve a purpose, mission, and vision. It does not exist to make a profit. It should be noted that some businesses, too, say they exist for a purpose or mission first, with profit being secondary.

It is said that social entrepreneurs can identify solutions where others see only problems. They truly believe in teaching individuals how to fish instead of simply giving them a fish. Entrepreneurs recall the old adage that if you give a person a fish they will eat for a day, but if you teach them how to fish they will eat for life, meaning they will be able to take care of themselves.

THE BEGINNINGS OF SOCIAL ENTREPRENEURSHIP

In the July 14, 2008, issue, *Crain's Chicago Business* describes social entrepreneurs as "Entrepreneurs who try to fix social problems—and profit." The five examples cited in the beginning of this chapter illustrate this point. But where did the recent push for social entrepreneurs really begin? Although numerous individuals have been cited as starting the movement of social entrepreneurship in modern times, there are several who deserve to be credited.

One of them is Al Whittaker, who founded the company Opportunity International in 1971 in Latin America. Mr. Whittaker, who was the former president of Bristol Myers International Corporation, thought that giving the poor a working chance was important to society and the economy. Almost simultaneously, David Bussau, an Australian entrepreneur, began a similar program in Indonesia. In 1974 their two organizations merged. The initial purpose of Opportunity International was not finding work for the poor, but helping them to create or expand their businesses by providing loans and job training directly to poor people. Once the initial loans have been paid back, the businesses have grown or expanded and the cycle of chronic poverty, which Colin Powell stated is "the greatest moral challenge of the 21st century," has been altered. Opportunity International now serves over one million clients annual 14. What is amazing is that 98% of the loans are paid back with market-rate interest and on time. This fact contradicts the long-held belief that poor people are not a good credit risk because they do not pay back their loans.

Al Whittaker, like Dr. Yunus, who you will read about shortly, knew that poor people need access to credit in order to break the cycle of poverty. Research has shown, for example, that there is often food available where people are going hungry—the real impediment is access to funds to buy the food. Microfinance or microcredit is a way to empower individuals to break the cycle of poverty.

MODERN-DAY SOCIAL ENTREPRENEURS

A few examples of current social entrepreneurs will assist in illustrating the point that you can cause social change while doing good in the world and making a profit.

Albina Ruiz and Ciudad Saludable

When Albina Ruiz was attending college in Peru, studying to be an industrial engineer, she could not help but notice the garbage piling up in the streets, which inevitably led to health and environmental problems. Albina came up with an idea for a new community-managed system of garbage collection. It was her dream that if her idea worked in the test area, which was El Cono Norte in Lima, it could be replicated throughout Peru. The situation in El Cono Norte was that 16 million individuals lived there, producing 600 metric tons of garbage daily. The local authorities could only collect and process about half this amount. People had no choice but to throw the garbage that was not collected into the streets, vacant lots, and rivers.

Albina's idea was to have small-business people from the community, micro-entrepreneurs, be responsible for collecting and processing the garbage. This idea led to another community problem being helped—that is, the number of individuals who were unemployed. Albina initially helped these micro-entrepreneurs (a majority of whom are women) become established and set the monthly fee for service at $1.50. She even helped with the marketing to convince individuals, families, and households to use this service and pay on time. The end result was the creation of Ciudad Saludable, which develops solid waste management systems, generating employment and leading not only to cleaner cities but also to a better quality of life for all.

Albina is also educating individuals about protecting the environment. Some of the micro-entrepreneurs have created other profitable businesses by making things such as organic fertilizer out of the garbage they collect. Finally, because of Ciudad Saludable's education and marketing, 98% of their clients pay for garbage pickup, whereas the government has a pickup payment rate of 40%. Albina Ruiz is a social entrepreneur who has affected change on at least four levels in her community:

- Collecting garbage systematically by establishing micro-entrepreneurial businesses
- Reducing unemployment
- Generating understanding of the importance of the environment
- Encouraging on-time payment for services

Dr. Muhammad Yunus and Grameen Bank

Another social entrepreneur, who also happened to win the Nobel Peace Prize in 2006, is Dr. Muhammad Yunus, founder of the Grameen Bank. Dr. Yunus believes that every individual has the right to credit. To him it is a fundamental human right. His overall goal was to help poor people escape poverty and its cycle by providing loans to them on terms they could meet. He also thought it important to provide a few basic financial principles, thus allowing them to better help themselves in their businesses and lives.

Dr. Yunus is an economics professor and Bangladeshi banker. He began helping destitute basket weavers living in Bangladesh in the 1970s through small loans. He soon realized these small loans had a huge impact on a poor person's ability to break the cycle of poverty, thus helping the individual to avoid the usurious rates so often found with other lenders. Dr. Yunus knew that a financial institution had to be created to lend to those who had no collateral or other resources. He recognized that the existing financial institutions were not interested in making small loans at reasonable interest rates because they thought the repayment rate from poor people would be low. Dr. Yunus thought the opposite and was right.

On October 1, 1983, the Grameen Bank was opened to make loans to the poor people of Bangladesh. One of its focus groups was women borrowers, who did not have to have collateral but only the ability to prove they were poor and that their family owned less than one-half acre of land. Both the liberal and conservative ends of the spectrum were resistant to the idea and made an outcry. To these naysayers, much success is the answer. Billions of dollars have been loaned to millions of individuals. Repayment is ensured because the bank uses a system of what it calls solidarity groups, which are groups of individuals applying together for a loan and holding each other accountable for paying it back. The success that the Grameen Bank and Dr. Yunus has seen has been replicated in 100 countries in both the developing and even the industrialized world. It has been said that Dr. Yunus's idea has been the single most important development in third world countries in the last 100 years.

Mimi Silbert and the Delancey Street Foundation

Finally, Mimi Silbert is a social entrepreneur, having founded the Delancey Street Foundation in San Francisco, California, in 1971. Her dream was to have a place where former felons, substance abusers, and others who had hit rock bottom would have an opportunity, through their own efforts, to turn their life around. This vision, which began with a one thousand dollar loan and four residents, has now blossomed into the reality of a large organization grossing $20 million annually and serving individuals in other locations, including Los Angeles, New Mexico, New York, North Carolina, and Stockbridge, Massachusetts. What is amazing is that the Delancey Street Foundation has never accepted any government funding and has helped more than 14,000 people who now lead crime-free and drug-free lives fully integrated into society.

The foundation does not cost the client any money. It funds itself through revenue generated by the businesses it operates. According to its website:

> Delancey Street is considered a pioneer of social entrepreneurship development in America—developing business skills to help solve social problems. Since 1972, Delancey Street has created 12 successful ventures that have trained residents in marketable skills, created positive interactions

between residents and customers in the community, and helped support the organization financially. These include:

- Crossroads Café, Bookstore & Art Gallery
- Catering & Event Planning
- Delancey Coach (Corporate Private Car Service)
- Digital Print Shop
- Handcrafted Furniture, Ironworks, Plants & Glass, Ceramics
- Landscaping
- Moving and Trucking
- Paratransit Van & Bus Services
- Restaurant
- Screening Room
- Specialty Advertising Sales
- Christmas Tree Sales and Decorating

While our enterprises' pooled earnings provide about 60% of our annual budget, our emphasis has always been people before profit. Our goals of

1. Teach residents to interact positively with the public;
2. Help educate the public about the positive changes ex-felons and former substance abusers can make;
3. Teach marketable skills to the formerly unskilled; and
4. Earn income.

Mimi Silbert is an example of an individual who saw a problem and built a business to solve it that, as she says, focuses on the people it serves, not on the profit gained in solving the problem.

Compassionate Capitalism

Another term that is used to describe social entrepreneurship is *compassionate capitalism*. As Jack Kemp, chairman of Empower America, and Chris Crane, CEO of Opportunity International, state in an article published in *The Washington Times*, compassionate capitalism is really venture capitalism that energizes the spirit of entrepreneurship among the working poor.

Dr. Govindappa Venkataswany, or Dr. V. as he is often called, and David Green know this first hand. To them compassionate capitalism is giving sight back to millions of individuals who would be blind if not for their intervention. It began, according to The New Heroes website, with Dr. V. realizing as a young person that "intelligence and capability are not enough. There must be the joy of doing something beautiful." At an age at which most of us retire, Dr. V. mortgaged his house and set up a hospital to perform free or low-cost cataract surgery on poor Indians. During his first year, he performed 5,000 surgeries.

Upon learning about Dr. V's effort, David Green was inspired, too, recognizing that at the end of life it is not how rich we have been or are, but how many people we have helped along the way. Working with Dr. V., he opened a lens factory manufacturing lenses at the cost of $10 per pair instead of the $150 usually charged. To these two men, compassionate capitalism is taking a small profit from each item served but having a high sales volume. By doing this, not only can a profit be achieved, but lives can be transformed; in this particular example, people can see. Dr. V. and David Green are social entrepreneurs making a difference in the lives of hundreds of thousands by restoring their eyesight and allowing these individuals to return to their communities as full and productive contributing members.

It should be noted that in all these examples, not once was it mentioned that the individuals running these companies were not being paid a salary or that they did not have employees. The important differentiator is that these individuals' primary value is people and social change, with profit being a secondary concern.

FINAL THOUGHTS

Although there has been much success, many social entrepreneurship ventures depend on foundation and various grant money, which blurs the line between traditional philanthropy and traditional business. Throughout the United States, most universities and colleges teach courses on social entrepreneurship, and it is believed that a clearer path of opportunity for social entrepreneurs to succeed will become apparent.

Dietlin's Discussion Directives

1. Provide a definition of a social entrepreneur.
2. On what does a social entrepreneur focus?
3. Does social entrepreneurship focus on the short term, long term, or both? Provide an example.
4. How does social entrepreneurship differ from nonprofit work?
5. Name a historical social entrepreneur and describe the change he or she affected.

Chapter 11

Philanthropy by Celebrities and Athletes

WHY TALK ABOUT CELEBRITIES AND ATHLETES?

Celebrities such as actors, musicians, athletes, and other high-profile personalities are entrepreneurs. We often forget this, but it is true. As these individuals build their careers, they are selling some natural skill set they possess. It might be their acting ability to carry a role in a movie or television series, their voice in recording songs and selling records, their ability to act and dance in theatrical performances, their athletic skill on a field of play, or their creativity in writing songs, books, movies, and plays, but in each and every case these individuals we call celebrities, athletes, or high-profile personalities have a gift that reaches far beyond their immediate network and circle of influence.

Nonprofit organizations and their leaders often have strange ideas about what getting one of these celebrities or athletes involved with their group means and what it might lead to for the nonprofit organization.

WHY OPRAH AND BILL GATES AREN'T YOUR DONORS

As I mentioned in Chapter 2, when I meet people and tell them that I work in the philanthropic world, they often ask me how they can get Oprah or Bill Gates to be a donor to the nonprofit organization at which they work, volunteer, or serve as a board member. I tell them they can't unless they have a preexisting relationship. Sometimes it is the nonprofit staff and at other times it is their volunteers who think that if they get a famous person involved with their cause, then fundraising and all other aspects of securing the financial future of the nonprofit organization will become easier. Often, board members and other leaders of charities think that if they can get someone famous to attend or serve as honorary chairperson of the annual gala, become a spokesperson, or make a large donation, many other contributions will flow to the nonprofit organization. This type of thinking is indicative of individuals wanting someone or something else to lift the responsibility for fundraising from those who are truly responsible: the board and the staff.

Securing a high-profile personality will bring to your nonprofit organization some increased awareness of its mission and vision. The challenge is that the benefit is usually not sustainable, meaning that the success achieved is brief. It is hard to translate a successful event with a high-profile personality into continuing support.

FOUNDATIONS ESTABLISHED BY CELEBRITIES AND ATHLETES

A number of celebrities and athletes have established foundations to support causes they care about. Almost everyone knows about Oprah's Angel Network, Newman's Own Foundation, the Sundance Institute, the Shoah Foundation, and the Jolie Pitt Foundation, founded, respectively, by Oprah Winfrey, Paul Newman, Robert Redford, Steven Spielberg, and Angelina Jolie and Brad Pitt. Tiger Woods, Lance Armstrong, Andre Agassi, Peyton Manning, Kristi Yamaguchi, Brett Favre, Mia Hamm, Billie Jean King, Roger Clemens, Vijay Singh, and Jeff Gordon have all established foundations, too, as have many other athletes.

Some of these foundations are very specific, such as the Shoah (Visual History) Foundation, started by Steven Spielberg in 1994 after he made the film *Schindler's List*, which won numerous Academy Awards. This foundation exists for the sole purpose of gathering video testimonies from survivors and other witnesses of the Holocaust. It is very specific because its founder, Spielberg, wants to record the oral history of those who were affected or witnessed this tragedy in world history.

Alternatively, Newman's Own Foundation has given over $250 million to charities worldwide for various educational and charitable purposes. In other words, its founder, Paul Newman, did not want to limit his foundation's donations to a specific subject or area.

The foundation established by Tiger Woods makes grants promoting the health and education of children and even runs its own learning center in Anaheim, California, whereas Lance Armstrong's foundation has fundraising events and sells the well-known and very visible yellow rubber bracelets to be able to provide grants to a number of cancer causes. Each is different, yet each high-profile personality, be it celebrity or athlete, has a cause he or she cares about and supports. Therefore, it can be difficult to get them involved with your nonprofit organization or cause.

"BUT WHAT IF I STILL REALLY WANT THEM TO BE INVOLVED?"

A number of individuals, even after learning the challenges involved in securing high-profile personalities for charitable activities, still want to have them involved with their nonprofit organization, annual gala, or golf outing. This is not necessarily a bad idea, but be forewarned: it takes a lot of work. The primary challenge comes in gaining access to the high-profile person. The best way to gain access is to know the individual or someone who does know him or her and will ask on your behalf.

High-profile personalities will get involved with a charitable activity for one of three primary reasons:

- They personally support and are passionate about the cause.
- They have been asked by someone close to them who either supports the cause or is inclined to recommend they become involved.
- They see it as a business opportunity—in other words, as another business revenue stream—because a number of high-profile personalities are paid for their appearances.

It sometimes surprises nonprofit organizations that they will have to pay to secure a celebrity or high-profile personality to attend an event or lend their support. But remember that these individuals have businesses to run, and what they are selling is themselves and their skill set.

WHAT TO BE AWARE OF WHEN USING A CELEBRITY OR ATHLETE TO RAISE MONEY

Nonprofit organizations need to recognize that bringing in high-profile personalities to raise money is a risk. The presence of a celebrity or athlete may help sell tickets, but it may raise the awareness of the celebrity or athlete and not necessarily of the nonprofit organization. There are also costs involved, as well, such as paying the following:

- A fee to secure the high-profile personality
- The celebrity or athlete's entourage (i.e., individuals who travel with the celebrity, such as a band if they are a musician)
- Travel, transportation, and other expenses
- Special arrangements, such as certain food in the green room, special rooms, and so on

OTHER THINGS CAN HAPPEN, TOO—SUCH AS THE WHITE HOUSE CALLING

The nonprofit organization must also understand that things can happen that cause a high-profile personality to cancel at the last minute. One of the first times I saw this happen was when Alison Krauss, the Grammy-winning bluegrass artist, was called to perform for President George W. Bush at the White House. She had been scheduled to appear at a luncheon for a nonprofit organization that she cared about, but had to cancel in order to go to Washington, DC.

Another time I saw this happen was during Feeding America's annual conference. The band Emerson Drive was scheduled to perform. Unfortunately, a few days before they were to arrive, one of the band members died. The performance was canceled, and a substitute band performed. Although there was great understanding, there was disappointment, too. Both of these examples were not events that were raising money, but think if they had been. Unforeseen circumstances happen all the time when working with high profile personalities, nonprofit organizations must be prepared for them.

SCRUTINY IS REQUIRED AND SHOULD BE EXPECTED

Careful scrutiny is always required when nonprofit organizations consider taking on a new initiative or involving a high-profile personality, company, or other nonprofit organization. For example, athletes and sports teams are always working to raise and improve their images within a community, and they do use their philanthropic, or charitable, efforts to help showcase them. Gaining the involvement of an athlete or a professional athletic team, when it is done right, can be of tremendous benefit to both the nonprofit organization and the athlete or team. However, when it is not done right, trouble can loom for all.

While most professional athletic teams set philanthropic goals, "It's kind of all over the map," according to Greg Johnson, executive director of the Sports Philanthropy Project, which has worked with teams in the NHL, NFL, NBA, and MLB (*Indianapolis*, December 25, 2007).

The *Wall Street Journal* in April 2007 printed an article that reviewed the tax filings of 85 foundations started by athletes; only 35 of them devoted more than 75% of the funds raised to charitable programs. The majority of the money of the rest of them went to administrative costs. One of the criticisms noted in the article was that athletes tended to hire family members and friends to operate and run their foundations. It was assumed the majority of these individuals did not have experience in working in the philanthropic world. In defense of the athletes, they probably believe that by hiring people who know them or have known them for the majority of their lives, their overall philanthropic goals will be achieved. Whether this is true or not can be debated.

What cannot be debated is the scrutiny that follows high-profile personalities in what they do. By involving them in charitable efforts, that scrutiny will follow the nonprofit organization as well. One only has to think of the criticism received by Michael Phelps in late January 2009 when photos appeared of him smoking marijuana from a bong. This event was reported on a Saturday. Imagine if he were the honoree or spokesperson for a charitable event that evening. At times the scrutiny that follows a high-profile personality will also be applied to a nonprofit organization with which they become associated.

> **LIFES Tip**
>
> Entrepreneurs considering establishing a foundation should see Chapter 12 for advice about using a community foundation to ensure success in achieving their goals.

SOME WHO HAVE GOTTEN IT RIGHT

Numerous high-profile personalities have done philanthropy the right way, by which I mean they were able to raise the profile of a cause or issue in a manner that created a movement of support. The following is a listing of names and causes. See if you can match who raised the profile of what cause (answers are provided in the footnote).

1. Katie Couric		a.	Diabetes
2. Michael J. Fox		b.	Spinal cord injuries
3. Christopher Reeve		c.	Colorectal cancer
4. Mary Tyler Moore		d.	Land mine ban campaign
5. George Clooney		e.	Parkinson's disease
6. Doug Flutie		f.	Save Darfur
7. Princess Diana		g.	Autism

Answers: 1, c; 2, e; 3, b; 4, a; 5, f; 6, g; 7, d.

How many did you get right?

It is important to remember that although a high-profile personality can bring awareness to a cause or issue, it can involve a great deal of work for the nonprofit organization. Both staff and volunteers can become burned out if not done right.

FINAL PIECE OF ADVICE

Caution is urged when wanting and/or deciding to involve high-profile personalities in your cause or issue. The best place to begin gaining support for the cause or issue is in your own community by talking to those you already know, especially entrepreneurs in your community. These are the individuals most likely to respond to a request from you. These are the individuals most likely to have their heart moved. These are the individuals who have the ability to make a transformational difference.

Dietlin's Discussion Directives

1. What are some of the challenges with involving high-profile personalities in nonprofit organizations?

2. Name some high-profile personalities who are attached to a specific cause or issue; name both the individual and the cause or issue.

3. What are some things to be aware of when wanting to engage a high-profile personality?

4. Name some high-profile personalities involved with a philanthropic endeavor.

Chapter 12

Private and Community Foundations

I am often amazed at the things I learn in the field of philanthropy every day. Sometimes I am stunned by the lack of knowledge that still pervades our society about how to get involved charitably and make a difference. At other times, I am struck by the amount of bad information that is dispensed by well-meaning individuals who are advisors and experts in other areas. Although those who have an interest in charitable efforts are simply trying to help others, including those who are less fortunate, the vehicles and complicated paths they embark on continue to amaze me. These individuals often seem to believe that they have to "go it alone." They are unaware or uninformed of the opportunities that exist to give directly to the cause or nonprofit organization they want to support in a way that creates the change they are seeking as well as the accountability they desire. Additionally, these same individuals seem to lack information about their local community foundations and the work they do and can do to achieve philanthropic goals, both for the individual and the cause or nonprofit organization they are interested in helping.

THE DIFFERENCES AMONG PRIVATE, OPERATING, AND COMMUNITY FOUNDATIONS

The term *foundation* is used liberally and sometimes not accurately in conversations that entrepreneurs and others have in discussing their philanthropic and charitable activities and goals. First, the term *philanthropic foundation* is used as a general descriptor for an entity created when funds are being donated by a corporation, family, individual, or community to support nonprofit organizations in a certain geographic area or program sector. However, each of these particular entities varies greatly.

Some basic definitions are helpful for further understanding what type of vehicle an entrepreneur should consider when contemplating creating or becoming involved with a foundation.

- A *private foundation* is defined by the Internal Revenue Service (IRS) as an entity having one source of funds; it usually makes grants to nonprofit organizations through the revenue generated from the earnings on its investments. Generally, private foundations make grants and do not run programs.
- An *operating foundation* is defined by the IRS as a private foundation whose main focus is to conduct research, promote the social welfare, or become involved with other programs as determined in its charter. Although some external grants are made occasionally to outside nonprofit organizations, the majority of an operating foundation's funds goes to programs it operates.
- A *family foundation* is defined by the IRS as a foundation that receives funds from one family. Additionally, the family members usually determine the grants that are awarded or the process to be used for awarding grants, often through their roles as officers or board members.
- A *corporate foundation* is established by corporations to handle contribution requests from nonprofit organizations; depending on the corporation, requests could be local, statewide, national, or even international.
- A *community foundation* is defined by the IRS as a foundation that serves a specific geographic area and the nonprofit organizations located within that area. Historically, community foundations have been started through the generous bequests of one or more individuals in the community.

> ### LIFES Tip
> When most entrepreneurs speak of a foundation, they want to start a private foundation or a family foundation. But look before you leap: there is a lot more to running a foundation and administering a grants program than meets the eye.

SO, YOU THINK YOU NEED A FOUNDATION

When I meet high-profile personalities and they learn what I do, one of the first things they usually tell me is how they are involved with nonprofit organizations. I always thank them for what they are doing to make their community and the world a better place. The next part of our conversation usually involves them sharing with me that they have started a private foundation or that they want to start their own private foundation. Most of the time by this point in the discussion, it becomes apparent they have received some bad information from a well-meaning advisor.

One of the first times I witnessed this phenomenon was when a high-profile musician approached my company wanting to start a private foundation with the goal of putting music back in the schools. It was a very noble endeavor because the musician felt schools needed to have music teachers, musical instruments, and music classes. The potential client was a referral from a friend, and by the time I was brought into the situation, the paperwork had been filed for the corporation to be established (remember that this is a first step in forming a nonprofit organization).

I remember sitting with the musician and his family members, along with the accountant, and the attorney, discussing how the newly formed foundation was going to secure funding. As the conversation ensued, it appeared that major corporations throughout the country had offered to provide assistance to this musician if he started a foundation. Upon hearing this information from these corporations, the musician had assumed their involvement would mean cash donations, believing these corporations as well as others were going to fill the coffers of his foundation. The musician didn't realize that he would need to put substantial resources into this foundation himself. He had received, at worst, bad advice and, at best, incomplete advice.

LIFES Tip

To start a private foundation, it is recommended that you begin with a donation of at least $5 million, if not $10 million. Although this number seems enormous, it is the best way to ensure that you as an entrepreneur will be able to achieve the results you are seeking. It should also be noted that it costs about $100,000 to establish a private foundation.

I LOVE WARREN BUFFETT!

Yes, I do really love Warren Buffett, because in one day he changed the philanthropic landscape. On Monday, June 26, 2006, Warren Buffett announced that he was going to give more than $30 billion to charity. However, he was not going to create a new foundation or charity with his name or his family's name on it. Instead he was making this donation to an already existing nonprofit organization whose work he admired—the Bill and Melinda Gates Foundation, basically doubling the Gates Foundation's fund balance. In one day, Warren Buffett transformed the way a lot of individuals think about philanthropy, legacies, and making a difference. He did not have to give the money to another nonprofit organization to achieve his goals. Mr. Buffett has enough money to start any number of private, operating, family, corporate, or even new community foundations. However, just as he is shrewd in business, so too is he astute about his charitable work. He knew what he wanted to support and looked for a nonprofit organization that was doing it well. My guess is that when Mr. Buffett passes away, there will be additional gifts to the Bill and Melinda Gates Foundation, as well as other nonprofit organizations, but I highly doubt he will be creating any new private foundations.

Warren Buffett will definitely be remembered not only as one of the icons of the business world, but also the philanthropic world. When years from now one thinks of the leaders who changed the direction of philanthropy, Warren Buffett's name will be added to those of John D. Rockefeller, Andrew Carnegie, and Henry Ford.

To complete the picture, it should be noted that Mr. Buffett and his children have established several private foundations. The first was the Buffett Foundation, renamed the Susan A. Buffett Foundation in honor of Mr. Buffett's late wife. Each of Warren Buffet's children has established a foundation, too. His daughter, Susan, established the Susan Thompson Buffett Foundation. His son Howard, who is set to take over as chairman of Berkshire Hathaway, the investment company his father founded, started the Howard Graham Buffett Foundation, while Howard's brother, Peter, established the Novo Foundation. In addition to the $30-plus billion Warren Buffett is giving to the Bill and Melinda Gates Foundation, he is also making donations totaling $1 billion to the charities his children have started.

AN OVERLOOKED WAY TO MAKE A DIFFERENCE: UTILIZING COMMUNITY FOUNDATIONS

Most entrepreneurs I speak with find philanthropy overwhelming. I think it is because of the appearance of the lack of structure and overall rules and regulations. Although philanthropy has worked well for years, it is a process that works a lot on the honor system. That is not to say there are not rules, regulations, laws, and policies that govern the nonprofit world, but for the most part, in my opinion, it is largely still the wild, wild West, with new ideas still being implemented, vetted, and tried. Many truisms exist, but long-held beliefs are being challenged by entrepreneurs, the Baby Boomer generation, as well as the Gen X-ers and Gen Y-ers, often called the Millennials, not to mention the changes caused by advances in technology and the globalization of the world.

A resource that works well in the philanthropic world is community foundations and the community foundation is a vehicle entrepreneurs should use more fully to conduct and achieve their philanthropic endeavors. Community foundations exist to help individuals in a geographic area achieve their philanthropic goals, hopefully within that community. The first community foundation in the world, the Cleveland Foundation, began in 1914. It was started by a banker at the Cleveland Trust Company named Fredrick Goff. Like many of today's entrepreneurs, Goff was frustrated with philanthropy and sought to create a dynamic organization that had a structure similar to corporate America but that would respond to community needs appropriately. Today, the Cleveland Foundation has more than $2 billion in assets and serves the greater Cleveland area, including Cuyahoga, Lake, and Geauga counties.

Community foundations have three basic types of funds, each of which is briefly explained here.

- An *unrestricted fund* is administered by the community foundation's board, officers, and staff; an entrepreneur (or for that matter anyone) can make a donation to the unrestricted fund of a community foundation knowing that someone else will make the decision about how the funds are allocated within in the community.
- A *donor-advised fund* is established through a gift by the donor to the community foundation; this gift, usually at the $10,000 level or more because it is usually endowed and will exist in perpetuity, creates a fund through which the donor can advise where he or she

wants the funds to be awarded annually. For example, if a donor wanted to clean up the environment, the community foundation would annually find an organization that works to clean up the environment, with some years perhaps being focused on air quality and others on water, land, or noise pollution cleanup.

- A *donor-designated fund* is again established by a gift from the donor to the community foundation; the donation, again usually starting at the $10,000 level or more because it is usually endowed and will exist in perpetuity, creates a fund that allows the donor to select a particular nonprofit organization, program, or cause that will receive gifts from this fund. In other words, the donor gets to designate the area to which the funds are to be directed.

In all three instances listed, donors receive a tax deduction for their philanthropic donation. Although many community foundations have established other types of funds, these are the basic ones.

I highly recommend entrepreneurs consider working with community foundations for their philanthropic and charitable endeavors for the following reasons:

- It is the most cost efficient and often most effective way to achieve the philanthropic results you are seeking.
- Community foundations have their finger on the pulse of the community and can provide a wealth of information about the issues, challenges, problems, and other needs of the geographic area in which they operate.
- Administrative operations are handled by a professional team well versed in the policies, rules, and regulations that must be followed.
- Finally, even if the cause you care about ceases to exist, your wishes will be honored by a professional staff that will seek out an alternate opportunity to affect the type of change that was your original intention; please note this usually occurs after a situation has been resolved or a disease cured and, if the donor is still living, always in consultation with him or her.

Two great community foundations that I have worked with are The Chicago Community Trust and the Santa Fe Community Foundation. Both are doing outstanding work for the communities they serve.

The Chicago Community Trust and Affiliates, as it is officially known, began in 1915 when Albert W. Harris along with the board of directors of the Harris Savings and Trust Bank started the foundation. The first award was distributed in 1916 in the amount of $5,000 to United Charities. Since its inception, The Chicago Community Trust has been part of the social fabric and ever-changing nature of the city, its residents, and communities. In 2006, The Chicago Community Trust gave more than $77 million to almost 1,200 area nonprofit organizations from its more than $1.5 billion in assets.

The Santa Fe Community Foundation was founded in 1981 with an initial gift of $5,000, with half of the donation made by the city of Santa Fe and the other half by the Gannett Foundation. Today, 27 years later, they have $30 million in assets. The Santa Fe Community Foundation has done an outstanding job in fulfilling its organizational tagline, which is "We make it easy to care for Santa Fe." In the pamphlet entitled "A History of the Santa Fe Community Foundation," longtime Santa Fe gallery owner Al Wadle stated, "I have found the secret to eternal life . . . when you give to create endowments at the Santa Fe Community Foundation, you live forever." The strategy of the Santa Fe Community Foundation is to attract donors, invest their gifts, and make grants from the interest while keeping the corpus growing for the future.

Community foundations are a great place for entrepreneurs, including high profile personalities, celebrities and athletes, to begin becoming involved in the philanthropic world in a strategic and meaningful manner. It is a way for not only entrepreneurs but their entire family to be involved in charitable activities and to learn about what is taking place in their community. It is convenient and easy, allowing an entrepreneur the freedom to make donations, some of them even transformational, to the community. It also frees an entrepreneur from the administrative costs, both in terms of financial dollar sand time, that usually accompany the creation and running of private foundations.

LIFES Tip

For those individuals involved in the nonprofit world as staff or leaders of nonprofit organizations, it is highly recommended that you meet with the community foundations in your geographic area and make them aware of the good work you are doing. If you don't share with them the differences and transformations you are making in the community, they will likely not know about you and definitely will not be able to recommend you to a potential donor who might be an entrepreneur wanting to make a difference.

Dietlin's Discussion Directives

1. What is a private foundation?
2. What is a family foundation?
3. What is an operating foundation?
4. What is a corporate foundation?
5. Name the first community foundation established.
6. What does a community foundation do and where does it operate?
7. Explain the differences between a donor-advised fund and a donor-designated fund.
8. Does your city or town have a community foundation? Are you familiar with it?

Chapter 13

Final Thoughts

I believe philanthropy is the noblest of all the professions.

I have often stated in the many presentations I make that in order to survive the challenges of the 21st century, nonprofit organizations will have to engage entrepreneurs in the life of their organizations. As discussed in the first chapter, when one peruses history, the transformation that has occurred in the world because of philanthropic activity has been caused for the most part by entrepreneurs and their vision of a better world. Through their active involvement, financial resources, and true engagement, entrepreneurs have changed the world. I frequently say and truly believe the first sentence of this chapter—that the field of philanthropy is the noblest of all the professions. I believe this because whether you are involved in the charitable world as paid staff or a committed volunteer, you are asking on behalf of those who cannot ask for themselves. You are asking and making a difference in the life of a child who is hungry, a senior citizen who cannot afford his or her medicine, a young adult who will not be able to go to college, an abused woman who needs shelter, animals trying to survive in an environment that is being destroyed, and so on.

Still no one grows up and says they want to become involved with the nonprofit world or be a philanthropist. A child does not tell their parents, "Hey, Mom and Dad, when I grow up I want to work in the nonprofit world." Instead we hear about individuals who want to start businesses, fly to the moon, or becoming a doctor, attorney, professional athlete, or teacher. We all have dreams, but usually they do not include becoming involved in charitable work. However, in my opinion this field is the noblest of all. If I were to ask you today who is the largest donor to Harvard University or the lead fundraiser, my guess is that you would not know. I could ask those same two questions about the Mayo Clinic, the Georgia O'Keefe Museum, Feeding America, the Joffrey Ballet, the Sierra Club, Carnegie Hall, the American Cancer Society, Michigan State University, or any other nonprofit organization; unless you were closely involved with them, you probably will not know the answer. Yet these individuals, donors, volunteers, and fundraisers, quietly go about their work to make a difference and thus transform the world and the lives of people in it.

Entrepreneurs make a difference every day. They can and do make a difference in the philanthropic world. It is the responsibility of all of us working in this field professionally to be sure they are engaged. It is the responsibility of the entrepreneur to give back, because I believe in that old saying, "To those to whom much has been given, much is expected." Go make a difference in the world!

Dietlin's Discussion Directives

1. How will you make a difference?
2. What will you do?
3. Make a plan for this day.
4. Make a plan for this week.
5. Make a plan for this month.
6. Finally, make a plan for the year and then for the rest of your life!

Entrepreneurial Stories

JULIE AZUMA

Julie Azuma started Different Roads to Learning in 1995. The company sells learning products for children diagnosed with autism and other developmental disabilities, including Asperger's syndrome. In 1999, she created DRL Books Inc., a publishing company for books and manuals that were missing in the repertoire of books available to parents and teachers of these children. DRL Books is primarily a business-to-business company. In August 2005, she began the Mind and Memory Store, which is dedicated to mental fitness and short-term memory retention. The three companies provide services to over 30,000 customers.

Julie received a BFA in apparel design from Washington University in St. Louis. She had a 30-year career in the apparel industry as a designer and merchandiser working at corporations that have included Givenchy Sport, Collegetown, Jordache, and Mast Industries, a division of The Limited.

In 1994, when her older daughter, Miranda, was diagnosed with autism at the age of six, Julie left the apparel industry to begin a niche business. At the time, there were limited resources to help autistic children. Therapists were constantly requesting materials and tools that were unavailable to most parents. Julie was able to find a core group of products that would help children with language and help parents shape their behaviors.

In February 2005, Julie was featured on a CNBC series about the autism epidemic. In April of the same year, she was named one of *Inc.* magazine's 26 Favorite Entrepreneurs, and was featured on the MSN version of *Road Trip Nation* in the summer of 2006. She was a guest speaker at the Syracuse Women's Entrepreneur Conference in 2004 and 2006. In 2007, she was featured in the magazine *Professional Woman*. She was the keynote speaker for Red Eight, a group of Asian American entrepreneurs, in 2007.

She has been honored for her involvement in the Asian American community and has received various awards, including the Martin Luther King Jr. I Have a Dream Award by New York State Governor George Pataki. She has received community service awards from the Office of the Public Advocate of New York City, the Cosmopolitan Lions Club, and the Organization of Chinese Americans. In 2007 she received the first Lotus Award from the Coalition of Asian Pacific Americans.

In the autism community, she was given the Robert Ambrey Award from Eden II. In 2008 she was honored by the New York Families for Autistic Children. The Elija Foundation honored her for her company's work in autism with the prestigious Chariot Award in November of 2008.

For over 25 years, Julie has been actively involved in the Asian American community. She is currently the chairperson on the board of Asian Women in Business and of the Foundation Board at Eden II, an agency that works to educate and serve individuals diagnosed with autism, and is on the board of the Japanese American Association. She is a past member of the board at the Coalition for Asian American Children and Families and has served on the local board of the Japanese America Citizens League, Asian Americans for Equality, and Pan Asian Repertory Theatre. She has also served on the Coalition of Asian Pacific Americans, the Day of Remembrance Committee, and the Justice for Vincent Chin Committee. She is currently in Cambridge's *Who's Who*.

Little Notes Do Matter

In speaking with Julie Azuma you immediately realize that she is a person who knows who she is and what she wants in life. When I asked her how she defines philanthropy, Julie stated that "Philanthropy, in my mind, is someone who is able to give a ton of money, over $10,000 to a single organization." She further states that "Charity may be more of an organization that fills a void or a need, whereas philanthropy sounds like the Metropolitan Museum [in New York] or funding a library, something that might be icing on the cake instead of filling a need."

Her philanthropic experience began more than 25 years ago, when she began making monetary donations to Asian American nonprofit organizations. As Julie states, "I just did it. There's not a specific memory of when there was a decision made to support a specific goal. There were many goals at the time for the Asian American community and if I had some disposable income that wouldn't keep me from a new pair of shoes, I would give to a cause, event, or organization."

Although Julie cannot recall exactly what her first donation to a nonprofit organization was, she does vividly recall donations of about $50 to several organizations. In her mind these were small gifts, but to her astonishment they were surprisingly appreciated by the recipient organizations. She told me, "I didn't realize that a $50 gift can make an organization so happy so I continued to do it on an ongoing basis for several groups. I became committed to these groups in my mind because it made them so happy."

In the late 1970s, Julie began working with a community organization for the redress of wrongs and reparations for the 110,000 Japanese and Japanese Americans who were interred in camps during World War II. As she stated, "This was the real beginning of wanting to work in the community. When redress was won during the Reagan era, I became active on several boards and steering committees. Later I was involved around the movement relating to the death of Vincent Chin. I was asked to be on one of the benefit committees and on boards . . . and my community awareness grew from there."

On June 19, 1982, Vincent Chin, a 27-year-old Chinese American, was attending his bachelor party in suburban Detroit. After an altercation occurred in the nightclub he and his friends were patronizing, Vincent was followed and beaten by two men with a baseball bat. He died four days later, a mere five days before his wedding was to take place. This incident was a perfect example of the anti-Asian sentiment that was taking place in America. The outcome of the trial created an outrage in many communities, including the Asian Pacific American community. Initially, the two individuals responsible for the beating pled guilty to manslaughter and were sentenced to three years probation each and a $3,000 fine. Later, juries acquitted the two men in federal civil rights cases.

Julie's interest in philanthropy developed when she wandered into giving to nonprofit organizations. She is from Chicago, where there is an active Japanese American community, and was seeking a similar organization in New York with which to join and become active. In New York City, she found those types of communities with the Japan Society and the Japanese American Citizen's League, becoming members of both. This initial step grew into her current roles in other Asian American organizations, where, as she puts it, "there was more latitude in the ability to reach out to the larger community."

Julie's two areas of interest for her philanthropic and charitable work are the Asian American community and autism organizations. As she stated, "These were both populations that were relatively unknown and completely underserved when we began contributing." Julie also shared that, "I spend less time with organizations now but am trying to give more to make up for my inactivity."

Julie gives because of several reasons. The first is that she understands the obligation of serving on a board. She also recognizes that most board members in her community don't realize that part of their responsibility as board members is to either raise or donate money. She further states, "I also have personal relationships with a number of organizations in both the Asian American and autism community. The autism community becomes more of a sponsorship opportunity but it is also based on acquaintance-ship and friendship in the same manner as our ties to the Asian American community."

As shared in her bio, Julie Azuma founded the online retailer Different Roads to Learning (DRL) after realizing in 1994 that her daughter, Miranda, was severely autistic. DRL now offers more than 350 products and items to individuals, families, and friends affected by autism. Check it out at www.difflear.com.

Julie does not base her donations on results but rather on need. If she believes a nonprofit organization is well funded, she may reduce her commitment or stop giving for a while. For Julie, there is no results-oriented performance requirement or measurement tool; however, she will not contribute to nonprofit organizations that are about to go under. She needs to feel that the work being done is ongoing in order to consider making a donation.

Julie is a donor who believes she is reactive in her philanthropic efforts. As she states, "There are people who send that extra little note on their letter requesting funds and these notes do make a difference. There are also people I know in the community who expect us to make a donation of some sort. There are very few rare times when I'll think, gosh I want to give to a new organization. I'm already committed to several and something has to be outstanding to entice me to make a further commitment."

She readily acknowledges that being an entrepreneur affects her philanthropic decisions. Julie notes that sponsorships are much easier for her to accommodate because of the opportunities available for her company as well as the recognition.

Like many other entrepreneurs, Julie stated that other entrepreneurs she knows do not talk about giving. Instead they discuss the business climate or what company has been bought or gone under. She also shared, "I have met many people, usually from the financial and professional sector, who give in a true philanthropic way for scholarships, schools in third world countries, and helping parent groups in need of education and information."

Julie told me that apart from financial giving, she and her husband share their apartment with organizations that are in need of a place to meet or a place for networking. Their home is much like a community center; Julie often meets people who say that they've been to her apartment whom Julie has never met before. For some of the smaller events (with fewer than 40 people), Julie and her husband also provide food and drink if they are going to be a part of the event. The apartment provides an atmosphere that promotes networking in a relaxed environment.

Julie's Advice

- Have a true interest in the organization that you're going to commit to and realize this is the beginning of a relationship. It will be most likely an ongoing involvement.
- Take a look at their past work and the potential of the nonprofit organization. How many people will the organization impact? Will they be able to enhance lives in a way that meets your interests?
- Don't feel that the commitment will never stop; you are in control of the giving. If the organization's goals begin to differ from your expectations, you can always move on.

SUZY BOGGUSS

Suzy has a twinkle in her eye as she discusses her latest studio album, *Sweet Danger*. It's a line from one of her signature songs, but it's also the philosophy with which the Illinois-born singer manages her career, and the stepping-off point for a collection of her strongest songwriting and most evocative vocals to date. "I've been so fortunate to meet all these great people in all genres of music," she says. "To learn from them and grow is amazing. How could I not make music with the friends I've made over the years?"

One of those friends is legendary jazz producer and keyboardist Jason Miles, with whom Bogguss coproduced *Sweet Danger*. Miles has worked with the biggest names in jazz and popular music, including Miles Davis, Luther Vandross, Chakka Kahn, and Sting. He became friends with Bogguss over a decade ago when he was producing a children's album of Elvis Presley covers and asked her to contribute a track. The two shared a love of music that wasn't defined by boundaries or classification. They became fast friends and stayed in touch over the years.

A chance conversation after a show in New York led to their collaboration on the new album. "I love the sweetness of making a snap decision and the danger of living with the consequences," Suzy says. "When I went to New York that first time and we started to record, I called home because I was freaking out. I thought 'Oh my God, what is this music?' I didn't know what it was. I didn't know how to control it. As soon as I hung up and went back into the studio, I just let go, enjoyed the process and followed the music wherever we needed to go. Then I was elated. I came home with these tracks that were new and different and that was so exciting. I couldn't wait to get started writing the rest of the album."

But she still doesn't know what it is. Certainly the songs, seven of which Suzy wrote, stand alongside the best she's ever recorded. They could easily have been included on one of the hit-maker's seminal recordings from the early 1990s. But the production, while unquestionably current, hearkens back even further to albums by the likes of James Taylor, Paul Simon, or Joni Mitchell.

The new record is just the latest collaboration in a career that has always been adventuresome. Bogguss teamed with the late, great Chet Atkins on *Simpatico*, an album that received near universal praise. She also teamed with Ray Benson of Asleep At The Wheel on *Swing*, an album full of swing tunes soaked in jazz.

"Maybe the *Swing* album gave me the inspiration, but I feel like I'm still learning about my voice and what makes it appealing. I like to swoop and swell and even soar, but I just don't want to yell anymore. That's not my gift. I never wanted to be a vocal acrobat, I sing songs."

Like most explorers, she offers no apologies for chasing her muse wherever it leads her. She's always listened to her head and her heart when picking music for her albums. She's guided by a desire to be true to herself while communicating with her audience.

She says, "What I'm really trying to do is make music that people like. That's why I started playing in bars in the first place. That's why I listened to people when they told me I should sing another person's songs. I believed them. We were talking to each other. We were communicating. That's what's so great about the Internet now. It's what we used to do with artist co-ops and mailing lists only now you can reach millions of music fans instead of hundreds." Connecting with her audience has been a fundamental part of her career since she graduated from Illinois State University with an art degree and began touring the coffeehouse and club circuit.

After five years crisscrossing the country in a camper truck, Bogguss landed in Nashville and immersed herself in the creative community. She found like-minded writers who believed in songs with style and substance. Her big break came when a talent scout from Capitol Records saw her perform at Dollywood, Dolly Parton's theme park in East Tennessee's Smokey Mountains. A tape of her music that she sold at the park reached the hands of a label executive, and three weeks later she was signed.

Her strong, supple voice and straightforward style were a clarion call for country fans looking for music with meaning. Songs such as "Aces," "Drive South," "Someday Soon," "Outbound Plane," and "Letting Go" soon took her to the top of the country music charts. Along the way she won raves from critics and her peers in all genres. She won the Country Music Association's Horizon Award in 1992 and Album of the Year Award in 1994, ASCAP country and pop awards for her songwriting, and in 2005 a Grammy for her contribution to the best folk album, *Beautiful Dreamer: The Songs of Stephen Foster*.

The only way to describe her career arc would be as an evolution. One project inevitably led to the next. That's one of the reasons she's so excited about *Sweet Danger*. "The whole process was so natural," she says. "From my friendship with Jason through the whole writing and recording process. It was challenging at first because this was new territory for me, but when I let go and surrendered to the experience it happened so easily. I left New York sort of mesmerized with the whole process. Everybody just wanted to make something—to create."

The joy and creative freedom she felt imbues every note of *Sweet Danger*. Always a sublime, controlled singer, she hits a new milestone with this collection. By stretching, testing, and challenging her limits, she's captured the best vocals of her career.

Like all of her previous work, the new record is filled with songs of emotional integrity. She covers Chicago's "If You Leave Me Now" and creates a totally new vibe by stripping the song down to its emotional core and rebuilding it with a tight acoustic ensemble. Verlon Thompson's "No Good Way To Go" is an inner dialogue on how to end a relationship, half sung and half spoken with smoldering sexuality. She turns to husband/songwriter Doug Crider for "In Heaven," the emotional centerpiece of the album. The song, which deals with love, loss, letting go, and moving on, is especially poignant because it was written about close friends of Bogguss and Crider. It also has an incredible, instantly memorable melody. She remains consistent in her unwillingness to be defined by the expectations of others. She's always been the type of artist to boldly listen to her instinct and chase that wily muse where it leads her. Suzy Bogguss has always taken, and will always take, the road less traveled—and that has made all the difference.

It Just Feels So Good Doing It

I remember the first time I met Suzy Bogguss. It was at the home of our mutual friend, Beth Nielsen Chapman, a singer and songwriter who, like Suzy, lives in Nashville. The purpose of the meeting was to discuss how each of them could become more strategic with their philanthropic activities. As celebrities in the music industry, they are often approached to do something charitable for a nonprofit organization or requested to donate something. Requests can range from a letter asking for an autograph to be auctioned at a nonprofit gala to performing a concert to help raise funds. Their challenge was that it is often hard to tell a "good" charity from a "bad" charity. In other words, they were wondering how to assess the requests and how to ensure they align with their values and passion. Suzy told me that one of the worst feelings is to be performing at a special event and realizing that you're not well informed about the organization because you have been on the road for two to three weeks and are exhausted. We all have been at events where the keynote speaker or entertainer did not get the name of the organization or the event correct.

I worked with both Suzy and Beth to develop a tool that would help individuals identify and assess their current activities, determine what they are passionate about, and select nonprofit organizations that align with their values. Suzy, who is very charitably minded, was readily identifiable as a committed philanthropist always willing to jump in to help a cause. Throughout her life, she supported nonprofit organizations and charities either through her gift of music, such as performing at a benefit for a nonprofit organization, or by acting as a spokesperson, volunteering to help, or providing financial support. Suzy is always willing to consider causes and requests for help, especially in her local community. Two organizations that are very important to her are the Vanderbilt Ingram Cancer Center and the Second Harvest Food Bank of Middle Tennessee. But Suzy has a big heart and is interested in and cares about other causes as well. These include health- and disease-related nonprofit organizations, such as those addressing cancer, breast cancer, and antismoking efforts, and nonprofit organizations protecting and preserving our nature habitats and national parks. Suzy also cares about her local community and the nonprofit organizations located within Nashville and the surrounding cities.

Suzy once told me that although at times she is extremely busy, she finds herself always wanting to give back. She always is looking for a way to make a difference and does this in both her professional life and in her personal life, where she serves on the board of directors of the Second Harvest Food Bank of Middle Tennessee.

Bringing both her music and her love of helping others to the people in her life and career is important to her, and she does it very well.

Suzy's Advice

- Make sure that you are passionate about the cause with which you are getting involved.
- I think a person can be drawn in and cultivate this passion, but I recommend getting involved in increments so that you can feel the fit as you commit to the project.

JOHN AND RITA CANNING

John A. Canning, Jr., is chairman of Madison Dearborn Partners, LLC (MDP), which specializes in management buyout and special equity investing. MDP manages over $14 billion of committed capital and portfolio investments. Prior to founding MDP in 1993, Mr. Canning spent 24 years with First Chicago Corporation, most recently as executive vice president of the First National Bank of Chicago and president of First Chicago Venture Capital.

He currently serves on the boards of directors of the Economic Club of Chicago, Exelon Corporation, Milwaukee Brewers Baseball Club, Northwestern Memorial Hospital, TransUnion Corporation, and Children's Inner City Educational Fund. He also serves on the boards of trustees of the Big Shoulders Fund, the Field Museum, the Museum of Science and Industry, and Northwestern University.

Mr. Canning is also a commissioner of the Irish Pension Reserve Fund, a trustee and chairman of the Chicago Community Trust, and a director and chairman of the Federal Reserve Bank of Chicago. Mr. Canning has an A.B. from Denison University and a J.D. from Duke University.

His company, Madison Dearborn Partners, based in Chicago, is one of the most experienced and successful private equity investment firms in the United States. MDP has more than $14 billion of equity capital under management and makes new investments through its most recent fund, Madison Dearborn Capital Partners V, a $6.5 billion investment fund raised in 2006. Since its inception in 1992, Madison Dearborn has invested in more than 100 companies across a broad spectrum of industries, including basic industries, communications, consumer, energy and power, financial services, health care, and real estate.

Rita Canning graduated from University of Illinois, Champaign, with a B.S. degree from the College of Commerce and Business Administration. She is chairperson of WINGS (Women In Need Growing Stronger) and founder of the Palatine Home of the Sparrow, which are transitional shelter programs for abused and homeless women and their children. She opened a

10,000-square-foot resale store for WINGS and recently opened the first domestic violence shelter in Chicago's northwest suburbs. Rita serves as vice president of the Canning Foundation, which funds such programs as the Canning Scholars, which provides scholarships to over 100 inner-city children to both elementary and secondary private schools. She helped to create and continues to fund the Holy Angels Outreach Program, which provides assistance to those in need in the Ida B. Wells Project homes. She is also a member of the women's board of Northwestern University, the women's board of the Field Museum, a director of Harris Bank–Palatine, a director of the Buehler YMCA, and a trustee at Harper College.

She has received the Sears Distinguished Leader Award for exemplary volunteer contributions, the Woman to Woman Making a Difference Award from the Illinois state treasurer's office, The *Business Ledger*'s 2003 Influential Women in Business Award, and the WINGS 2004 Shining Light Award.

Giving Done Selfishly

While "giving done selfishly" seems like an unlikely title for a section in a book about philanthropy, it is exactly how John Canning describes what he does. When I asked him and his wife, Rita, why they give away so much money, he says it is because he is selfish! He wants to make a difference in the lives of others and this is one way to do it, and he feels good about it. Both of them want to affect lives, and for them that is the payback. All of these are selfish reasons, according to John. Although this might appear to be a most unusual perspective, it accurately reflects why a lot of entrepreneurs get involved with charitable efforts. They selfishly want to make a difference.

When you first meet Rita and John, you would never guess how far reaching their work is and how deep their hearts. Their depths of caring are immeasurable and are evidenced by the work they do and support philanthropically. Both grew up in humble surroundings, and their humility continues today.

As a couple, Rita and John were philanthropic, but they both readily agree that initially their philanthropy was not strategic. They were donors—and continue to donate—to many civic, culture, arts, and other organizations in the Chicagoland area, such as the Field Museum, the Museum of Science and Industry, WINGS, Northwestern Memorial Hospital, Northwest Community Hospital, Northwestern University, Harper College, and many others. However, they knew they wanted to be more strategic about causes for which each of them felt a true passion.

John and Rita serve on numerous nonprofit boards of directors, finding another way to give back to various communities.

With their giving somewhat lacking in strategy, they met one night for dinner and decided to establish a foundation that would focus on two areas. For John the focus was inner-city schools; for Rita, it was domestic violence issues. They both agreed they wanted to make an impact on these issues.

When I asked them how their deep involvement with philanthropy began, they told me a story. Rita and John read an article in the *Chicago Tribune* about Eric Morse, a little boy who died violently at the age of five. Eric was a good kid. He didn't steal, went to school, and was not involved with drugs. And that is what led to his death. Gang members wanted him to become involved with drugs by buying, selling, and trafficking. When he said no, they took him to the roof of one of the buildings in the Ida B. Wells Project to make an example and threw him off. Rita and John were outraged and knew they had to do something. They wanted to help Eric's family. The story had haunted them and they needed to get involved. They went to the police station in that area of the city and were directed to a school Eric attended named Holy Angels. Sister Sarah, who is the "Bing Crosby of Nuns" according to Rita, greeted them and explained that it was not possible to help Eric's family. The father was in prison and the mother was involved with drugs. However, Sister Sarah shared that she had seven children who needed scholarships to attend school. Would Rita and John consider providing those scholarships and making a difference in these young lives? Rita laughed during the interview, stating she remembers seeing one of the children, Antonio, leaning on his forearms and staring through the window of the office with a look of hope on his face. Rita and John immediately agreed to provide the seven scholarships. That answer was transformational to Rita and John, changing their lives in ways they could not even imagine and becoming the first step in their focused efforts in philanthropy.

After receiving the scholarships, the students and their parents or legal guardians asked to meet John and Rita. Sister Sarah arranged for an introduction and party on February 14, Valentine's Day. It seems it was the most appropriate day Sister Sarah could have chosen, because John and Rita fell in love on that day not only with the students, but with what they were doing. This experience led John and Rita to annually provide 100 scholarships to students at two elementary schools and five or six high schools. They even provide collegiate scholarships at times.

This in and of itself is amazing, but John and Rita shared something else they do. John personally interviews each of the 100 students selected to receive a scholarship, as well as his or her parents. The criteria John and Rita have selected for their recipients is the following: no drugs, no alcohol, and no trouble in school. A student doesn't have to get straight A's but does have to make an effort. The students' report cards are sent to John and the students' parents and if they get an F, the student and his or her parent or legal guardian need to meet with John to explain why this grade occurred. Overall, this program has worked exceedingly well, with most of the students being successful. But there have been a few bumps along the road, such as when one of the first scholarship recipients was murdered while visiting friends in his old neighborhood after his graduation from college. Senseless acts of violence started Rita and John down this path to transform lives, and senseless acts of violence strengthen their resolve to try again and again to help those who only need a hand up.

The other area of focus for Rita and John's foundation is domestic violence. Although Rita never was exposed to the types of situations the women in abuse shelters face, she empathizes with their stories and lives, and is motivated to do better each day for them. Rita started on this path by wanting to volunteer at a domestic violence shelter. That was all she thought she wanted to do. However, none were available for her to provide her services as a volunteer. When she realized there was no domestic violence shelter in her immediate area to provide service to women who were in sometimes impossible situations, she decided to start one. Rita and John are big believers in not duplicating efforts, but in this case, there appeared to be a need for a new domestic violence shelter to be established. The domestic violence shelters in the surrounding areas, such as WINGS (Women In Need Growing Stronger) in Mt. Prospect and Greenwood, as well as the Home of the Sparrow and the Elgin Community Crisis Center, were turning away 100 to 200 women per month. Rita quickly realized there was a need for another domestic violence shelter. She did her homework and began getting to work, while still sending financial contributions to all of the agencies that were serving this population. Even though Rita knew another domestic violence shelter was needed, she did not withdraw her support away from those in existence. Instead she was supportive of these nonprofit organizations while finding and securing land, obtaining the appropriate zoning permits, and funding, building, and staffing the new domestic violence shelter.

Her real fight was not with the other domestic violence shelters, but with neighbors in the community. As she explains it, she had to fight everyone to get this domestic violence shelter for women built. It took her four years to secure the property, there were two or three lawsuits, and once it was built, the state of Illinois did not deliver on its $975,000 payment. As John noted, "Rita built that domestic violence shelter without any money!" It is true that she got donations and support from everyone she knew. But because the state had not provided the promised funding, they were near the end, meaning they would have to close the shelter. So, Rita went to inform David Hill, chairman of Kimball Hill Homes, whose company had built the domestic violence shelter and who with his wife Diane was very supportive, of the problem. Rita was not looking forward to the meeting, but while waiting to see David, she came up with an idea. When she met David, she explained the situation and said to him, "If you and Diane put in a million dollars, John and I will put in a million dollars!" David looked at her, laughed, and called her bodacious. Rita said that she did not know what that word meant, and immediately after the meeting called John and asked him what it meant. John laughed when he shared, "I told Rita I don't know who described you that way but it is the perfect word! You are bodacious!"

Bodacious, according to the online Merriam Webster dictionary, means outright, unmistakable, remarkable, and noteworthy.

Rita noted that for three months she did not hear anything; even when they were with the Hills socially, the request was never brought up. Rita really thought they were going to have to close the domestic violence shelter. Then one day, when Diane and Rita were at a meeting together for another nonprofit organization, Diane casually said as they were walking out, "By the way, David and I will give you the million dollars." Rita stated that she immediately burst into tears, so overwhelmed with what this meant to WINGS, the women it served, and their children.

Today, John and Rita actively raise money together for WINGS, with John asking his many colleagues and associates in the professional world for financial support. As Rita told me, "It is 100% of John's contacts that provide the financial support to WINGS."

Rita and John are that rare couple who have each found a niche in the philanthropic world to support and then support each other in those endeavors. They also reach out to the community to get others involved in the causes about which they are passionate. Rita and John revealed that John, serving as co-chair of the Big Shoulders Fund, had initiated a program for schools to be adopted. He asks an individual or corporation to commit $150,000 each year for three years to the operational fund, meaning it is unrestricted. He also asks that a board be formed at each of these schools, with the focus being to bring in outside expertise. John stated that when he looked at these schools, the individuals on the boards were well meaning but were usually parents or community people without access or influence to what was needed to support the school. To date 65 schools, all private, have been adopted and funded, with expertise being brought in. "What does the outside expertise mean?" I asked John. He said schools have been wired for technology (some of them even have wireless technology), computers have been purchased, supplies ordered, and so on.

John also took it a step further, asking the Kellogg School at Northwestern University to mandate a community service requirement for its college students, and it did. Students from Northwestern University's business school adopt a class and then begin interacting with and teaching the students, exposing them to things that don't exist in their lives currently.

A final push for helping children in the inner city are John and Rita's efforts with the Children's Inner City Educational Fund. Through their vision and leadership, they raise funds with others to support noncapital projects such as cross-cultural exchanges. An example of this is two schools, such as Holy Angels School and Healy Elementary School, that have their students interact. This might not seem like a big deal, but Holy Angels is composed of 100% African American students, whereas Healy Elementary is composed of 100% Chinese students who speak six different Mandarin dialects. By ensuring the funds are available for this type of program, John and Rita continue to affect the lives of thousands of students.

When I asked John and Rita whether they have any disappointments with their philanthropic activities, they both said no. There are some things they wished had worked out differently, but mostly they are honored to be able to do what they do and to make connections. Both acknowledge that there are contributions that are expected from them in the community, and they willingly make these. However, for Rita joy comes from making connections that have an impact. For example, Rita has been able to connect a local community college, Harper College, with the local hospital, Northwest Community Hospital, in such a way that it is a win-win situation for everybody. John shared that his regret is that they waited until their late 40s or early 50s before they started to become very active in philanthropy.

John and Rita's Advice

- Set metrics regarding what you are trying to achieve with your donation.
- Take risks.

- If something you are funding is not successful, stop doing it.
- Get involved by going to see what you are funding in progress.
- Get involved, as you will have better control and knowledge [of whether] the money you are donating is going to where it is intended.
- Do your due diligence before getting involved.
- Give to your passion.
- Have a narrow focus.
- Recognize reciprocal giving; if you are asking someone to donate to something you support, they will likely ask you to support a cause about which they care.
- You can't force philanthropy on your children; they have to come by it themselves.

RICHARD DRIEHAUS

Richard H. Driehaus has enjoyed enormous business success, earning a reputation within the investment management industry as an investor extraordinaire. In addition to his business career, he has focused much attention and energy on a wide variety of philanthropic and community-service–oriented projects, individually and through the efforts of the Richard H. Driehaus Foundation and the Richard H. Driehaus Charitable Trusts.

Mr. Driehaus founded Driehaus Securities LLC in 1979, followed by Driehaus Capital Management LLC in 1982, and Driehaus Mutual Funds in 1996. He is the Chairman and Chief Investment Officer of Driehaus Capital Management LLC, and he is also the architect of the firm's overall investment philosophy and responsible for reviewing all domestic and international portfolios. In 2000, Mr. Driehaus was named to Barron's "All-Century" team of the 25 individuals who were identified as the most influential within the mutual fund industry over the past 100 years.

From 1968 through 1973, Mr. Driehaus developed research ideas for the Institutional Trading department at A.G. Becker & Co. In 1973, he became

Director of Research for Mullaney, Wells & Co. In 1976, he became Director of Research and a money manager for Jesup & Lamont.

Mr. Driehaus earned his BSC degree from DePaul University in 1965 and received an MBA from its business school in 1970. In 2002, he was granted an honorary doctoral degree by DePaul. Thankful for the solid education he received there, he has given back to his alma mater in many ways. In fact, Mr. Driehaus has conveyed his gratitude to other Chicago-based educational institutions and religious orders that helped shape his life. They include St. Ignatius College Preparatory School, St. Margaret of Scotland, and the School Sisters of Notre Dame. Other institutions that have benefited from his generosity include Holy Trinity High School, Cristo Rey Jesuit High School, St. Bede's Grammar School, Loyola's St. Joseph Seminary, and Sacred Heart Schools.

Mr. Driehaus' diverse philanthropic interests include funding economic opportunity initiatives to teach financial literacy to those in need, historic preservation of architectural landmarks, and support cultivation of the arts including design, fashion, theatre, music, and dance.

Life began for Richard on the southwest side of Chicago in an Irish Catholic community called Brainard. He lived comfortably in a traditional bungalow with his parents and two sisters, Dorothy and Elizabeth. As a child, he did not know about entrepreneurs. His father, Herman Driehaus, was a mechanical engineer who worked for Goodman Manufacturing, a heavy coal mining equipment manufacturer. His father worked very hard and had a number of patents to his credit, but was never able to fulfill his dream of building a custom English Tudor style home in the more upscale Beverly neighborhood. Richard remembers being confident the move was going to happen. His father had hired an architect to design the home, which was estimated to cost over $50,000. However, it became apparent that a lack of financial resources would prevent the family's dream from being realized. Richard overheard his father and mother debate the possible move to Beverly every night at the dinner table. He couldn't help but wonder, "Why didn't his dad have the money to buy the new house? He had a good job and of course, the patents." After overhearing a number of these discussions between his parents, a 10-year-old Richard made the bold move of asking his mother, "How much money does Daddy make?" His mother answered $10,500 per year. Richard decided right then that when he grew up he was going to be able to make enough money to afford a house in Beverly.

Young Richard began plotting a course to accomplish his goal. As a newspaper delivery boy, he had learned of a number of career paths but recognized that he was not that interested in math, science, electronics, or technology—even in light of Sputnik and the space race. Richard also knew he did not want to be a doctor or an accountant and definitely did not want to be an attorney as he thought he could not defend guilty individuals. He also considered his hobby of coin collecting but realized this would not help him achieve his goals.

One day, when he was 12 years old, Richard was reading a local Chicago paper and came across a page with as he puts it, ". . . corporate names, numerous columns, and numbers showing lots of fractional changes in small print." They were the New York Stock Exchange quotations explained his father, who admitted he did not know much about stocks. He suggested Richard talk to his paternal Uncle Ade, who worked as an accountant for Westinghouse and regularly bought stocks. Richard conferred with his mother who agreed to calling her brother-in-law, both unaware this would ignite Richard's passion and his life-long career in investment management.

As Richard recalls, one of the best pieces of advice he received from his mother was that *before you invest, you have to investigate*. So Richard read the stock listings and monitored stocks such as Sperry Rand and Union Tank Car Company, but he felt he needed to learn more. He went to the Chicago Public Library on a regular basis and read many publications including the *Wall Street Journal, Forbes* magazine, and *Fortune*. He saw stocks going up and down and began to realize that if a company did well, the stock prices would follow over time—some of the stocks he researched had increased 1,000%. Richard began thinking that if he invested $2,000 then, within 10 years he would be a millionaire. After making his first investments with money earned from his paper route, it proved more difficult to get a 30% return per year than he originally thought!

Richard recalled what he had learned early on from the Sisters of Notre Dame nuns who taught him at St. Margaret of Scotland school. They taught him that *a person is responsible for their own actions*. He admits that he was not a good student though. He laughingly shared a favorite quote by Mark Twain who said, "I never let schooling interfere with my education."

Richard never did buy that house in Beverly. Instead his investment success allowed him to buy homes and office locations in downtown Chicago, St. Thomas USVI, and Lake Geneva, Wisconsin, dedicating the home in Wisconsin to his father. But he never forgot the importance of giving back.

REACH DOWN TO REACH UP

By all accounts, Richard Driehaus is a very successful and effective entrepreneur who is well known and respected. The idea of giving back and helping others was instilled in him from an early age. Richard's earliest philanthropic memory is from the Catholic Church—he remembers the small envelopes in which he would place his weekly donation for mass on Sundays and the Holy Days. He also recalled special visits from priests in other parts of the world who would come to his school or church to give sermons on their various missionary work. Richard even remembers the Catholic school teachers collecting funds to help poorer parishes.

When I met with him to discuss his very active role in philanthropy, one of the first things he shared was his belief that nonprofit organizations need to figure out how to measure effectiveness, or in his words, ". . . at least make the attempt [to measure their effectiveness]." Richard recognizes that it is difficult to measure the work of nonprofit organizations and often even more difficult to determine if success has been achieved. However, he firmly believes that it is a good idea to rely on a means of measuring and determining the best practices. Philanthropy, according to Richard, commonly overlooks the budgetary discipline and efficiency that are necessary to measure the effectiveness of a nonprofit.

Richard believes he is so intent on measurements because he comes from an industry that is in some instances *over*-measured. As he says, ". . . perhaps measured to death." Richard cautions against being too "left brain" in analysis, but recognizes it is also imperative for nonprofit organizations to observe what is happening in the world and be practical about the implications. From a business perspective, if funds are limited, it is even more important to employ best practices.

Richard fondly recalls questioning his mother why he needed to learn Latin, as he viewed himself as "practically oriented not academic." He has always wanted to know how something he was learning applied to the real world and his life's ambitions. He applies the same logic to his philanthropic endeavors, looking at the practical side of who and what is being served.

Richard says he is not as attracted to sponsoring large nonprofit organizations such as educational, health care, and food institutions. He believes sometimes the problems are too big to be solved by philanthropic efforts and would be better served through government funding. Instead, he prefers to focus on other areas where the results can readily be seen. Richard also knows that giving away money is hard work. While some chuckle at this statement, those who know philanthropists realize how much time and effort is placed into their philanthropic work.

The Richard H. Driehaus Foundation was started in the early 1980s with a $1 million donation of TCBY stock (one of his most winning stock picks). One of his first philanthropic efforts through the Foundation began when DePaul University approached him for funding. The University's President, Brother Ryan, approached Richard and simply asked, "Can you help DePaul?" Because Richard values education, and because his DePaul University education gave him a solid foundation of business knowledge, it has been important to him to give back to his alma mater.

Several of his charitable endeavors have been devoted to the university through his focus on the College of Commerce and the Charles H. Kellstadt Graduate School of Business. He has endowed The Richard H. Driehaus Center for Behavioral Finance and has established a Professorship in Behavioral Finance. He has also endowed the Driehaus Center for International Business Studies, a program designed to foster a global business perspective.

He was recently involved in the establishment of DePaul's Czech Management Center (CMC) in Prague, and serves on its Board of Directors. In addition, The Richard H. Driehaus Foundation has provided scholarships to full-time MBA candidates. He served on the Advisory Board for the Department of Finance, and has spoken at various college events as well as hosted career development events for business undergraduate and graduate students. In recognition of his contributions to DePaul University's business curriculum, Richard was named "Financial Executive of the Year" in 2000, and in June 2002, he was granted an honorary doctoral degree. He is currently a member of the DePaul University Board of Trustees.

An important tenet in Richard's philanthropic philosophy is the belief in giving individuals the chance to create their own success, a reflection of his gratitude toward those who gave him opportunities to prove himself throughout his career. He has funded economic opportunity initiatives to benefit people living in poverty. One such program is Opportunity International, which makes small business "micro" loans to people in small villages around the world. He also made a most unusual gift to St. Xavier University, on Chicago's southwest side. He donated Gilhooley's Grande Saloon to the school, along with the entire shopping center in which it is located. He requested, and St. Xavier agreed, that a hospitality curriculum be established for students to learn how to run a food/drink establishment, to provide service, and to learn bottom line financial responsibility.

Richard often seeks to make donations that leverage resources in the form of challenge grants. For example, he provided a donation to the Garfield Park Conservatory in Chicago that allowed them to hire a grant writer. Through the grant writer's efforts, the Lila Wallace Readers Digest Foundation made a gift of $1.1 million toward the restoration efforts. His Foundation has also supported the development of a financial literacy program designed to help low-income families learn how to create and preserve wealth and an initiative sponsored by the South Shore Bank to develop Individual Development Accounts, which dollar-match low-income family's saving plans.

Richard also has a personal interest and commitment to design excellence and historic preservation as indicated by his involvement in a wide variety of projects, through his personal gifts, The Richard H. Driehaus Foundation, and his charitable trusts. His commitment to this area stems from a focus on the "built environment" and his belief in the need to bring progressive design principles to people and projects that otherwise could not afford them. This is something The Richard H. Driehaus Foundation is known for, a unique niche in philanthropy.

The philanthropic acts that are most memorable to Richard allow him to match his passion in architecture and landscape design with his charitable efforts. Through the University of Notre Dame and his trusts, Richard has helped establish the Richard H. Driehaus Prize for Classical Architecture that grants a $200,000 annual prize to an individual who has made an extraordinary contribution or achieved great success in the field of classical architecture.

Richard supports the annual award for achievement in the writing and implementation of Form-Based Codes, which is sponsored by the FBCI through his Richard H. Driehaus Charitable Lead Trust. It is hoped that this coding will affect zoning by designing more livable spaces with greenery and trees.

According to the Form-Based Codes Institute, "Form-based codes are a method of regulating development to achieve a specific urban form. Form-based codes create a predictable public realm primarily by controlling physical form, with a lesser focus on land use, through city or county regulations." In other words, form-based codes advocate constructing buildings that adapt to the elements.

With respect to historic preservation, Richard's projects have included the restoration of the Ransom Cable House in Chicago (the current headquarters for Driehaus Capital Management LLC) and the award winning restoration of a 1905 Georgian Revival style country house in Lake Geneva, Wisconsin. In 2008, he completed a massive five-year restoration of the historic Nickerson Mansion, originally built between 1879 and 1883. Considered the grandest residence ever built in Chicago, it is now home to The Richard H. Driehaus Museum showcasing period decorative arts from his personal collection. Additionally, The Richard H. Driehaus Gallery of Stained Glass adjacent to the Smith Museum of Stained Glass Windows at Navy Pier in Chicago, features important stained glass pieces from the Driehaus collection.

Richard is also involved in the activities of the National Trust for Historic Preservation, Landmarks Illinois, the Wisconsin Trust for Historic Preservation, and several preservation organizations in the U.S. Virgin Islands. He has been involved in the preservation and restoration of historic homes in the Bronzeville and Prairie Avenue districts of Chicago, and with a variety of religious-oriented restoration projects. Through Local Initiatives Support Corporation (LISK), the Foundation sponsors annual awards to architects for Excellence in Community Design in low to moderate income communities. Other Foundation activities have included a design competition to produce universally accessible designs for the Chicago Public Schools, the development of design alternatives for mixed income housing in Chicago, award sponsorship for non-profit housing design, and support of design programs at the University of Illinois at Chicago's College of Architecture and the Arts.

Richard has made his mark in the field of fashion as well. The annual Richard H. Driehaus Prize for Fashion Excellence gives students from the four Chicago area design schools an opportunity to showcase their latest creations and receive monetary awards for excellence. Richard arranges the underwriting for the Red Hot Chicago Fashion Gala, an annual display of designs from Chicago's best and brightest young professional designers. He has personally set up a loan program, through the Apparel Board, to allow fledging designers an opportunity to borrow money to purchase materials for orders they receive.

Richard's personal philanthropic style is to work with smaller nonprofit organizations to make a bigger difference. His attitude is, "Let's try and see if it works." However, he does not believe a philanthropist should ignore the larger endeavors. During the fundraising phase for the creation of Millennium Park, John H. Bryan, then CEO of Sara Lee, met with Richard to ask for his support of the Park. Richard wanted to see the space next to the Frank Gehry outdoor concert venue become something unique and special, so he directed his $1 million donation toward a sculpture garden and an endowment for special shows in that garden. Later on, at the request of Ed Uhlir, head of the Millennium Park construction, he sponsored a design competition.

As a wine connoisseur, Richard has a unique way of supporting non-profit organizations. Richard likes to purchase the wine for charitable events both ensuring good wine is available, while also satisfying his personal desire to drink great wine.

Richard shared that his giving can be sparked when he is touched by a story or a special need. Once while listening to National Public Radio (NPR), he heard the story of a police officer named Lisa Nigro who couldn't bear the plight of homeless people in her Chicago neighborhood. After work she would fill a little red wagon with food and drinks to feed the homeless—it was the beginning of the Inspiration Café, based on a Boston model to provide homeless people with a place that served good food in a lovely social setting. Richard was so moved by the story that he funded the Inspiration Café in Chicago's Uptown neighborhood.

Richard finds enjoyment in supporting smaller performing arts groups in which his donations of $2,500 or $5,000 can be a transformational gift. His support of the arts is based on his belief that the arts provide a much-needed balance to people's busy lives. The Richard H. Driehaus Foundation has a primary focus on smaller theatre and dance companies in Chicago, in the neighborhoods, as well as downtown. A sampling of the groups and projects he has supported include Pegasus Players, Trinity Irish Dance Company, Chicago Shakespeare Theatre, Poetry Society of America, Hubbard Street Dance Company, and Redmoon Puppet Theater. In addition, the Foundation sponsored an annual juried award for eight years to support three promising individual Chicago artists.

When asked if Richard thinks there is a difference between philanthropy and charity, he responded "yes." To him, philanthropy is bigger with a larger appeal, goal, or ambition. It can be a new area to explore, have long-term sustainability, and it can be a more comprehensive way of aiding others. Philanthropy, according to him, is harder than charity. He feels charity can at times be viewed as a handout and as a result may not be as appreciated by the recipient. He also believes that if we tie philanthropy and charity together, meritocracy would prevail. One of the challenges Richard shared is his belief that people assume they must attain a certain level of personal success before they can make a philanthropic impact. He would urge people against applying that logic. Richard believes that philanthropy enhances ones personal fulfillment. As he says, "It allows me to escape from my business." Richard believes his business also benefits when he can take a break to be involved in meaningful philanthropic work.

Richard says that the entrepreneurs he knows do not formally or informally talk about philanthropy, but they are often willing to support a philanthropic endeavor if approached by a friend. According to him, everyone works together to make sure Chicago and its various nonprofit organizations are supported. Richard explained that philanthropy does not have a direct access point to intersect with his business. He does note, however, that he is aware of his reputation for making charitable donations and doing good things. Richard recognizes that because of the favorable press pieces written about his philanthropic acts during the past 20 years, he is viewed in a good light by others. He also knows that when he chooses to speak up about an issue, his voice is heard and credibility is lent to an issue or a cause. To him, this is also a form of philanthropy.

When asked where he envisions the philanthropic world to be in 25 years, he said he expects more people to be giving away money. He envisions people trying to make a bigger impact beyond just giving. Richard also hopes that the larger nonprofit organizations are able to become more responsive and not so dominant in the philanthropic arena. He can also envision a return to the early days of philanthropy where a small number of individuals contribute a larger amount.

Another unique philanthropic interest of Richard's is providing the funding for awards. Richard is committed to giving awards that are really special and distinct. He jokes that no honoree needs another fake walnut plaque.

Richard has no regrets about his philanthropic activities. He recognizes there are things that could be done better, but he is also appreciative of the successes. As a risk taker he is not afraid to fund controversial initiatives or projects. Although, Richard does caution entrepreneurs against working so closely with a nonprofit organization to the point that the organization becomes dependent. He shared several examples of when he thought he was doing the right thing, but ended up creating a dependency.

Richard has two young children and while they are too young to be directly involved, they are aware of the importance of philanthropy in their father's life. And because Richard expects his Foundation to operate in perpetuity, it can be expected his children will have the opportunity to be actively involved in the philanthropic world. Through his personal gifts, his foundation, and his charitable lead trust, Richard has funded many capital projects and programs. Each philanthropic interaction is unique, which is a direct result of Richard's enthusiasm for funding creative projects and initiatives. He hopes his children share his passion for giving back.

From Boys and Girls Hope to the Boys and Girls Clubs. From Old Town School of Folk Music to the Sherwood Conservatory of Music. From Beverly Area Planning Association to the St. Petersburg International Center for Preservation. All of these, and many, many other organizations, have benefited from the generosity of Richard H. Driehaus.

To learn more about the Richard H. Driehaus Foundation please visit their website: www.driehausfoundation.org.

Richard's Advice

- Determine what you hope to accomplish. How do you measure it? Think about how you share your experience as an entrepreneur and add value to the nonprofit organization.
- Remember, there will be lots of trial and error; philanthropy takes time and effort and you will need to determine how to go about getting involved.
- Learn about the nonprofit organization before you invest your money or your time—*before you invest, you have to investigate.*
- Be mindful about your commitment to the nonprofit organization. If you over-invest they can become dependent on you. If you under-invest, you won't make the difference you had hoped.

GARTH FUNDIS

Garth Fundis, one of the most respected producers in Nashville since arriving in Music City in the early 1970s, has worked with country music's cream of the crop, including Sugarland, Alabama, Don Williams, and Trisha Yearwood. Perhaps one of Fundis's finest moments was reining in the reckless and self-destructive energy of Keith Whitley. Although the talented performer eventually died of alcohol poisoning, Fundis was able to provide a sanctuary in the studio for Whitley that allowed him to create some of his best work while still in the midst of a chaotic personal life. This type of relationship is not uncommon for Fundis, who is known as a patient and nurturing producer capable of bringing out the best in the artists with whom he chooses to work.

With over three decades of active involvement in Nashville's music industry as an independent record producer and engineer, Fundis's credits include numerous multiplatinum, platinum, and gold RIAA sales achievements; and CMA, ACM, Billboard Music Awards, and Grammy nominations with artists such as Trisha Yearwood, Keith Whitley, Don Williams, Crystal Gayle, Sugarland, Alabama, Colin Raye, Waylon Jennings, Emmylou Harris, New Grass Revival, Doc and Merle Watson, Townes Van Zandt, and others. In 2001, Fundis was elected chairman of the board of trustees for the National Academy of Recording Arts and Sciences (NARAS), and he has served as trustee and president for the Nashville chapter. He served on the boards of the Grammy Foundation and MusiCares. Alumnus and board member of Nashville's Leadership Music, Fundis is owner of Sound Emporium Recording Studios, the site of many of Nashville's landmark recordings.

When Business Practices Meet Nonprofit Practices and It Works

The first time I met Garth Fundis, he asked me a memorable question. We were in his office in Nashville discussing a strategy I was exploring for my business. Garth leaned across his desk and asked me if I ever worked with nonprofit organizations. I stated I did and that actually they were the largest part of my business. He then asked me if I had ever heard of the Grammys. I replied that I had, and it was at this point that Garth shared with me that he was the immediate past chair of the board of the National Academy of Recording Arts and Sciences (NARAS), the official governing body of the Grammy organization.

As noted in his bio, Garth is a prolific and well-respected record producer. When asked if he always considered himself an entrepreneur, he said that he realized it later in life when thinking about his upbringing. Garth came from a family of Kansas farmers, and he likens his record-producing business to that of his ancestors and farming. When he makes a record, he believes he is planting seeds in the music industry to see whether they will germinate, with the end result being records sold. His family members did the same thing when they planted seeds to see whether a crop would grow. Patience is required in both situations. He believes his entire family was entrepreneurs. Garth shared that his parents farmed the land but that both also worked odd jobs to keep up.

Growing up he had great music teachers. Garth went to a high school with only 250 students in the entire school. These music teachers realized the potential in Garth. As he laughingly stated, "It sure beat farming!" He grew up in a town 10 miles away from Kansas University, which had a music summer camp that Garth attended during junior high and high school. He was a vocalist and in high school played brass instruments such as the trumpet, trombone, and tuba. Garth shared that for the first time at this camp, he realized he was immersed in a culturally diverse population. For the first time, he was exposed to students who were musically as good as or better than he was. The competition was good for him because he realized he would really have to work at being good in order to compete in the music industry.

While attending college at Baker University near Kansas City and Washburn University in Topeka, Garth was a music education major, but soon the love of music and being in a rock band called him to leave school. He explored the music scene in Memphis with the band but ultimately made the move to Nashville. He became the protégé of Allen Reynolds, who was a successful songwriter/producer for Don Williams, Crystal Gayle, Garth Brooks, Kathy Mattea, Emmylou Harris, and others.

Although Garth has worked with some of the largest names in the country music genre, including Don Williams, Keith Whitley, and Trisha Yearwood and Sugarland, he began his career as a "go-fer," or intern, in the business. In 1971, he started working as a recording engineer.

His first producing credit came as an associate producer on a record Don Williams was recording. For those of you who know the song recorded by Don entitled "I Believe in You," Garth Fundis was responsible for bringing that song to Don. Garth progressed through the ranks from go-fer to engineer to coproducer to producer. Garth realized that as an engineer one of his greatest assets was that he was a good communicator between the producer and the artists. He was in effect a translator. He was learning the business inside and out.

After years in the business, Tom Schuyler asked him to come to RCA as the vice president of artists and repertoire (A&R) at RCA; this was Garth's first exposure to corporate America. His comment to me was, "There were so many meetings!" He recognized the need to work within his and other departments, but what surprised him was the territorialism and strife. He was amazed that even with all the resources available, being successful didn't always happen. You had to constantly battle through the obstacles.

After a couple of years, Garth was invited to open a record label for Jerry Moss and Herb Alpert called Almo Sounds. Garth ran it for three years. But it was at a time in Nashville when the number of record labels went from six labels to twenty-four almost overnight. Eventually, Garth went back to being an independent record producer.

> A record producer is in essence the coach of the talent or talents and the overall arranger of songs in the album. Record producers may work for a company or can have a company and business of their own, as Garth does.

From 1971 to 1991 Garth worked with Don Williams, Keith Whitley, and Trisha Yearwood and others, but then he had an opportunity to buy the recording studio in which he had worked for years. The Sound Emporium had been for sale for a couple of years, but there had been no offers. Garth also knew rain was leaking through the roof. The then owner was Roy Clark of *Hee Haw* fame.

Garth first went to his accountant, expecting him to say this was a crazy idea. But the accountant did not. Although his first offer was rejected by Roy's accountant, Garth finally talked to Roy directly, assuring him the two staff members would be kept on and reminding Roy that he had already taken about all he could out of the building in terms of tax deductions; the deal was soon accepted. Garth then went to the banks, which had a hard time believing he was purchasing a recording studio for a price that was less than the appraised value. It took a while to convince them. Finally, he did and purchased the Sound Emporium. The first thing he did was fix the roof, and then he added an office in the front and pulled the two buildings together. He also refurbished Studio B as well as made an office for himself in the back out of the way so that other producers coming to use the building would not be interrupted by Garth's presence.

Garth was fairly confident about owning a recording studio because he had done everything at the Sound Emporium from cleaning the gutters to sweeping the floors to making records. He reminded his staff that they were in the service business, noting that individuals and other record producers were going to be using the studios, in essence renting studio time, and that the goal was to give them a good experience. As Garth says, "The Sound Emporium might not be the fanciest recording studio, but it is clean, professional and the equipment works." In the recording business, repeat business is essential. Artists become comfortable, especially if they have a productive experience. As Garth jokingly said, "Musicians and artists are superstitious," meaning if they use a particular studio and have a hit record, they will want to go back and use the same facilities.

As Garth was having success as a producer and a studio owner, he was invited to run for the board of the local NARAS chapter in Nashville.

NARAS has recognized and celebrated music for 50 years through the Grammy Awards. The Recording Academy has a rich legacy and ongoing growth as the premier outlet for honoring achievements in the recording arts and supporting the music community.

The Grammys themselves are the only peer-presented award to honor artistic achievement, technical proficiency, and overall excellence in the recording industry, without regard to album sales or chart position.

Initially in his philanthropic journey, Garth could give away studio time as an item to be auctioned off at charitable events. For example, he donated time for a youth symphony to use the recording studio. It was the first time these young orchestra members had been in a studio and they had an outstanding experience. But Garth shared what he learned: once you do something like this, the nonprofit organization keeps coming back and almost expects the donation automatically.

Another philanthropic experience began in 1994 after his brother passed away in his late 40s due to complications from multiple sclerosis. The local multiple sclerosis chapter approached Garth to be on the board of directors, and he agreed. It was at a time when he wanted to be sure to do something to honor and remember his brother. However, the experience made him realize it was not a good fit. This nonprofit organization did not really meet his goals bcause they were really looking for cash, something that Garth as an entrepreneur at this point in his life was not able to provide to a great extent. He could serve and provide in-kind donations, but not large sums of cash. What surprised Garth was that the group did not tell him when he was being recruited what they really needed. They did not share the financial expectations of board members. As I told Garth, the nonprofit organization was probably thinking that once a board member was recruited the nonprofit organization would convince him or her that this was a worthwhile endeavor to which the individual would want to give money. As Garth and many others have shared, it would have been better if they had been more up-front.

Record producers generally get paid twice a year based on royalties. There are good years and bad years, ups and downs.

NARAS was different. First, it is a 501(c) 6 rather than a 501(c) 3; however, there are two 501 (c) 3 organizations related to the NARAS organization: the Grammy Foundation and MusiCares. After having first having served as a governor on the local Nashville chapter board, and eventually as the chapter president, Garth was able to attend the annual national meeting. As chapter president, he sat in the back row. But even though he was in the back row, he was able to communicate with the trustees. The trustees were individuals who were the "who's who" in the music industry from New York, Los Angeles, Memphis, Atlanta, Austin, Chicago, and the other chapters. Garth realized at this point that if it were not for his service on the local NARAS chapter board, he likely would never have had another way to get to know these individuals. Garth ultimately became a trustee at the national level of the NARAS board.

Garth shared that as he continued to become more and more involved in the nonprofit world, his wife, Ann, herself very philanthropic, would give him books on nonprofit organizations and how to be a good board member and leader. Garth read these books with interest, realizing his responsibility as a board member. He was also one of those rare people who actually read the bylaws, minutes, mission statement, case statement, and strategic plan. In meetings, when decisions were being made that could not, for example, be made by the board of directors but needed to be made by the entire membership, Garth would raise this as a point of order during the meeting. As he laughingly said, "It would send the lawyers scurrying to read the bylaws and charter." Garth also realized that in order to get a proposal approved by the board one did not simply bring it up at a meeting for a yea or nay vote but that one had to do one's homework beforehand, securing consensus around the table before the actual vote took place. He became a politician, so to speak. He was very astute regarding the process and was able to get things through the board process. Others saw this and would come to him with their proposals. Once again he saw his role as being a translator, a communicator, or a coach.

In 1998, Garth was elected chairperson of the NARAS national board. He was excited. Garth had watched the Grammy Awards show since he was a kid, and here he was chairing the nonprofit organization that brought that peer award program into existence and everyone's living room. Sixty days after assuming the chair position, however, he received a FedEx package from the offices of attorney Gloria Allred. It landed on his desk with a thud. It detailed a complaint from a high-ranking employee alleging sexual discrimination, harassment, and even assault. Garth stated that after reading it he sat stunned in his office for about 30 minutes, not moving but pondering what to do. Garth summoned all his business expertise and dove in. Between meetings with the attorneys and other board members, hours, days, and weeks slipped away. This was also time away from his family. But Garth, and his family, were committed to seeing this lawsuit through to the end much like he sees the producing of a record through to the end.

Once the lawsuit was settled, Garth was asked by the board to serve as the temporary president/CEO of NARAS while he also continued as chairperson of the board. While this is a bit unorthodox, it worked. And if you knew Garth, you would realize it was absolutely the best solution. Garth temporarily moved to Los Angeles for seven months, coming home to Nashville on the weekends, but he did not make a record for two years. A new president of NARAS was hired in December 2002 and Garth's term as chairperson of the board ended in May 2003, but he served another two-year term as the chairperson emeritus.

Garth said that although the nonprofit experience did not add directly to his business's bottom line, it changed him. He had associated with likeminded individuals and had access to people he would never have met otherwise. Many of these people have become friends. Because of this access, his business has changed as well.

Garth continues his charitable work and currently serves as the facilitator for Leadership Music, another nonprofit organization.

Garth's Advice

- Choose something you understand.
- Give unselfishly of yourself to that cause.
- It is about the organization first; any credit you receive is admirable but it is not the focus.
- Use your head . . . trust your gut.
- Don't take things at face value.
- There may be bigger problems than originally anticipated.
- You can't quit.

CAROLYN GABLE

Carolyn Gable proves that dreams can be achieved: as an individual who rose from waitress to CEO, as a single mother parenting seven children ages 9 to 34, and as the founder of the Expect A Miracle Foundation, a visionary foundation serving the needs of single parents and their children.

Carolyn Gable is president and CEO of New Age Transportation, Distribution & Warehousing Inc., a 30-plus million dollar enterprise based in Lake Zurich, Illinois. The corporate headquarters includes an 85,000 square foot warehouse. Her 23 years of experience in the transportation industry include working with such clients as Time Warner Cable, Cox Communications, McCormick & Co., Flavor Savor, and Insight Communications.

Carolyn's entrepreneurial business success has been featured in both local and national media outlets, including ABC's *20/20, Good Morning America, The Wall Street Journal, Crain's Chicago Business, Chicago Tribune, The New York Times, Ladies Home Journal, Chicago Sun-Times*, and the cover of *Business Week*. In addition, Carolyn has been honored to receive awards in recognition of her business and philanthropic achievements:

- 2008 Business Star Award from the Women's Business Enterprise National Council (WBENC)
- *Enterprising Woman* magazine's Top Women Entrepreneurs in North America
- Daily Point of Light Award from the Points of Light Foundation
- Regional Ernst & Young Entrepreneur of the Year Award in the service category
- Chicago Entrepreneur of the Year Award presented by the University of Illinois, Chicago
- Women of Achievement Entrepreneur Award from the YWCA of Lake County
- National Luminary Award presented by the Mothers In Business Network and the International Alliance of Working Mothers

Expect a Miracle!

The true magic of Carolyn Gable cannot be explained by listing all the awards she has received as an entrepreneur or by reading a standard bio of her accomplishments. Carolyn Gable is not your typical CEO. To understand the impact and the importance of her work today, we need to take a short trip back in time.

When I first met Carolyn Gable, I was greeted with a warm smile and immediately felt welcomed. The positive energy she radiates is undeniable, and she made me feel as if we were lifelong friends. Because I was already familiar with her success in business and her charitable work, I began by asking when she knew she was philanthropically inclined. She immediately steered the conversation to stories of her childhood, and more important, her family's lack of philanthropy.

Carolyn is one of six children, and they grew up like most families in a financially strapped household where having a cola was a treat. Carolyn fondly recalled her mom bringing home a pizza and six colas. Each of her siblings plus Carolyn would make that cola last by drinking it slowly. It might last a day or two, but to be sure no one else drank from the wrong bottle, each sibling put his or her name on the bottle and marked a line where the soda was when it was put in the refrigerator. Every time a sip or drink was taken, another marker line would be added to the bottle indicating where the soda was now.

Although her parents were not philanthropic, to Carolyn, being philanthropic is just a natural part of her. Carolyn's first memory of acting charitably was when she was about 10 years old. There was a woman down the street from where Carolyn lived who had brain cancer. Carolyn reached out to her and provided help such as shampooing the woman's hair, babysitting her children, and doing the dishes. Another childhood story involved watching an *I Love Lucy* episode with her older sister Maureen. The episode, dealing with homeless people, resonated with Maureen, causing her to exclaim "That's you! You are the friend of the homeless, friend of the friendless!" Later, when Carolyn was in beauty school in Des Plaines, Illinois, she would go to a home for foster children, Maryville Academy, and take care of the kids' hair.

While her philanthropic journey seemed well on its way, her career path was off to a slower start. After graduating high school, she spent the following year as a beautician. Still feeling unfulfilled, she entered the restaurant industry as a waitress. It was during this period of her life that her philanthropic nature morphed into providing excellent customer service. Over the next 12 years, Carolyn perfected her people skills: managing difficult kitchen staff and demanding bartenders and, of course, providing excellent service to her customers with a warm smile. Carolyn is quick to point out that being a waitress is the ultimate customer service job, and it provided her life training and a better education than any Harvard degree.

Carolyn has outstanding people skills, to which anyone who has ever been a waitress can relate, but it was difficult to raise two small children on an income comprised mainly of tips. Wanting a better life for herself and her children, she walked into an employment agency looking for a change. Landing an interview at a transportation company, she was offered a job as a customer service representative. Dedicating the next two years to learning the business by day, and still waitressing at night, her hard work materialized into a sales position. Using her customer service skills, she quickly excelled in the position. Five years later, in 1989, she launched her own company, New Age Transportation, out of the basement of her home.

Carolyn's rise to success was hardly typical, especially in the male-dominated logistics industry of the late 1980s. Yet, almost 20 years later, this single mother of seven children has developed New Age Transportation into a thriving business, with over 60 employees and clients ranging from *Fortune* 500 companies to small local businesses. The recipient of numerous awards, including the Chicago Entrepreneur of the Year Award from the University of Illinois, Chicago, and the feature of many media stories, including *Good Morning America* and *20/20*, Carolyn has not stopped in her quest to help people realize their dreams.

Last year, Carolyn wrote *Everything I Know as a CEO I Learned as a Waitress* to inspire others who want to achieve their dreams. Her book describes the skills she learned while waiting tables and why she credits them for her success today. From honoring honesty to paying attention to details and having fun, these values are a reflection of her strongly held personal beliefs and the foundation for conducting business at New Age Transportation. Further, Carolyn is currently providing inspiration through speaking engagements and weekly videos posted to her website, www.carolyngable.com.

Because her formative teenage years were spent living in a single-parent household and she is a single parent herself who relied on food stamps to help make ends meet, she has lived the struggles that many face today. As a result of the success of New Age Transportation and her passionate advocacy regarding the plight of single-parent families, in 2001 she created the

Expect A Miracle Foundation. Chartered to help working single parents provide their children with extracurricular activities such as organized sports and special tutoring, the Foundation has enriched the lives of more than 3,000 children nationwide.

Carolyn believes the children of today are the promise of a better future for all of us. Although the children who are beneficiaries of the Carolyn Gable Expect A Miracle Foundation send letters of gratitude, many letters describe an upsetting reality: they can't play outdoors because the communities they live in are so dangerous. Carolyn explained that when the children are not in the summer camps and other planned activities, they may become involved with gangs, which is destructive to our communities and societies. Furthermore, she believes a percentage of these children will be abused both physically and sexually. The staggering number of children in these situations is daunting, evidenced by a volume of requests totaling over $100,000 annually. Yet Carolyn continues her quest to change the lives of children, obtaining inspiration from their letters explaining how happy they are to partake in organized activities in a safe environment.

In addition to the Foundation, Carolyn continues to lead by example through her participation in the Principal for a Day program within the city of Chicago. Launched in 1998, Mayor Richard M. Daley's Principal for a Day program relies on local business leaders to foster a long-term relationship with a participating school within the Chicago public school system. The school Carolyn supports is Social Justice High School in the Little Village neighborhood on the south side of the city. Carolyn had a great experience meeting these young adults and learning their stories, but she didn't realize the magnitude of their struggle until the day was over. Expecting to hail a taxicab to take her to her next appointment, the reality set in when the principal explained that taxis do not come to that part of the city. Carolyn was incredulous, thinking "How could this be?" This scenario bothered Carolyn, and days later when she was speaking to another group she shared that there are kids in the city of Chicago who are afraid to walk to school for fear of the violence that exists and advocated for everyone to get involved and make a difference.

Her personal involvement with these students goes beyond a few personal appearances and making cash donations. A couple of weeks before Thanksgiving 2008, Carolyn learned that many of the students would not be able to celebrate Thanksgiving in the traditional sense (over 95% of the students are from low-income families). Carolyn's own life experiences provided firsthand knowledge of these struggles, and she immediately mobilized a team of employees to organize a donation. At the end of the school day on the day before Thanksgiving, Carolyn and her team of employees handed out 400 Thanksgiving dinners—complete with a frozen turkey and all the trimmings—for every student and his or her family to enjoy.

Carolyn also learned that the school did not have adequate supplies. This, too, bothered her, but she figured she would tackle one problem at a time, and the problem she was now focused on was the violence issue in the school's neighborhood.

A few months after serving as principal for the day, Carolyn received an email from the Little Village school principal thanking her for the school supplies. Carolyn knew she had not sent the supplies but thought maybe she had forgotten something. So Carolyn asked her assistants, and they informed her that neither the company nor the Foundation had sent the supplies. Carolyn was a bit puzzled and embarrassed, assuming she was going to have to call and tell the principal he had made a mistake. However, before she could make that call, she learned from her employees that upon hearing of the situation at the school they took it upon themselves to collect and send the supplies. Her employees had learned from Carolyn what could be done and helped those in need, with the end result being that the school was the recipient of a miracle.

Carolyn built her company, New Age Transportation, into a successful corporation, which allows her to focus on helping others through the Expect A Miracle Foundation. She uses the analogy of her company being a train and the Foundation providing the direction. In other words, she allows the company to be the source of her life's work, which is manifested in the success of the Expect A Miracle Foundation. Carolyn, a very spiritual woman, believes metaphysics plays a part in giving, too. When you give, you attract more and are thus changed. It is about the laws of the universe, says Carolyn.

When I asked her whether being philanthropic has helped her business, she immediately said, "Yes." She notes that when you give it comes back tenfold, as it states in the Bible; it is part of the laws of the universe. However, she also believes you have to be in a place to receive. Carolyn believes the universe rewards. Problems create opportunities, and learning leads to greater learning.

Finally, one of Carolyn's favorite sayings comes from a Johnny Cash song written by Billy Joe Shaver: "I'm just an old chunk of coal, But I'm gonna be a diamond some day!" This is what philanthropy is about to her.

Carolyn's Advice

- The Universe rewards, so get involved.
- Find a way to help even if you don't think you know how.
- If you can't give money, do something such as smile at someone, shovel a driveway, help with groceries, or simply give them a hug.
- Get out of your skin; it is not about you.

DEBORAH GIBSON

For more than 20 years, Deborah Gibson has proven she's an entertainer of immeasurable talent. From singer, songwriter, and musician to actor and dancer, she embodies what it truly means to be an entertainer.

Born and raised in Brooklyn, New York, the celebrated singer started her personal love affair with music at the ripe age of two and a half. "I'd put my ear to the speaker in my bedroom and run back to the piano and play—left and right hands." Known the world over as "the Original Pop Princess," Deborah has come a long way from her early days of classical music training.

Deborah exploded on the pop music scene at the tender age of 16. A music prodigy, she quickly became the youngest person ever to write, produce, and perform a number one single ("Foolish Beat"), a record she still holds today in the *Guinness Book of World Records*. To date, Deborah has sold more than 16 million albums worldwide.

Refusing to simply ride out the wave of her initial success, Deborah has since invested more than 20 years into the music industry. Releasing a string of well-received albums—*Out of the Blue* (1987), *Electric Youth* (1989), *Anything Is Possible* (1990), *Body Mind Soul* (1993), *Think with Your Heart* (1995), *Deborah* (1996), *M.Y.O.B* (2001), and *Colored Lights* (2003)—as well as a greatest hits collection, Deborah has successfully worked the music industry from all angles. In 1988 Deborah co-hosted Nickelodeon's first ever Kids' Choice Awards with Tony Danza.

After conquering the pop world, she set her sights on the theater. Deborah took a star turn in the Broadway production of *Les Miserables* as Eponine. She broke box office records in the London West End production of *Grease* as Sandy, and then took the stage in the U.S. Broadway tours of *Grease* and *Funny Girl*, playing Rizzo and Fanny Brice, respectively. Gibson also wowed critics as Belle in Disney's *Beauty and the Beast*, Gypsy Rose Lee in *Gypsy*, the Narrator in the national tour of *Joseph and the Amazing Technicolor Dreamcoat*, Cinderella in the national production of Rodgers and Hammerstein's *Cinderella*, Velma Kelly in *Chicago*, and Sally Bowles in the Broadway revival of *Cabaret*.

Continuing to dazzle with entertainment magic, Deborah bridged the gap between pop music and Broadway with her one-woman show *Pop Goes Broadway*. She brings the best of both worlds to the stage, singing some of her biggest pop hits and reprising her starring roles on Broadway. Critics said "'Pop Goes Broadway' is the best show Atlantic City has seen in quite some time . . . it's totally entertaining" during her three-week engagement in May 2008 at the Concert Venue at Harrah's. Phil Roura of the *New York Daily News* said, "she has mastered her craft to the point where she just doesn't perform a song—she embraces it and delivers it with her own special stamp of approval."

Deborah recently returned to her Broadway roots for a successful run of *The King and I*. Steven Stanely of *StageSceneLA* said, "From the moment this Broadway vet steps onto the stage, there is magic in the air, and no one can doubt that this Anna will enchant the King from their first meeting." Les Spindle of *Backstage* said, "Gibson exudes grace and warmth as the patient but determined Anna. She brings renewed luster to beloved songs such as 'Hello Young Lovers,' finding the passion in Rodger's eloquent lyrics and Hammerstein's lush melodies." Cary Ginell said, "Utilizing a meticulously cultivated British accent, Gibson is excellent in her portrayal of Anna." Gibson is now the composer and co-lyricist on a new musical in preproduction for Broadway: *The Flunky*, written by Jimmy Van Patten.

The "Original Pop Princess" is ready to pass the torch to the next generation of musical sensations. Her passion to mentor and foster young performers and songwriters led her to create Deborah Gibson's Electric Youth, a series of performing arts camps and songwriting/recording intensive classes.

AWARDS AND ACHIEVEMENTS

Winner of ASCAP Songwriter of the Year, 1989
Nominated for Favorite Female Music Performer, People's Choice
    Awards, 1990
Rock Producer of the Year, American Songwriter Awards, 1990
Nominated for Best Pop Female Vocalist, American Music Awards, 1990
Artist of the Year, New York Music Awards, 1990
Song of the Year ("Lost In Your Eyes"), New York Music Awards, 1990
Best Pop Female Vocalist, New York Music Awards, 1990
Debut Album of the Year (*Out of the Blue*), New York Music Awards, 1989
Debut Artist of the Year, New York Music Awards, 1989

Yawn the Biggest, Smile the Widest!

Almost everyone has heard of Deborah Gibson, the 1990s pop star who then was referred to as Debbie Gibson. Her music, songwriting, and acting continue today, but what she is most enthused about is her philanthropic work and the establishment of the Deborah Gibson's Electric Youth organization.

To understand how she decided to start an organization with a charitable component, I asked Deborah about her first philanthropic memory. She responded by saying she recalls always being willing to give of her talent and time. She remembers going to nursing homes and performing on a regular basis when she was eight years old. Deborah fondly recalls that her parents were both working and had no free time for what one might think of as traditional philanthropic work, but they were always willing to drive her and, on occasion, her sisters to activities that had a charitable and a performance component. Deborah believes this activity she did as a young person is what most performers are able to do quite readily—use their talents and give of their time to charitable endeavors. According to Deborah, "It is a valuable thing to do."

Deborah grew up in a working class family but clearly remembers her father's example of helping others. Deborah shared that her dad, when taking her to an audition, would on occasion see a homeless person on the street and say to Deborah, "Let's go buy that person a slice of pizza." She cites this and other examples from her parents while she was growing up as teaching her that you are supposed to help other people.

Deborah also told me that when she was 15 years old, she was perusing a magazine and saw an advertisement by the Christian Children's Fund asking individuals to sponsor a child. The advertisement said that for the price of a daily cup of coffee, you could change a child's life. Even though Deborah did not drink coffee, this advertisement tugged at her heart. She decided to sponsor two children in Malaysia through the money she earned babysitting and teaching piano. The sponsorship continued for many years, and when Deborah was 19 she traveled to Malaysia to meet them. They were of course very excited to meet their sponsor, who also happened to be one of the top pop stars at that time. Deborah enjoyed talking to them and learning more about them and their lives. At one point, she even brought them on stage during a concert to accompany her when she was touring in their part of the world.

Deborah also shared that when the parents of one of the children had another daughter, they named their newborn child after her. To Deborah this was the ultimate expression of thanks.

Throughout her life and career as a pop singer and Broadway star, Deborah recalls fondly that she was involved with and continues to be involved with many other nonprofit organizations, including the Make-A-Wish Foundation, Starlight and Starbright Children's Foundation, the Children's Miracle Network, and various animal rights organizations.

However, in 2008, Deborah's heartfelt philanthropic work really began. It was then she founded Deborah Gibson's Electric Youth (www.deborahgibsonselectricyouth.com), an organization that, according to its website, is focused on providing a nurturing, creative, disciplined, and fun atmosphere for young people who are serious about embarking on a career in entertainment.

In discussing Electric Youth with me, Deborah said, "I set up my nonprofit organization, Gibson Girl Foundation, to provide scholarships to help kids. I wanted to help broaden kids' interest and lift their spirits. The funding is for private music lessons and any other arts programs they wish to attend at the camp." Electric Youth is open to youth between the ages of 10 and 20 who are serious performers, with classes offered in songwriting, music theory, improvisation, vocal technique, scene study, dance, pop performance and styling, and camera and audition techniques. Deborah is directly involved with the camps and gets some of her friends to join her, including, recently, Jason Alexander, Lorenzo Lamas, and Wayne Brady.

When I asked Deborah what inspired her to start this nonprofit organization, she said she thinks one of the reasons was recalling her father's youth. Her dad grew up with three other boys living in a foster home. The four boys formed a singing quartet that eventually performed on television shows such as *The Ed Sullivan Show* and *Name That Tune*, ultimately winning a station wagon for the foster home on the latter. She realized that by being in a singing and performing group, her father and the other three boys were able to stay out of trouble. It also provided them with a common focus and kept them together, even though they had no parents or family.

One of the goals of the Deborah Gibson's Electric Youth organization is to allow children to be focused and stay out of trouble, as a number of the attendees are children with a difficult home life. Deborah also wants music to be part of their life and has already seen results. As she readily shared, "The kids thrive at the camp. Their self-esteem and self-empowerment increases. The camp and its activities elevates the energy of a kid and is supportive." When I asked Deborah if these outcomes surprised her, she answered, "No, because music did this for me." She did, however, recognize that she did not know the degree to which music and performance had empowered her. Deborah recalled that she and her three sisters were always doing shows or they were being "dragged" to an audition of hers. She further told me that her youngest sister was painfully shy as a child, but that "by being around this type of activity she [her sister] came out of her shell."

Deborah is energized by the kids who have attended the first two camps. As she says, "Their individual experiences are amazing!" She also loves to see their faces as they labor and become truly exhausted doing what they love: "You see the kids yawn the widest and smile the biggest!"

Deborah also told me the story of one of the first winners of the camp, a 16-year-old girl who was Armenian and came from an Armenian community. As a matter of fact, this young girl had attended school all her life with only other Armenian children. When she came to the Electric Youth camp, she was depressed, but she came with an idea for a song. She attended the songwriting session and was able to channel her feelings and ideas into a powerful song that allowed her to express what she was feeling. Deborah witnessed a transformation occur during the songwriting session. Through attending the camp, the young woman met 120 other young people who were different than the kids in her immediate home community, and she now keeps in touch with them. This young woman has an entire new community of friends.

The website of Deborah Gibson's Electric Youth noted that "Mishavonna, a Camp Electric Youth alumni from last summer, has made it to American Idol's Hollywood week!" According to Deborah, "Mishavonna is a superstar vocalist, musician and a sweetheart and we here at Electric Youth are so proud of her!!! Go get 'em Mishavonna!!!"

During our conversation about philanthropy, I asked Deborah if she had any regrets or desires for "do-overs" about things she had done for charitable efforts. She immediately responded that she did not have any regrets, but she had learned some lessons about her philanthropic focus. Deborah shared that she prefers to keep what she does for others personalized. She says the big, celebrity-filled events don't need her help as much as the kids she personally mentors. This is where she wants to spend her time.

As you might guess, one of the things Deborah continues to be proud of in regard to her philanthropic efforts is starting the Electric Youth organization. She says that every day and every thing she does is for the camp: "It is pretty much nonstop." She is happy because she started it from the ground up even though she did not know anything about starting an organization that had a charitable component. When others would ask her how she would get it done, in other words, how she would succeed, her response was always, "I will know what to do when the time comes." And she did.

Her ultimate thrill was being at the first camp orientation of Electric Youth and seeing the kids with their parents. She told me she shook her head and incredulously asked herself, "How did I get here?" She then took me back to the beginning, sharing that this vision of hers was and continues to be all-encompassing. Deborah said that at the beginning she went through every business card she had and started thinking of every person she knew, recalling especially those who had said, "If you ever need anything, just call." She particularly remembered a producer at the show *Entertainment Tonight*. Without calling any agents or public relations people, she picked up the phone and dialed his number directly. When he answered, she told him about her vision and what she was doing in building the Electric Youth organization, asking if he was interested in the story. He told her he would call back in 10 minutes and hung up. Ten minutes later he called back and said *Entertainment Tonight* wanted to do an exclusive. Deborah laughingly shared that although she does not nor cannot ask for anything for herself, she finds she is shameless in asking everyone she encounters for help with the kids and the camps.

Given all of her experiences in the nonprofit world, I asked Deborah whether she sees a difference between philanthropy and charity. She stated that although both are important, she believes philanthropy is wider reaching. It is building something that is a legacy and will most likely continue for years and years. Philanthropy, to Deborah, has more roots and a solid foundation. Charity, on the other hand, is a one-off, meaning it is about providing immediate help in a particular situation. The Deborah Gibson's Electric Youth is definitely viewed by Deborah as a philanthropic effort!

Deborah's Advice

- When doing charitable or philanthropic work, pull out all the stops; pull in every favor.
- Do what you love, and the rest will follow; in other words, be gutsy!
- Trust your instincts; create a society that is right and meaningful.
- Donate your time and talent as well as your financial resources.

LETICIA HERRERA

Leticia Herrera is president of ECI, a Chicago-based company she founded in 1989. ECI is a professional, full-service industrial, construction, and commercial maintenance firm providing comprehensive cleaning, maintenance, and restoration services for private businesses, public agencies, institutional owners, and others. The company employs approximately 50 people and is one of the few firms specializing in fine stone and metal restoration, particularly in the areas of high-image, high-traffic impression, intricate lighting systems, and other areas requiring special care and attention. ECI has established itself among the top industrial maintenance and restoration firms in Chicago.

In her role as president, Leticia oversees all phases of the firm's operations and is directly involved with clients to develop long-range preventive maintenance and restoration programs designed to reduce repair and replacement costs and maximize the useful life of buildings, equipment, and their components. She also directs all marketing and strategic planning for the company.

Her professionalism and persistence have catapulted ECI to a prestigious level, working for such highly respected institutions as the Museum of Science and Industry, the Shedd Aquarium, the Oriental Theater, the City of Chicago, the State of Illinois, United Airlines, Northern Illinois University, and the Field Museum, to mention a few. Leticia is also highly regarded for her ability to build partnerships with a number of construction and property management companies and building owners, including R.R. Donnelley, U.S. Equities Realty Inc., W.E. O'Neil, the Tribune Company, and Alter Asset Management Group.

Prior to founding ECI in 1989, Leticia owned and operated Biblioart Inc., an import company specializing in the purchase, sale, and marketing of Spanish art that she founded in 1980. With ECI, Leticia combined her love of buildings and fine architecture with her love of art to assemble and train a team of people who bring a standard of excellence, commitment, and integrity to their work. Working with geologists, metallurgists, sculptors, and other stone and metal specialists, ECI has made an art of the provision of building restoration and maintenance services.

A dynamic woman with a commitment to her Latino heritage, Leticia mentors other minority and women entrepreneurs and is an advocate for the advancement of youth. She is currently on the board for the United States Hispanic Chamber of Commerce, the Women's Business Development Center, and the Mexican American Chamber of Commerce. Her leadership and energy has been recognized by Latino, women, professional, and business organizations with numerous awards, including the Small Business Person of the Year Award by Illinois Governor George Ryan in 2000. ECI was also recently recognized as one of the fastest-growing inner-city businesses in the United States by the Initiative for a Competitive Inner City (ICIC) and *Inc.* magazine.

Philanthropy of the Heart

I first met Leticia Herrera when I worked for the University of Illinois at Chicago. She had recently been inducted into the Chicago Area Entrepreneurship Hall of Fame, the oldest hall of fame to honor entrepreneurs in the Chicagoland area. As stated in its annual program booklet, "Those inducted into the Chicago Area Entrepreneurship Hall of Fame embody the entrepreneurial spirit of Chicago area businesses: a determination to succeed, an unsurpassed commitment to excellence, and the rare ability to meet challenges and recognize opportunity through innovation, proactiveness, and risk taking."

Leticia's first business was a lemonade stand when she was seven years old. She laughingly shared that it was probably her most profitable venture because her mother bought all the ingredients. In other words, Leticia sold the lemonade and kept all the profit. This was a very enterprising start for a young entrepreneur. Today, Leticia owns and operates ECI. Founded in 1989 originally as a janitorial and cleaning services company for commercial buildings in Chicago, ECI from its beginning to its present-day form has embodied the entrepreneurial spirit.

Leticia also embraces the entrepreneurial spirit in her philanthropic endeavors. She believes an individual needs to give beyond writing checks and instead practice what she calls "philanthropy of the heart." Leticia and her siblings are first-generation Americans; their parents came from the small town of Durango, Mexico, to the Chicago area. Although philanthropy is part of the Mexican culture, it is not part of their vocabulary. Leticia believes that when Mexicans hear the word philanthropy, they think of Donald Trump and the Kennedy family. She stated that often in the Hispanic community and culture, philanthropy, even just saying that word, is not necessarily something everyday people can relate to. Leticia, however, believes that philanthropy is "priceless" like the MasterCard television commercial and cannot be measured. She revealed that recently she had purchased Halloween costumes and given them to children she knew did not have a costume. Although it was not an effort organized through any nonprofit organization, Leticia truly believes and espouses that this is philanthropy. Time, according to Leticia, is the most valuable thing a person can give to the charitable endeavors in the world. Time is what is most needed, according to her, and it is the underestimated philanthropy that is taking place in this country and the world.

She further believes that those individuals who serve as a foster parent to a child, who visit a senior citizens home, or who volunteer once a month are all philanthropists, even if they don't write a check or make a donation. Again, it is what she calls philanthropy of the heart. As she stated, "We don't consider helping others to be philanthropy, but it is." She further believes the federal government should consider a tax credit for those who give of their time, stating that it might lead to even more individuals becoming involved in charitable activities.

Leticia's earliest memories of philanthropy come from her grandmother, who told her and her siblings to help those who most need it. She believes that in the Hispanic community it also comes from the Catholic Church, where giving is a given and occurs on a daily basis. Leticia shared that many philanthropic things are done in the Hispanic community but are not necessarily considered by individuals to be philanthropic but rather what you do to help others. In other words, according to her, the word philanthropy is not part of the Hispanic culture or language in a formalized manner. Leticia gave the example that if a visitor came to her family's hometown of Durango, Mexico, and there was only one enchilada or taco left, the visitor, meaning the outsider, would be given it to eat, even if everyone else in the town was hungry. This would be done to make them feel a part of the community and welcomed. This to Leticia is true philanthropy and the embodiment of the Hispanic culture.

> Leticia uses another example, asking the question, "Why aren't people taking someone home for Thanksgiving dinner, even if your family does not know this person? Why isn't this a tradition that is honored as philanthropy?"

What is surprising is that something like this actually happened to Leticia. She recounted a time when she went to Durango and was invited to the home of the man who takes care of her father's "ranch," which according to Leticia consists of a few head of cattle. Upon arriving at the home, Leticia realized how poor the family was because the house had a dirt floor. As poor as they appeared, however, they gave her a chile relejano—the only chile relejano they had. Although she was very reluctant to eat it, because she knew the family would not partake and that they did not have any other food, she knew she had to in order to honor them. As she retells the story, Leticia gets teary eyed because she states that as they sat and watched her, pure joy was on their faces. To her this was the ultimate example of being charitable and philanthropic.

Leticia also believes we do not give enough credit to those who are giving from their need, not their surplus. The example she shared was that if you have $10 million and make a donation of $100,000, you are giving 1% and are recognized as a great philanthropist. But what about the person who has $100 dollars and gives $10 (10%) to charity? Such a person is not seen as a great philanthropist but has actually given more in terms of a percentage of what he or she possessed than the wealthier individual.

Leticia also recognizes that our society is a little out of balance with our philanthropy. Part of the American dream is to chase the "almighty dollar." But as she cautions, "There is a price to be paid to get that dollar."

Leticia thinks we need to be more in touch with our community and, as entrepreneurs, share our knowledge and experiences too. Entrepreneurs need be reliable community citizens so others can count on us.

She strongly believes that everybody can be a philanthropist because we all have the power to change someone's life through a smile or a hug, through being a listening ear or a person who gets called into action. This, to Leticia, is the beginning of being philanthropic: the giving of oneself for the betterment of others. She challenges entrepreneurs and others to think of philanthropy as a team effort, with some able to give money and others able to give time. The key according to her is being able to care and serve in the role of caregiver. As Leticia states, "You need to care to give." She also encourages individuals to put the philanthropic word into action. She would ask individuals to find a balance or middle ground whereby all can be involved in charitable activities and feel like contributors. There is value in both giving dollars and giving "touch" to humanity. One thought Leticia shared with me is how wonderful it would be if senior citizens became associated with animal shelters. Think of a world where older individuals go to animal shelters to touch and pet dogs and cats. It would be a win-win situation for all.

Leticia also believes that through giving of one's time or financial resources, you are showing you care. In other words, giving is caring. And by giving you make dreams come true for others. Again, Leticia thinks that everyone has the ability to be a philanthropist because everyone has the ability to give.

When I asked her what a philanthropist receives when he or she gives, Leticia immediately responded with, "Joy that you can't buy. Also honor and respect. When I was eating that chile relejano I felt like Princess Diana. I didn't feel superior as I knew they were giving from their heart and full of joy but I was on top of the world."

Although some might think that if a person doesn't give financially, he or she doesn't care, Leticia has a different thought. She believes if an individual offers an opinion or his or her time and causes a transformation to happen, that action is philanthropic because the opinion comes with your knowledge, wisdom, and expertise. Leticia also thinks that taking the time to make a call on behalf of someone or some organization, writing a letter, reviewing a resume, paying the toll for some-one behind you, or buying a candy bar for a child you don't know is philanthropy.

Leticia's wish is for philanthropy to become a household word in all communities for all citizens.

Finally, for all entrepreneurs, Leticia has some advice: "Share you failures, too, because those are the times that have made you a success even though you initially failed. You are a success the moment you take a chance and risk to make your dreams come true!"

Leticia's Advice

- Wake up: you are a philanthropist as we are all born philanthropists; it is innate.
- The more you give, the more you will get back.
- Good news: you don't have to give dollars to be a philanthropist.
- Agree to serve on a board or volunteer.
- Talk to children and adults about giving, sharing, and caring because these all are philanthropy.

BILL IMADA

Bill Imada is the chairman and chief executive officer of IW Group Inc. (formerly Imada Wong Communications Group), a Los Angeles–based marketing communications company specializing in the North American Asian markets. Currently his firm has three offices and employs more than 60 people from over a dozen countries.

Bill has over 20 years of experience in marketing, public relations, advertising, and cross-cultural training, and has served as a consultant to more than a dozen *Fortune* 500 companies. Some of his current clients include American Airlines, Farmers Insurance, McDonalds USA, MetLife, Nissan North America, PhRMA, U.S. Census Bureau, Wal-Mart Stores, and WellPoint. IW Group Inc. is a part of the Interpublic Group of Companies (NYSE: IPG). The firm is a minority-owned and operated agency and is ranked nationally in both public relations and advertising.

Bill has a bachelor's degree in business administration from California State University, Northridge, and is a graduate of the Coro Foundation's leadership training program in public affairs. He is a graduate of the AMBEP Program at the Tuck School of Business at Dartmouth.

A frequent speaker at various conferences and conventions, Bill has presented to the Association of National Advertisers, the National Association of Minorities in Cable, the Retail Council of Canada, the Public Relations Society of America, the National Association of Realtors, and numerous corporate and nonprofit organizations throughout the United States, Canada, and Asia.

Bill serves on the boards of several regional and national organizations, including the Advertising Educational Foundation, the Asian Business Association, and the Center for Asian American Media.

Taste the Street

Bill Imada and I met through working together for the Asian and Pacific Islander American Scholarship Fund (APIASF) and immediately realized we were kindred entrepreneurial spirits. We were entrepreneurs who recognized that when you own the business, you do everything from faxing the faxes to licking the stamps. It is something, we both agreed, that a number of individuals who want to be entrepreneurs do not recognize.

The IW Group is Bill's second company after a stint in the corporate world. Bill's first company was a partnership and did reasonably well, but as with a lot of business partnerships, did not survive long term because of the divergent interests of the two principals. Bill then went to work in corporate America for an advertising and public relations agency. It was when he was working with his client, Anheuser-Busch Companies, that he was drawn back into the entrepreneurial world. As Bill tells it, an executive vice president at Anheuser-Busch Companies became a mentor, encouraging him to once again start his own business. Bill initially resisted, but was later convinced by this executive vice president to make the leap of faith. So, 19 years ago, IW Group began with Bill and three business partners he recruited as well as securing Anheuser-Busch Companies as their first client.

Within two years, all three business partners had left the company and Bill was on his own, flying solo; the executive vice president was still his mentor, however, encouraging, pushing, and at times cajoling Bill to the next level. The company was very successful, and 8 years after starting his second business, Bill went to meet with the executive vice president to thank him for his support and for opening up his rolodex over the years, referring Bill and his business to companies such as Bank of America and Prudential Insurance. The mentor was puzzled and asked Bill why he was thanking him. Bill replied that because of his kick in the pants and support, Bill now had a very successful business. Bill asked what he could do to thank the executive vice president, to which he replied, "Help 10 other people." Bill said, "We can do better than that—we will add a couple of zeroes and help 1,000 other people."

To date, Bill and the IW Group have helped 1,000 other people and have now set a goal of helping 10,000 people.

When I asked Bill whether he grew up in a philanthropic family, he replied no, not in the strictest sense. Like many other families in the area, he grew up without money and with limited means. He does, however, recall his family giving money to school fundraisers such as the newspaper drives and to the Boy Scouts as well as the temple. He remembers his mother making things to donate and his father, who was a gardener, donating his time to the temple to improve the landscaping and keep up the grounds. But philanthropy as a concept was not something that was central to everyday life and activities.

Bill is a third-generation American: his grandparents emigrated to the United States in the early 1900s, and his parents were both born in the United States. Three of his four grandparents were born in Japan and one was born in Hawaii, but all are of Japanese heritage. Before World War II, his maternal grandparents sent their two daughters, one of whom was Bill's mother, back to Japan for educational purposes. It was a time when immigrants to the United States labored and did not have the resources to provide for babysitters or daycare for their children. The Japanese culture also thought that an education in Japan while living with extended family relatives was better for the children. Bill's maternal and paternal families are from the Hiroshima area, and that is where his mother and aunt were sent to live and attend school. After the bombing of Pearl Harbor by Japan, all communication stopped between the United States and Japan, and his maternal grandmother had no word about the fate of her daughters for six long years. Sadly, Bill's aunt was working near the epicenter of the atomic bomb drop in Hiroshima in August of 1945 and was killed. His mother survived because she was at a distance from the bomb's blast.

After the bombing of Pearl Harbor, his grandparents moved to Ontario, Oregon, which is on the Oregon–Idaho border. This community, unlike some others, welcomed the Japanese and Japanese Americans because they needed laborers to harvest the potatoes in the fields while the young men from their community were fighting the wars in Europe and the Pacific. During this time, his maternal grandmother met an army general and told him the story of her daughters, who had been born in America and were Americans, being stuck in Japan and there being no communication. The army general was incredulous and promised her that after the war, he would bring them back to the United States. He kept his word. Happily, and one year ahead of other Americans who were living in Japan during this time, Bill's mother, his grandmother's remaining daughter, was brought back to her country by this general.

Although Bill was born in Ontario, Oregon, he grew up in southern California. When Bill was in high school and college, he became active in philanthropic activities. Bill recalled that one time during college, he decided to give up his traditional Thanksgiving and go to the Methodist Church in Hollywood in order to volunteer to feed the homeless. The church was huge and was packed with many people needing a meal. Bill found it personally upsetting that all of these individuals who were showing up for this Thanksgiving meal were hungry and did not have the means to feed themselves. It was a moment of revelation for Bill about how some people have to live in order to survive.

Bill confided that he often recalls this scene to remind himself that no matter how bad things seem at times in business or his personal life, his problems are small in comparison with those who cannot find or secure food to feed themselves.

I asked Bill whether he believes there is a difference between philanthropy and charity, and he responded, "Yes." Philanthropy sounds more scientific to him and not people-oriented. On the other hand, charity, although he doesn't like the word, is an act of kindness: of doing something without thinking and not negotiating. Bill shared with me a recent incident that happened during a dinner out with three friends that illustrates the latter. Over the course of the meal, a homeless person came into the restaurant and approached Bill's table asking if he could have five dollars to buy a sandwich. Almost immediately, his dinner companions all said to ignore this man, and the owner of the restaurant quickly came to the table to try to get the man to leave. Bill, however, asked them all to stop so they could hear the homeless man state his situation. The homeless man stated that he needed five dollars in order to buy a sandwich down the street at the Subway shop. Bill offered to buy the man a sandwich and excused himself from the table for a few minutes. Upon going outside the restaurant, the homeless man again asked for the five dollars, to which Bill replied he would buy him a sandwich but not give him the money. Bill said he would be happy to walk to the Subway shop with the man to purchase the sandwich. We probably all know how this ended: the homeless man only wanted the five dollars and did not want a sandwich purchased for him. At this point, Bill went back into the restaurant to continue dinner with his companions. What is interesting is the discussion that ensued upon Bill's return to the table. His dining companions questioned whether what he was doing was actually pitying the man instead of doing charitable work. To his companions, attaching conditions and strings to a donation is more an act of pity than charity. As you can imagine, a lively discussion took place, with many opinions being offered.

Bill believes that being philanthropic absolutely helps and benefits his company. He trusts in that old adage that what goes around, comes around. Bill said that if you work hard and do good things, people want to be around you. He also states that he does not want personal recognition for the donations he makes. He makes the donations because it is the right thing to do. This belief has been something he is working to educate his staff about. When his staff questions why the money given to charity can't be used to increase salaries or purchase equipment, he responds by telling them that the community does so much for them that it is important to help the community in their various missions and visions. Bill also noted that the company's philanthropic efforts are often the differentiator when a choice is being made by a client between Bill's company and another potential vendor. He told me that he has often been asked by a prospective client, "Are you and your company doing something to give back to the community?" To which Bill can readily reply, "Yes!"

An example of this situation occurred when the American Cancer Society (ACS) chapter in the Los Angeles area approached the IW Group about a campaign. Bill knew the campaign was too large for the IW Group to handle alone but wanted to be supportive of the effort. He used his entrepreneurial skills and asked three of his competitors to join his company in the ACS campaign. They agreed. When Bill reported back to the American Cancer Society that the campaign would be possible through the combined efforts of his company and his three competitors, they were thrilled but shocked. Bill thinks that not only in tough economic times, but always, entrepreneurs should be creative about how to support the endeavors of nonprofit organizations. The ACS campaign concluded successfully.

Bill's company also uses this strategy with large corporations in America. For example, a vice president from Farmers Insurance, which is one of IW Group's clients, came to him and said that children are dying because parents are not installing and using child safety seats correctly. The vice president went on, further stating that Farmers Insurance needed help in educating the public but only had a budget of $5,000 to $10,000. Bill and his staff, who think entrepreneurially, got busy. They enlisted the help of General Motors, Wal-Mart, and McDonalds as well as the local police. All four of these entities as well as Farmers Insurance worked together to disseminate information about how to keep children safe in cars by providing a demonstration in the parking lot of Wal-Mart using cars from General Motors and safety seats provided by Farmers Insurance, with food and drink made available from McDonald's and the procedures taught by the local police. In the end, more than 1,000 families were educated and many safety seats distributed, saving numerous children's lives. Bill calls this connecting the dots between philanthropy and public relations and encourages other entrepreneurs to think this way as well.

Bill also shared with me a story that altered his thinking about how to become involved with communities. He stated that a Vietnamese woman approached him about naming her restaurant in America. She wanted to call it "Taste of Saigon Street." Bill told her that this image and name wouldn't sell in the United States because most Americans view Saigon as a dirty city. The woman countered by saying, "But the best way to get a flavor of any city is on its streets." Bill now says "You've got to taste the street" when you are learning about any neighborhood, community, or community organization. Philanthropy and charity is more than just writing a check: you need to see, touch, hear, and feel what the community sees, touches, hears, and feels. In other words, taste the street!

Finally, Bill believes some old adages keep people and potential entrepreneurs from succeeding. Examples he gave included the following:

- We need to think outside the box.
- We need to level the playing field.
- Let's not reinvent the wheel.

Bill elaborated on each as follows. When we say "think outside the box" are we ready to do it? It is important to first think "inside" the box before thinking "outside" the box—in other words, do you have the answers internally to begin looking externally at helping others?

Regarding the playing field, according to Bill it will never be level and that is why there will always be a need for philanthropy. As long as there are economic disparities, the field will never be level. Great entrepreneurs recognize this, and as Bill told me, the best entrepreneurs will create a skateboard to navigate through the challenges of an uneven playing field.

Finally, in reference to the adage of not reinventing the wheel, Bill told me that telling people they shouldn't reinvent the wheel stifles great ideas, including in the world of philanthropy. Bill related a situation that happened to him when a Japanese public relations student said to him that this saying is something that puzzles most non-Americans. According to this person, if someone could come up with a better wheel, they should do it. In philanthropy, Bill believes we need to think big and consider different ways to help others so they can help themselves. At times, let's reinvent the wheel.

Bill's Advice

- People support what they help to create; get your staff involved in creating the philanthropic program.
- Don't let conventional wisdom and old adages weigh you down when doing philanthropic work.
- A lesson for getting involved in philanthropic endeavors is that the best opportunities are outside your comfort zone.
- Entrepreneurs believe that barriers are only temporary distractions; these distractions are obstacles that are meant to be overcome. You can also try to find a philanthropic opportunity in foreign situations.

AL JOHNSON

Entrepreneur and tireless philanthropist, Al W. Johnson of Chicago was the first African American to be awarded a General Motors franchise; he later became a leading independent Cadillac dealer. Johnson was born February 23, 1920, in St. Louis, Missouri. He received a bachelor of science in business administration from Lincoln University and a master of science in hospital administration from the University of Chicago in 1950. In 1945, he became an assistant administrator of Homer G. Phillips Hospital, a St. Louis teaching hospital, and began selling automobiles part-time to supplement his income. He became knows as "the man who sold cars from a briefcase" because African Americans could not be hired to sell inside a dealership.

His persistence in pursuing his dream of being an automobile dealer was rewarded in 1967 when he became the first African American to be granted a General Motors Oldsmobile franchise, more than 15 years after he began petitioning General Motors. In 1971, he obtained a Cadillac franchise, and the next year he became an independent dealer. Al Johnson Cadillac gained independent status from the Motor Holding Division of General Motors on July 31, 1972. In 1979, Al acquired a Lincoln/Mercury agency. Other business enterprises included Stellar Inc. and the Pyramid Trotting Association. By 1995, Al had sold his companies and has subsequently devoted his time to civic involvement, making significant contributions to hospitals, schools, recreation facilities, and charitable organizations across the nation.

Johnson has received numerous recognition awards, including the following:

- Man of the Millennium, University of Illinois Chicago's College of Business Administration
- Inductee, Chicago/Northwest Indiana Entrepreneurship Hall of Fame
- Chairman Emeritus, Center for Urban Business, University of Illinois at Chicago
- Inductee, 2004 St. Louis Gateway Classic Sport Foundation's Walk of Fame
- Certificate of Appreciation, Southern Poverty Law Center
- Honorary Doctorate of Law, Mary Holmes College
- Honor of Entrepreneurial Excellence, Howard University
- Lifetime Achievement Award, St. Louis American Newspapers

He has served in the following capacities:

- Founder, PUSH Foundation
- Member, Executives Club of Chicago
- Board member, LaRabida Children's Hospital
- Board member, Ingalls Memorial Hospital
- President, Variety Club, Childrens Charity of Illinois
- Life member of the NAACP
- Advisory board, General Motors Black Dealers Association

How a Car Salesman Became One of Chicago's Most Generous Philanthropists

When I first met Al Johnson, he was serving as an advisory council member at the College of Business Administration at the University of Illinois at Chicago, where I worked as the assistant dean of development. What I noticed right away about Al is that while he might not say a lot during a meeting, when he spoke, everyone listened. Al was the senior statesman on the advisory council and a wise man.

I met Al years after he had sold his business and was enjoying a life of retirement. But to know Al Johnson is to realize he never could retire. Al was the first African American in the country to have a General Motors (GM) dealership. It was an Oldsmobile dealership, and by the end of his career he also had a Cadillac dealership. Al loved cars! He also loved what selling cars could bring him, which was a life of opportunity.

Al Johnson was born in St. Louis. As an only child, he was brought up well, attending and graduating from the Lincoln University with a bachelor's degree in business administration in 1942 and then attending the University of Chicago, where he earned a master's degree in field hospital administration. Al soon found himself working as an assistant to the administrator of the hospital at the Homer Phillips Hospital located in St. Louis, Missouri.

Al's father was a physician and part of the Mound City Medical Group, which built the Homer Phillips Hospital.

Al chose to not become a doctor because of the long hours he saw his father work both in his office and in the hospital doing his rounds, as well as on house calls (at this point in history doctors made house calls). Although Al ended up working more than 20 years at the hospital, he readily recognized that his income would top out at $9,000 to $12,000 annually. Al knew he wanted a lifestyle that was beyond what that salary level could provide.

In 1953, Al did something that would ultimately change his life: he purchased a Buick Super with a rumble seat—as he puts it, the last one they made of that kind. Although Al already knew he loved cars, he soon discovered that a friend of his was selling cars on the side to African Americans and splitting the profit with a salesman at the dealership, so he thought, "This is something I can do." However, Al is quick to point out that the one thing he could not do was split the profit from work he did with someone just because he was not allowed at that time in the car show room because of his skin color. Al decided he wanted to sell cars but was going to make a different offer.

If you know Al, you know he always goes to the decision maker, so he secured a meeting and spoke with the owner of Nolting Oldsmobile, which was located in Kirkwood, Missouri. He told Mr. Nolting he wanted to sell cars and he would do it by using the GM Car Book. Basically, Al planned to sell cars the same way dealers order cars. Instead of the dealer deciding on the interior fabric color or trim metal, however, the purchaser would be able to customize his or her car. The car would be built to the purchaser's exact specifications. Mr. Nolting asked Al how many cars he thought he could sell in a month. Al responded by saying he could sell 18 to 20 cars a month. Mr. Nolting laughed, because the entire dealership sold only 60 cars per month, but he gave Al a chance.

In the first month of selling cars, Al earned $2,500 in commissions. According to him, it shocked the owner and the entire dealership. I asked Al if he resigned at this point from his hospital job, and he said no, because it was a built-in customer base. He knew that doctors, nurses, janitors, housekeepers, and cooks all needed cars. He figured if they trusted him as the assistant administrator at the hospital they would trust him to sell them cars. In that first year, 1953, Al made $60,000, which according to him would be approximately $300,000 in today's dollars. Al did not quit his hospital job until he got a car dealership.

Al had always wanted an Oldsmobile dealership, and to make that dream come true he began meeting with the leaders of General Motors. Like his customers, the GM leadership liked Al. One of them actually said to him, "If ever we break down bigotry and racism in the auto industry, you'll be our man." It is important to point out that up until this point in time no African American had ever owned a car dealership. Little did Al know he was going to be the first one!

It began in 1967 when Al was on his yacht in Lake Michigan. He and some friends had brought their yachts to Chicago from St. Louis to vacation for a few days. Al was on the third day of his vacation when early one morning he heard knocking on his stateroom door. He answered it, still dressed in his pajamas, and there was the district manager of Oldsmobile. The district manager told Al he had great news for him: Al was going to be the first African American to own a GM dealership, and it was going to be an Oldsmobile dealership. The dealership was located in Chicago, and he was going to have to move. But the district manager informed Al they had to leave immediately to go to St. Louis, Missouri, to sign the papers. Al's response was, "No." Although he was interested, he told the district manager he was on vacation with his friends, both those on his yacht and the others in the flotilla, and could not leave them. He told the district manager, "Make me the 21st black man to own a dealership" and then proceeded to shut the door on him.

Selling cars on the side afforded Al the lifestyle he wanted and the ability to purchase a yacht.

As you might guess, General Motors was not going to take no as the answer. The next day, the same district manager showed up and knocked on Al's door, again in the early morning hours. Al answered it, again dressed in his pajamas. The district manager told Al that he had to say yes; otherwise, the district manager's future growth in the corporation would be affected if he wasn't able to deliver. Al reiterated that he could not go to St. Louis to sign the papers because he had guests. The district manager told him he had a plane ready to go and that if they left in the morning they would be back by dinner time. At this point, according to Al, a friend of his stepped forward and said, "Al, this is a big deal. You need to do this." This is how Al Johnson made history and became the first African American to own a GM dealership.

In 1967, Al got the Oldsmobile dealership. At that time, he was the first and only African American to own one. Shortly after Al got the dealership, a lawsuit came about that prohibited General Motors from being involved in selling cars both retail and wholesale. As a result of the lawsuit, four years later in 1971, he had the opportunity to purchase a Cadillac dealership and earned the nickname of "Cadillac Al," meaning when you bought a Cadillac in Chicago you bought it from Al Johnson's store.

You might ask what prompted GM to sell a dealership to a minority. The answer was twofold: forward thinking and a federal lawsuit. General Motors recognized that the African American community purchased cars and was currently only 12% of the total sales. There was an opportunity for sales growth. The federal lawsuit settlement had said that General Motors could not sell automobiles both via wholesale and retail. GM had to divest its retail stores, and who better to sell them to than their most valuable salespeople? Chicago, as luck would have it, had five General Motors retail stores, and Al bought one of them.

The purchase of the Oldsmobile dealership, and later the Cadillac one, is what prompted Al's permanent move to Chicago. It also began his journey into the philanthropic world. Al stated that when he had some extra money, he began giving it away. In other words, he lived and still lives by the motto of whenever you have a surplus of money, you should start giving it away or paying back for the success you enjoy. Candidly Al said, "You know you should return some of it when you are blessed." For Al, it began with serving on the board of the Better Business Bureau and providing financial support for the public radio station. He also worked with Jesse Jackson to start

Operation PUSH (People United to Serve Humanity), which today is the Rainbow/PUSH Coalition organization. Since those early days, Al has given money to hundreds of nonprofit organizations, from the Center for Urban Business to the University of Illinois at Chicago to his local neighborhood organizations in Chicago and California, where he has a winter home.

Even though Chicago is his primary residence, Al did not forget about his beginnings in St. Louis; he provides charitable donations to that community, too. Al has also passed on his commitment to giving back to his sons, especially his son Donald, who Al says is a giver.

Al's Advice

- Opportunity is always knocking from the nonprofit world. Nonprofit staffs are always making appeals to make a contribution. The real question to ask is, "Why would you not make a donation?"
- Personalities have a lot to do with giving; find people with which you like to work and help them with their charitable and philanthropic work.
- People that are humble are willing givers. Once you have earned your wealth, if you are grateful and humble, feeling very fortunate to have earned the money made, remember those who helped you. This should move you to give back and help others.
- People who use the word "I" in describing what they have done often aren't as charitable as others.

SUZANNE JURVA

Suzanne Jurva is a filmmaker and entrepreneur. She has been involved in all forms of storytelling, from Tom Hanks's IMAX film *Magnificent Desolation: Walking on the Moon* to producing for the smallest medium, the mobile phone. In between the two extremes of media and technology, Suzanne was a feature film executive at Dreamworks working on several Academy Award–nominated films, including *Saving Private Ryan, Amistad, Minority Report, AI, The Lost World, Gladiator, Prince of Egypt, The Peacemaker, Deep Impact, Men in Black*, and *The Lookout*.

Suzanne has recently completed a documentary film on virtuoso guitar player Billy McLaughlin and his struggles with focal dystonia. *Changing Keys* will help raise awareness of focal dystonia, dystonia, and all neuromuscular disorders and was produced with funding from the Dystonia Medical Research Foundation. It also recently won the top film award for documenties at the Houston International Worldfest Film Festival.

The Mr. Magoo of Charity

I first met Suzanne Jurva when I was working at Michigan Technological University. Suzanne is an alumnus and at the time was working for Steven Spielberg at Dreamworks SKG (see Chapter 9 for more details on our first meeting and interaction). I found her to be a gregarious, enthusiastic, and eager person willing to get involved with her alma mater.

When we sat down to talk about this book and philanthropy, Suzanne recalled her first childhood memories of philanthropy as her family's involvement with the Redford Jaycees (as a reference point, Redford, Michigan, is located 17 miles northwest of Detroit). She remembers her mother and father being active with this group, with it serving as their social club. Not only were her parents involved, but also Suzanne and her siblings did everything with other Jaycee children.

> According to its website, "The United States Junior Chamber (Jaycees) gives young people between the ages of 18 and 40 the tools they need to build the bridges of success for themselves in the areas of business development, management skills, individual training, community service and international connections."

Regarding specific philanthropic activities in her youth, Suzanne recalled that at the Jaycee Hall in Redford they fed the homeless as a charitable activity by creating baskets of food during the holidays. She also recalls her Aunt Edna's dedication to ensuring that a Girl Scout troop existed for the mentally challenged in the Detroit area because Suzanne's cousin, who was Aunt Edna's daughter, had been born mentally challenged. Suzanne laughingly shared that this troop was the one she belonged to when she was a Girl Scout. She thought it was a normal Girl Scout troop because her aunt, her cousin, and other mentally challenged young girls were involved and members. A final memory of philanthropy in her youth is her aunt supporting the work of Eunice Shriver through efforts at the Hawthorne Center, which provided community activities for the mentally challenged.

When I asked Suzanne why she gets involved with charitable endeavors now as an adult, she said, "It's fun and I can't imagine not doing it." However, she also explained that she likes doing things in creative ways and dislikes simply writing a check. Suzanne likens the way she approaches her charitable activities to that of Mr. Magoo, the cartoon character, who gets into a lot of messy and sometimes improbable situations primarily because of his nearsightedness but always manages to come out on the right side in the end. An example she shared was an incident that happened during the first Iraq War. Suzanne had decided she wanted to block out information about the war because it was too disturbing. She decided there would be no televisions or radios on in her presence during this time. However, according to Suzanne, God, the Universe, or Fate had a different idea because the first time she did turn on a television she knew the army general who was speaking about the war. It seems he had been one of her escorts during her participation in the Joint Civilian Orientation Conference-61. It was through watching and listening to this general that Suzanne learned about Operation Interdependence and decided she had to get involved.

Operation Interdependence helps in supplying, preparing, and posting military care packages to troops overseas.

As she puts it, "I contacted them in the middle of the night via sending an email, and they responded almost immediately. I completed a form and then realized I just agreed to created 50 care packages for our troops. I began sweating and did so for three days, thinking how was I going to create 50 care packages? In the end, over 1,800 packages were created!" Suzanne learned that by sharing with her friends, neighbors, colleagues, and just about anyone who would listen what she was doing, people were willing to help. As she says, "Suddenly, lots of stuff began being delivered to my home. In my living room were boxes of toothpaste, toothbrushes, gum, candy, and flea collars. Because of my work with the film studios, they began sending things, too. It was a maze of narrow pathways to navigate my living room." Although very grateful for everything, Suzanne realized she would need to repackage the donated items into the care packages desired by Operation Interdependence. She did this with the help of others, and upon finishing realized she had never done anything like this in her life and that it felt really good!

The reason flea collars were a requested item is that the soldiers would wear them on their wrists and ankles to prevent the fleas, which were everywhere, from biting them.

Another philanthropic activity in her adult life that was memorable was when Suzanne and her husband, Joe, who are both alumni of Michigan Technological University (MTU), decided in the late 1990s to name the hockey coach's office at MTU in honor of her Uncle Abby Maki, who was the captain of the hockey team in the 1950s when he attended college there. Suzanne's uncle had recently died, and they felt this would be an outstanding way to honor his memory by making a donation and naming this office.

More recently, one of the philanthropic moments that stands out for Suzanne was fundraising for her daughter's Catholic girls school. For the annual fundraiser and auction, Suzanne asked Tom Hanks, with whom she had worked on numerous films, including *Saving Private Ryan* and *Magnificent Desolation: Walking on the Moon 3D*, if he could provide a signed copy of a poster from his upcoming movie, *The Polar Express*. He agreed and pulled the first poster printed for the movie off the press, signed it, and had it delivered to Suzanne for the auction. As you can imagine, it was a hot-ticket item that raised a lot of money for the girls school.

I asked Suzanne if she had any regrets or frustrations from her interactions in the philanthropic world, and she shared that her ultimate frustration was that as a parent she is continually asked or required to raise money for her children's many school activities. Although the act of raising money itself does not frustrate her, it is the methods chosen that do. As she put it, "I am continually being asked to sell candy bars, cookie dough, popcorn, nuts, jewelry, wrapping paper, magazine subscriptions, and other items as well as participate in the Jog-A-Thon by raising money for it! While we are not given a goal of how much each individual student needs to sell, we are told to sell, sell, sell." Incredulously, Suzanne realized recently that even her 1-year-old niece who is in a daycare/preschool was expected to sell See's Candy! As a parent and an entrepreneur, Suzanne stated that she would rather be told how much is needed financially and provide that donation than have to deal with selling numerous items almost on a continuous basis, most of which are probably bought by the parents themselves. Additionally, as an entrepreneur, she would like to be told what the focus is for the year, meaning what the need is and what projects will be focused on, and then determine the financial amount needed to meet that need or project. Much to her chagrin, however, this is not how private schools seem to fundraise.

Suzanne and her husband, Joe, are also teaching their children about philanthropy and giving back. Suzanne shared that Joe is the co-head coach for the VIP Soccer Program, which has children with disabilities as its players. Their two children join Joe weekly to help this team, and as Suzanne told me, "This is the favorite part of the week for them."

In December 2008, the lessons to her children continued, and Suzanne witnessed what she calls a transformation in her 17-year-old daughter and perhaps her entire family. Her daughter was heading up the efforts of her religion class at her school to provide for families who might not have anything for Christmas. The school adopted over 40 families and gathered the items the archdiocese said each was to receive. Suzanne's family and another student were able to deliver the awaited Christmas boxes to three families. They arrived at the cathedral early in the morning and were given directions to the families in order to deliver the packages, which included gift cards from Wal-Mart as well as items such as clothing and toys. Although Suzanne admits the project started out a bit bumpy because of difficulties in locating the first family and in being organized and comfortable with what to do, it became a wonderful experience. Her daughter at one point was able to use her many years of studying Spanish to communicate with one of the families.

It was at this point they learned that another family was waiting for a bicycle that had not been delivered with the package dropped off earlier by someone else. While her daughter and Suzanne tried to explain that they would certainly take the message back to the organizers at the cathedral, Suzanne's husband, Joe, had an idea. He quickly ran down to the parked car to retrieve an American Express gift card he had been given from his workplace as a bonus. As they gave the card to the family waiting for the much-anticipated bicycle, Suzanne and her family hoped the card would be used toward the purchase price of the bicycle. Upon driving away from this last interaction with one of their assigned families, Suzanne realized the activity had been truly a teaching moment for her children and a transformational experience for her entire family.

Suzanne's Advice

- Philanthropy is necessary!
- Follow your passion and make sure it is fun; in other words, if it is not fun, why would you or anyone do it?
- The only way to understand God and creativity is by doing something different and more exciting.
- Include others; if someone else can do it, include them by asking them to participate.
- If you are not using it, get rid of it; donate it to someone else who could use it.

JANET KATOWITZ AND CAROLE MUNDY

Janet Katowitz has been earning a living in politics since 1980. Her extensive political organizing experience ranges from directing door-to-door fundraising and persuasion canvasses in New York, Massachusetts, Florida, Ohio, and Illinois to managing electoral campaigns in Michigan and Ohio.

As deputy director of political operations for the Michigan Senate Democratic Caucus, she was responsible for developing and coordinating time buying, direct mail, in-house polling, and field operations for targeted state Senate campaigns. When she wasn't being paid to do politics, Janet was active in her community, serving as a board member of Planned Parenthood and an officer of the Ingham County Democratic Party.

Janet developed winning media strategies for hundreds of political campaigns, from Alaska to Florida, New York to California, and from city council to Congress, governor, and U.S. Senator in her role as vice president and director of media planning for Joe Slade White and Company (1993 to March 2002). She also devised creative buying strategies for myriad corporate clients, for image building, air cover for lobbying efforts, and even boosting ticket sales for the Seattle Seahawks and Portland Trailblazers.

In March 2002, Janet and Carole Mundy joined forces to create Mundy Katowitz Media Inc. A lifelong political activist and expert shopper, Janet has combined both passions along with her exceptional phone skills and encyclopedic knowledge of television programming as a political media buyer since 1989. She is an expert at devising buying strategies that get the most out of every dollar invested, incorporating the research, the voter targets, and the overall strategy of the campaign.

Carole is a born news junkie. Long before *CNN* and her 10th birthday, Carole read "Doonesbury" and watched Dan Rather nightly and Tom Brokaw and Jane Pauley in the morning. Politics was a natural fit, having started in campaigns at the tender age of 9 and argued with the teachers at her parochial school over privacy and women's rights and the negative impact of the Reagan administration on education budgets.

She followed a fairly typical Washington path before pursuing political consulting as a media buyer—finally all those years in front of the TV paid off. In 1997, after suffering burnout and mononucleosis, she took a job on Madison Avenue and quickly realized that hawking movies did not compare to working with candidates whose values you share. She quit and jumped into her first company, Buyline Media Inc., with a used computer, an American Express card, and no clients. It wasn't as simple as "if you build it, they will come," but her nontraditional thinking and attention to detail encouraged clients to get out of their own headspace, and Buyline Media found an audience. Carole is both giddy and amazed that she has a job she enjoys that allows her to take her values to work with her.

We Are Only Going to Survive If We Help Each Other

Janet Katowitz and Carole Mundy met years ago when Carole applied for a job as an assistant media buyer. Janet was working, at that time, for Joe Slade White and Company, a media consulting firm located in Washington, DC, that provides services to Democratic political campaigns and liberal initiatives. On the same day Carole interviewed for the job, she and Janet bumped into each other that evening at a Women Opening Doors for Women reception. They decided it was fate, and Janet hired Carole. Carole went on to become media director at another Washington, DC, firm before opening her own media buying shop, Buyline Media Inc. A few years later, when Janet decided to leave Joe Slade White and Co., she contacted Carole, asking if Carole could sustain her in the lifestyle to which she had become accustomed. Carole, being both a risk taker and a bit of a cockeyed optimist, knew it would work out and said, "Of course," and thus Mundy Katowitz Media, a Democratic media planning and placement company, was formed in March 2002.

To both Janet and Carole, being an entrepreneur is liberating. According to Carole, it is like having a blank sheet of paper and writing a novel or a song. "The possibilities are endless if you just take the first step into the abyss and let go of expectations."

One of the primary business mantras at Mundy Katowitz Media is to treat people the way you want to be treated. This mantra is especially true with their staff, as these two women entrepreneurs work to make the political jobs their young employees have—sometimes their first paid political position—a good experience. The second belief is that if you train your staff and show trust and respect, you can help them reveal their potential and maybe learn a thing or two yourself along the way. The idea is to build out so when they move on, they will help the next person coming up.

A business partnership can be challenging, but Janet and Carole have found a way to make it work to great success. As they shared with me, Janet handles more of the human resources and operations sides of the business, whereas Carole excels in the financial and business sides.

Their business is changing rapidly as the way we communicate changes. As they stated, "Fifteen years ago we could not have conceived or even predicted the effect the information superhighway would have on everything including politics and everyday life." They further noted that with each cycle of new technology, their company needs to be nimble and to be able to respond immediately. An example they share is that with the advent of digital video recorders and online content, using television advertising to convey a political message is much more challenging than it once was. Although there are more households with televisions than ever, media buyers must look for programming that's somewhat impervious to timeshifting, as well as layer communications using a broad range of paid media. While Janet and Carole do recognize that the business model for political advertising will change, they also know there will always be some form of paid communication used in political campaigns.

> Janet and Carole also stated that the work they are doing is deconstructing people's views and perceptions of watching television.

One of the goals for success in their field is to be creative when putting together the communications plan. A favorite success story they shared with me is the use of an ancient medium—crop circles—in the midst of the most technologically advanced presidential campaign in this nation's history. In 2007, prior to the first presidential debate in Iowa, a healthcare advocacy client was looking for ways to increase its visibility. Mundy Katowitz Media presented a list of traditional communication options, along with the tongue-in-cheek proposal for a crop circle. To their surprise, the client selected the crop circle for its "outside the box" appeal. Mundy Katowitz Media began researching in earnest and managed to find a crop artist and a soy field, the size of 11 football fields, in the flight path of the Des Moines airport. Within two weeks, the crop artist carved the organization's logo in the field, where anyone flying into Des Moines, including the national press corps, would be greeted by the healthcare advocacy message. As you might imagine, quite a bit of media buzz occurred, to the benefit of the client. See page 225 for photo of the crop circle.

When we began discussing philanthropy, Janet and Carole both shared personal stories. Carole's philanthropy started at more of a one-to-one level. While growing up in upstate New York in a small college town, she witnessed her parents helping others, whether it was her mother collecting food and personal goods such as toothpaste or soap for a family services charity or watching her father stop strangers in need in the dead of winter and offering them a ride to go buy them a warm winter coat. The effect was not lost. "Regardless of your lot in life, you are no better or worse than the next person and you have a responsibility to others whether in dollars or deeds."

Carole is taking steps to establish a scholarship fund in honor of her mother, who passed away when she was young. The scholarship will benefit students from rural areas in Otsego County, New York, who are not A students but are B students who need some help to succeed. Carole feels that grades are not necessarily the best predictor of future success and that solid students may not compete for scholarships because they fear there is no point. Similarly, she suspects that small-town America sometimes is overlooked because resources tend to flow to larger metropolitan areas.

Carole is also a generous donor to Planned Parenthood and the social service centers in upstate New York. She attributes this in part to seeing the workings of Capitol Hill during the Clarence Thomas hearings. Women's issues and the assault on reproductive rights propelled her to be even more charitable to these types of organizations and causes.

Carole also believes it is our obligation to pay our fair share.

Janet grew up in a very political household, the daughter of devout atheists. She recalled laughingly discussing her unorthodox beliefs with the neighborhood kids when she was a child. They were horrified, and a few hours later, knocked on the door to tell Janet's father, "Mr. Katowitz, Janet doesn't believe in God." Mr. Katowitz responded by calling Janet to the door, patting her on the head, looking the children in the eye, and saying, "Good girl, Janet."

Janet views her philanthropic contributions as an extension of her political views. She cherishes the right to freedom of speech, especially in this post-9/11 world, and is amazed if not dismayed by how easily individuals are willing to give up their freedoms in the name of national security. Situations like these are what motivate her to give. Janet is a strong supporter of public television and radio, viewing these as independent voices in support of the right to freedom of speech. As she states, "I like to fund the 'other' voices."

When her mother died a few years ago, Janet and her siblings asked that in lieu of flowers, donations be made to Planned Parenthood because Janet's mom was an adamant supporter of women having access to birth control. She and her siblings felt that combining their mother's political views with philanthropy was one of the best ways to honor her memory while creating a legacy. Both Janet and Carole believe that individuals need to give money where their beliefs are, or as the saying goes, "Put your money where your mouth is."

When I asked them if they see a difference between philanthropy and charity, they both said they did. They see philanthropy as a bigger, sustainable, and long-term endeavor. It is also more philosophical to them as a way to provide for things that are falling short, such as women's rights. Janet and Carole also believe that philanthropic activity is formed by where you want to go; in other words, ask yourself this question, "What is your world vision?"

Charity, on the other hand, to them, is more immediate and a rapid response to an immediate problem. It is visceral in the sense that you see somebody and want to help. It is an immediate rush of emotion being put into action. But both Janet and Carole recognize that overarching lifestyle choices might lead someone to practice charity before they practice philanthropy.

Charity, according to Janet and Carole, can be schizophrenic, but the important thing is to get involved. A suggestion they made as an easy first step for everyone to consider is providing phone cards with minutes to the USO or Red Cross. Even if you don't have money, there are ways to be charitable. Begin by being creative!

Janet and Carole's Advice

- Find your passion and then figure out how you can contribute to it. Contributions are not necessarily monetary, so do not box yourself in before you start by thinking only in dollars.
- Create movement; you do not have to have anything in order to be involved—jump in and things eventually fall into a workable place.
- Philanthropy and charity can be paralyzing; think of it in smaller pieces and get involved. Keep trying until you find your niche.

MARSHA McVICKER

Errand Solutions founder and CEO Marsha McVicker has an extensive background in supply chain management, communications, strategy and channel development, financial analysis, and marketing. Prior to founding the company, she worked as a public affairs consultant and for more than six years as a communications director on Capitol Hill in Washington, DC. Marsha received her Supply Chain Management and Entrepreneurship MBA from the University of Wisconsin–Madison and was a logistics analyst for Jewel Osco, a division of Albertson's in Chicago, Illinois.

As a result of concepts covered in her academic study and her logistics experience, Marsha came to the realization that many concierge models in the market were inefficient and expensive. As a participant in the Weinert Applied Ventures in Entrepreneurship (WAVE) program at the University of Wisconsin, she was able to test the feasibility of Errand Solutions and develop the company's current model, which is both efficient and affordable. As a result, Errand Solutions received Wisconsin's first ever e-commerce technology development loan from the Wisconsin Department of Commerce.

Since then, Marsha has been featured in *i-Street* magazine and the *Chicago Sun-Times* as one of Chicago's "Women in Black," the 26 most prominent women in Chicago's high-tech community; she is profiled in two books, *You Need to Be a Little Crazy* and *Bounce*, by serial entrepreneur Barry Moltz. Marsha's accomplishments have also been published as a case study in the textbook *Mastering Management Skills* by R. J. Aldag and L. W. Kuzhara (Southwestern Publishing). Marsha has been interviewed by Robert Reich for National Public Radio's *Future of Success* series, and she has been featured or profiled in many publications, including the following: *Business Week*, *In Business* magazine, *Crain's*, the *San Francisco Examiner*, the *Miami Herald*, and 62 other nationally recognized publications.

Marsha is a proud member of the Entrepreneurs Organization (EO), SHRM, and the Chicagoland Chamber of Commerce, and she has been a guest lecturer at a variety of conferences and in academic settings, including the Kellogg School of Management at Northwestern University, the University of Chicago, the University of Wisconsin–Madison, the Women's

Business Development Center, the Premier Patient Services Conference, and Springboard, the platform for the top female-owned businesses in America.

As Errand Solutions' CEO, Marsha's focus is on creating and sustaining corporate growth, managing investor relations, and identifying expansion opportunities.

Coat Check Lines and Philanthropy

It is rare to meet someone in a coat check line after a National Association of Women Business Owners (NAWBO) luncheon and find an outstanding philanthropist. However, that is exactly what happened on a cool day in April of 2001. I met Marsha McVicker in a coat check line as we both waited our turns to retrieve our coats. We were both anxious to get back to work, but as we chatted, Marsha and I realized we had a very similar background because we both had worked in the Michigan political landscape but were separated by about four years. This meant we knew all the same people but somehow had never met each other, and now were both in Chicago waiting in a very long line with other attendees. Our conversation continued, and soon thereafter we were friends having lunches on a regular basis to discuss, among other things, business and philanthropy.

Marsha's first recollection of charitable acts is from her days as a young child living in Wisconsin. She vividly remembers her family delivering food to people who were shut in at Thanksgiving. She remembers her family helping with food drives, clothing drives, and bake sales. It seemed to Marsha that her mother was always involved in doing something to help others in their community.

As an adult, during her MBA program Marsha received a grant of $100,000 from her alma mater, the University of Wisconsin–Madison, to fully launch her business. During good times and bad, her company has always had a charitable component. When she first started, neither the business nor Marsha had any money to donate to charitable endeavors. However, Marsha wanted to be philanthropic. She decided to commit Errand Solutions to give back to the communities in which it operated. The plan, which still exists today, is for each client to choose a month during which 5% of all transactional revenue will go to the charity or cause of the client's choice. Because Errand Solutions has a large component of its business in the healthcare field, a number of the receiving nonprofit organizations have been healthcare auxiliary groups and boards. In all, Errand Solutions has given to more than 30 nonprofit organizations, including the Boys and Girls Clubs, AIDS organizations, the March of Dimes, Ronald McDonald

Houses, Jenner Academy, Joe DiMaggio Children's Hospital Foundation, and the United Way.

Furthermore, Marsha's company has taken it to another level by advertising its ability to help with philanthropic endeavors. Errand Solutions often is the philanthropic hub for its clients in their charitable work by doing such things as being the logistics staff for food drives, clothing drives, and back-to-school efforts. The company and staff are the behind-the-scenes individuals who coordinate activities that range from the printing of t-shirts for sponsored walks to the erecting of tents for celebrations, to name a few. In every way, Errand Solutions, its staff, and, most important, Marsha McVicker are involved in charitable work for the betterment of the communities they serve. Marsha also regularly updates her company board of directors on how the company is giving back to the communities in which Errand Solutions operates and serves.

Marsha believes to her core that being involved in philanthropic activities adds to the bottom line of her business. She personally knows that the good you project out in the world comes back to you and that, although it might not be obvious, a difference is made. She also knows that a giving culture leads to a service culture; given that Errand Solutions is in the service business, this is a good thing. Marsha does not have a metric for knowing this, but rather an instinct. That instinct has led her to know to incorporate a philanthropic or charitable component into the proposals she submits to potential clients. She revealed that when clients read that part of the proposal there usually are a few oohs and aahhs.

While most entrepreneurs do not talk about philanthropy (see Chapter 6 for a discussion of this issue), Marsha informed me that the Entrepreneurs' Organization (EO) recently started a forum for charitable efforts through the organization. EO focuses on the top 100 entrepreneurs under the age of 45 in a city. Some current activities include a trip to Mexico to build homes and a humanitarian trip to Cuba.

Marsha believes that most entrepreneurs give back because they are so used to sacrificing for their businesses by working hard before they reward themselves with money that sacrificing for charitable efforts is relatively easy. They know what it is like to be working for a cause or a belief. Entrepreneurs, according to Marsha, are very appreciative of success, and when it happens they usually know why they are successful. Most entrepreneurs have a large support group via their churches, mentors, and others and naturally get involved to support these efforts in order to give back and repay (see Chapter 1 for more information on repayers). Marsha is also one of those rare entrepreneurs who has a portion of her estate designated in her will to nonprofit organizations, including the University of Wisconsin–Madison, which, she never forgets, gave her the initial seed money to start her successful company.

Sadly, Marsha's father recently died from liver cancer after originally surviving a battle with colon cancer. Marsha's father was a mentor to her in both life and business, so she wanted to honor his life and memory in as many ways as possible. The first December after his death she decided to add a silent auction component to her annual holiday party, raising a few hundred dollars from her friends that she donated to the American Cancer Society. The effort has since grown from a small party at her home that raised a few hundred dollars to a full-out holiday bash held at a warehouse and requiring a ticket for admission that raises thousands of dollars. Marsha chose the American Cancer Society as the recipient of these charitable dollars because she liked the freedom they give to their donors to designate where the donation is directed. In other words, Marsha is able to designate the dollars raised in honor of her father to liver cancer research. She also shared that she was pleased to learn that the American Cancer Society operated with very little of the donated dollars going to overhead.

Marsha's Advice

- Start giving; the hardest part is to get it going. It is rewarding and easy. You can find a way to make a difference, and you will see a change in yourself, in your company, and in the way your clients treat you.
- Schedule your philanthropic donations and treat it like a business. In order to be effective, plan for it by putting it in writing and publicly acknowledging it.
- Find out what resonates with you charitably and make it public.
- Be contagious! One thing business owners are good at is marketing and evangelizing; do this with your giving to get others engaged in philanthropic work.

ALFREDO J. MOLINA

Alfredo J. Molina has dedicated his life to the service of others. Through his company's generous sponsorship of local and national charities, he seeks to improve the lives of those less fortunate. Gratitude, selflessness, love, and a firm belief in sharing compose the Molina way of life.

Alfredo J. Molina is chairman and CEO of the MOLINA Group, Molina Fine Jewelers, based in Phoenix, Arizona, and Black, Starr & Frost, based in California, America's first jeweler, established in 1810. His lineage of master jewelers dates back to seventeenth-century Italy.

Alfredo was born in Santa Clara, Cuba, in 1959. Eight years later, when the revolution forced the Molina family to flee the grip of communism, he settled in Chicago, where he learned the diamond and gemstone business from his grandfather. He came to Phoenix in 1980 with a dream of starting his own jewelry store, which came true in 1987.

Since its opening, Molina Fine Jewelers has built an unparalleled reputation, offering the rarest of gems and exclusive collections of fine jewelry. Arizona Business magazine has voted Molina Fine Jewelers first among jewelers in the state since 1998. When clients come into his salon, they are warmly greeted at the door and welcomed inside as if they were entering the home of friends. If it's hot outside, they are given a cool, moist towel to refresh themselves. If it's chilly, they are presented with a warm towel. They are then offered the finest chocolates or a piece of fresh fruit and the liquid refreshment of their choice. The atmosphere is one of refinement and relaxation. "We are not just in the jewelry business; we are in the emotion business," says Alfredo. "We are about the experience of buying fine jewelry. We do everything within our power to make that experience unforgettable."

This is especially true when it comes to buying fine diamonds. Alfredo recognizes the unique aura that diamonds possess when it comes to creating a quintessential and memorable moment. He knows that it is a moment to be savored and enjoyed. "You can ask any woman about the moment she received her first diamond and she will give you a step-by-step account of that encounter. It is the most emotionally charged gift that a woman can receive or experience," says Alfredo. "Therefore, we will do whatever is necessary to heighten that experience."

Molina Fine Jeweler's reputation for magnificent craftsmanship, value beyond price, and uncompromising discretion has made it welcome in international circles of nobility and influence. The company has drawn the notice of private clients around the world, who often call for consulting and commission work. "As a private jeweler, we practice the old-world tradition of: 'Have jewels, will travel.' While we welcome clients to visit us at our salon, we are just as delighted to pay a visit to them wherever they might be," says Alfredo. "The people we serve become the center of our universe and we strive to make that experience, no matter where in the world it is, unforgettable."

Alfredo's education and experience in the jewelry industry is extensive. He is a graduate gemologist of the Gemological Institute of America (GIA), master gemologist appraiser from the American Society of Appraisers, and a fellow member of the Gemological Association of Great Britain. He is an expert in the determination of country of origin of gemstones. He has served as president of the American Society of Appraisers, the Arizona Jewelers Association, and the GIA Alumni Association. He is a qualified appraiser for the Internal Revenue Service and an alumnus of the FBI Citizens Academy.

Alfredo devotes his time and many resources to the Arizona community. By staying in constant contact with the community, he feels that Molina Fine Jewelers is fulfilling a duty to its friends and supporters. Alfredo and his wife, Lisa, have chaired numerous charity events, including the Arizona Cancer Ball, the Samaritan Foundation Gala, the Symphony Ball, the Arizona Heart Ball, Crohns and Colitis, the Women of Distinction Gala, and Childhelp, Drive the Dream Gala.

Alfredo's list of community affiliations runs long, including the Arizona State University Presidents Club and the Dean's Council 100, University of Arizona President's Club, University of Arizona Health Sciences Center, Arizona Baseball Charities, Fiesta Bowl Committee, Boys & Girls Club, the Banner Foundation, the American Jewish Committee, and the Phoenix Art Museum.

In December 2005, Alfredo was honored in Washington, DC, as one of seven caring Americans and inducted into the Frederick Douglass Museum and Hall of Fame for Caring Americans on Capitol Hill. In 2008, he was inducted into the Jewelers Hall of Fame.

That's the Way I Like It

I think it is rare to conduct an interview and end up singing KC and the Sunshine Band's song "That's the Way (I Like It)," but that is exactly what happened when I met with Alfredo Molina. After singing a few lines, we both laughed and realized this song perfectly describes Alfredo and his wife Lisa's charitable endeavors.

When I first met Alfredo in 2005, he was being inducted into the Caring Institute's Hall of Fame. As his biography was being read, the list of his accomplishments in the philanthropic world was staggering. Alfredo and his wife Lisa were donating to 167 charities. According to best practices, that was about 164 too many. However, when you meet and talk to Alfredo, you learn of his passion to give back and realize that contributing to many, many nonprofit organizations and charities is the way he likes it.

Today, Alfredo, his wife, and their foundation support over 195 non-profit organizations.

I wondered where this passion for being supportive of others came from and asked Alfredo. He began by telling me his life's story. Alfredo was born in Cuba into a family of very renowned jewelers. His great grandfather was called the Golden Bull because he was not only a jeweler but also a cattle baron. Alfredo said, "I will never forget the first time I touched real gold. I had already worked my second year as a jeweler's apprentice under my grandfather's strict and demanding tutelage. My grandfather was from the old school where you never completed any task in a manner that met his approval! This was a Molina family tradition dating back some 400 years to my silversmith predecessors in Milan, Italy. That is, the oldest grandson learned the craft of fine jewelry manufacturing starting as a bench apprentice. My grandfather came to my mother on my birthday and simply said, 'Let me take the boy.' At the age of eight, my career as a jeweler began in early March of 1967."

Just a few months prior, Alfredo's family had fled Cuba. They emigrated to America and lived in a tiny apartment in Chicago. "Times were tough," as Alfredo told me. His father worked as a pipe cutter from 7 am to 3 pm and then worked nights as a janitor at Northwestern University to ensure the family had what it needed. This was a very different lifestyle for a man who had owned several hotels, restaurants, and a casino in Cuba before the communists confiscated his assets. It should be noted that Alfredo's father had left the jewelry business at the age of 25 when he developed irreconcilable differences with Alfredo's grandfather.

Times were tough during his work with his grandfather. As Alfredo told me, "The wooden jeweler's bench where I began my career was not built for comfort. It was a drafty space with thick wood floors where your toes were cold in the winter and your brow dripped sweat in the summer. I spent those first two years, every day after school, working amongst some 125 master jewelers, most of whom were in their 40s, all of us hunched over rows and rows of benches. These craftsmen created one-of-a-kind collections made of the finest metals and gemstones in the world and their designs were represented by the most exclusive jewelry firms of the time." Alfredo began learning his craft by taking pennies and rolling them flat to learn how to work the metal by engraving, shaping, sawing, and bead setting. He says he used pennies because they were plentiful as a learning tool as well as because copper has many of the same malleable properties as gold.

Alfredo went on, "Not until the second year had passed did I graduate from that menial apprentice work to real gold. Without saying much, my grandfather came to me one afternoon and plopped a small metal bin before me that was full of casting shot, which is granulated gold. I looked at him, and he managed a small smile before returning to his office. I turned my attention back to the gold and stared at it for a few seconds. Then I scooped my hand into the bin and ran it through the gold, letting it pour through my small fingers like sand. I felt an electrical sensation up and down my spine, and at 10 years old, I was hooked. The previous years of rolling pennies and missing all those kick-the-can games vanished in a red-hot surge of gold fever. I was the luckiest boy in all of Chicago! Without even knowing it, I had found my lifelong calling, a calling that would eventually lead me to every exotic corner of the planet." Now, some 40 years later, Alfredo is blessed with the opportunity to share his passion in bringing jewelry enthusiasts together with the finest and rarest gems in the world. As he states, "It is a distinct pleasure and honor to serve some of the most wonderful and fascinating individuals around the globe."

When Alfredo reflects on why he is so philanthropic and, as he puts it, "he can't say no to requests," he believes it is because of what happened to his family when they first arrived in Chicago and were living at the Wilson Hotel. Times were tough for the Molina family; Alfredo noted that the family's major source of protein at that time was garbanzo beans. It was an everyday staple being served at breakfast, lunch, and dinner. One day in the lobby of this hotel where they were staying, his father bumped into someone he had casually known in Cuba. This man, seeing the family had nothing, took them to a grocery store, purchasing groceries for them and, Alfredo suspects, the clothing they needed. Alfredo said that moment in time left an indelible imprint on him, forever changing the course of his life. It was the kindness of this stranger that caused Alfredo to know he was going to help others.

Alfredo has a deep desire to give. He feels blessed and lucky. He prays daily and gives thanks but never prays for material things. Instead, Alfredo prays for enlightenment and guidance. He noted that Lazarus is his patron saint and that when he is home he lights a candle to honor him. Alfredo tries to live a life of gratitude and is even thankful for the challenges he faces daily.

He believes the key to success is resilience, the ability to constantly be tested and weathered by the storm. This is when real growth occurs. Alfredo also attributes his success to having great mentors. He stated that one of the greatest things you can do is be a mentor. He also believes that if you concentrate on the negative there is no way to do positive things. Alfredo thinks, much like his friend Peter Thomas, that when negative things happen you need to try to compartmentalize them by placing them in a figurative or symbolic box. Then, if possible, hire someone else to deal with the box.

The three life philosophies that guide Alfredo's life and philanthropy are as follows:

- Everything happens for a good reason.
- Nothing has any meaning except the meaning you give it.
- On the other side of tremendous frustration is tremendous success.

Alfredo believes that he and his life are in a constant state of transformation and that his philanthropic activities help him reach the next level. Life, to him, is about constantly stretching. At the end of his life, Alfredo would rather look back and realize he was part of the "I Shouldn't Have Club" instead of being part of the "I Should Have Club."

One of Alfredo's favorite books, which he usually gives to everyone he meets, is *Rhinoceros Success* by Scott Alexander. It is a book about how to be successful, and as Alfredo describes it, there are about seven things the book teaches that each person should do:

- Develop and have a thick skin.
- Focus on what you want.
- Charge ahead; in other words, go for it.
- Do not stand still.
- Make things happen.
- Remember, you will be constantly tested.
- You will also be challenged and allowed to expand.

He also believes that many individuals live in a FEAR mode, meaning *f*alse *e*vidence *a*ppearing *r*eal. By living as a rhinoceros and without fear, Alfredo believes he and many, if not all, other entrepreneurs are afraid of nothing.

Alfredo and his wife, Lisa, give away about $3 million annually. When I asked him how they decide on the projects, charities, nonprofit organizations, and programs that they will fund annually, Alfredo's first response was, "How do you say 'no'?" But he did concede that there are criteria they follow, that the foundation and their personal giving over the years have become more strategic. The four areas on which they focus are children, education, diseases, and the arts. Alfredo shared that some of their projects and activities include endowing chairs at universities and colleges, whereas others are supporting a few families directly, meaning, for example, that they assist a single mom who might have an illness and needs a helping hand. Alfredo and Lisa also have a charitable board that reviews and monitors their donations. The members of this board do site visits to the nonprofit organizations and charities that are funded.

I asked Alfredo if they ever stop funding a nonprofit organization or individual, to which his response was, "When do you cut someone off?" He said it is hard to stop providing the funds to nonprofit organizations that are doing great work. Alfredo also shared that he personally never passes someone asking for money, such as a homeless person, without giving them something financially, by which he means $20, $50, or sometimes even $100. He went further, saying he does not care where the recipients spend the money, meaning on a meal or alcohol, nor does he worry about whether they are telling the truth. He simply knows he is supposed to give back and that by doing so he feels great. Alfredo told me about a study showing that when you perform an act of random kindness, serotonin and dopamine are released in your brain and allow you to feel a natural high. It is a good feeling!

Alfredo and Lisa lead by example, chairing many galas and other events annually and reaching out to others to let them know what wonderful opportunities exist for getting involved and possibly transforming someone's life. They also require their 50 employees in Arizona to be involved with at least two nonprofit organizations.

When I asked Alfredo if being charitable has helped his business, his immediate response was "Yes, absolutely! My giving has given back to me in multiples of thousands." Alfredo is also tremendously humbled by the affect his and Lisa's charitable giving has had on individuals. He sheepishly shared that every day someone says thank you. For Alfredo, that is greatly appreciated.

He encourages others to live a life of significance, not simply a life of existence. A life of significance will allow you, according to Alfredo, to be charitable to others in numerous ways.

Alfredo's Advice

- Find something you are passionate about and get involved; find your life's purpose in being able to give.
- Get personally involved by giving not only your financial resources but also your time.
- Give of your heart; your heart needs to be fed and giving is a spiritual happening.
- Giving is a privilege, and by giving you will receive more than you could possibly give.
- You will meet amazing individuals through charitable efforts.
- Through your charitable efforts you will discover what is important in your life and true happiness will be yours.

STEPHAN PYLES

Stephan Pyles, a fifth-generation Texan and a pioneer of new American cuisine, has created 14 restaurants over the past 22 years. The founding father of southwestern cuisine, he was the first person in the Southwest to win a James Beard Award for Best Chef and was the first Texan inducted into Who's Who of Food and Wine in America. *Bon Appétit* has credited him with "almost single-handedly changing the cooking scene in Texas," while *The New York Times* called Stephan "an absolute genius in the kitchen." In 2006, *Esquire* named Stephan "Chef of the Year" and included his newest restaurant, Stephan Pyles, in its list of best new restaurants. *Texas Monthly* named Stephan one of the "twenty most impressive, intriguing, and influential Texans for 1998," and in its February 2007 issue named his restaurant Stephan Pyles "Best New Restaurant of 2006." In late spring, he will open a new restaurant in the Arts District named Samar that will serve "international small plates" inspired by the cuisine of India, Spain, and the eastern Mediterranean. Stephan is cuisine consultant to American Airlines and the Dallas Museum of Art.

Stephan got his start at the Great Chefs of France Cooking School at the Mondavi Winery, where he served as chef's assistant and worked with Michelin three-star chefs such as Michel Guerard, Jean and Pierre Troigros,

Alain Chapel, Paul Bocuse, and Gaston LeNotre. In 1982, he met and worked closely with Julia Child and continued a warm friendship with her until her death a few years ago.

While chef and owner of Routh Street Café and Baby Routh in Dallas and Goodfellow's and Tejas in Minneapolis, Stephan was the recipient of numerous awards, including the AAA Five Diamond Award, *Nation's Restaurant News*'s Fine Dining Hall of Fame Award, *Restaurants and Institutions'* Ivy Award, and the American Academy of Achievement Award. He was the inaugural recipient of the James Beard Foundation's award for Best Chef in America–Southwest in 1991 and has been given the Outstanding Restaurateur of the Year award by both the Minnesota Restaurant Association and the Texas Restaurant Association.

In 1994, Stephan opened Star Canyon; during his tenure there, it was on the list of best new restaurants in *Esquire*, *Bon Appétit*, and *Town and Country*. It was nominated for Best New Restaurant in America by the James Beard Foundation, and was named one of the top 25 restaurants in the country. In 1997, Stephan opened AquaKnox, a global seafood restaurant, to critical acclaim; it was named best new restaurant by *Food and Wine*. Stephan sold Star Canyon and AquaKnox to Carlson Restaurants WorldWide in 1998. He opened for them a Star Canyon in Las Vegas at the Venetian Hotel and Resort and developed two new concepts for the company: FishBowl, an Asian restaurant, and Taqueria Cañonita, a casual Mexican restaurant. In 2001, he left the company and, in consultation, created such concepts as the nationally acclaimed Dragonfly restaurant at Hotel ZaZa and Ama Lur at the Gaylord Texan Resort & Convention Center in Grapevine, Texas. Additionally, he traveled extensively and researched food for the next five years.

He has cooked for dignitaries and celebrities ranging from Queen Elizabeth II and Mikhail Gorbachev to Mick Jagger and Sharon Stone. He has appeared around the world as guest celebrity chef and was one of five chefs worldwide invited to prepare dinner for Jimmy Carter's 70th birthday.

Stephan's first cookbook, *The New Texas Cuisine*, published by Doubleday, was named by *Bon Appétit* as one of the top 10 chefs' cookbooks of the 1990s and is now in its ninth printing. Stephan has also coauthored *Tamales*, published by Macmillan, and *New Tastes from Texas*, which is the companion piece to his Emmy-award winning nationally syndicated PBS television series by the same name. He also hosted a weekly cooking segment on the Texas ABC affiliate, which aired throughout the state. In addition, he has appeared on such national programs as *Good Morning America* and *The Today Show*. His fourth cookbook, *Southwestern Vegetarian*, was published by Clarkson-Potter, a division of Random House, in 2001.

Stephan is a founding board member of Share Our Strength, an international hunger relief organization, and in 1998 received the organization's Humanitarian of the Year Award. In addition, he serves as a life board member of the North Texas Food Bank and is on the board of Goodwill Industries. In 1988, he founded Dallas's Taste of the Nation event, which has raised over $2 million for local ministries and food pantries. He was cofounder of the Hunger Link, Dallas's perishable food program that links restaurants and hotels with shelters and other feeding programs.

Under the auspices of the Texas Hill Country Wine and Food Foundation, Stephan offers a $15,000 annual scholarship in his name to a rising-star culinary student in Texas.

Go with the Flow

"Don't try to make too specific a plan for anything; remain flexible" says Stephan Pyles, chef and owner of Stephan Pyles Restaurant, located in Dallas, Texas. This has been his life's mantra and has served him well. When I arrived at his restaurant and was escorted by him into his office for a private lunch, Stephan shared with me that he believes there are two paths that can be taken. You can either choose the journey and accept the destination or choose the destination and accept the journey. Stephan chooses the former: he chooses the journey and then accepts the destination.

His attributes his success to being in the right place at the right time, and then adds that he had some talent to be successful as a chef. However, Stephan is quick to point out that during the past several generations there was not a great interest in food in America. It was a time when the TV dinner had been invented and Americans were crazy about it. The selling point of the TV dinner was that it was easy and convenient for the housewife. However, most TV dinners had poor nutrition and bad taste, leading to a group of people who eventually did not know how to cook.

As Stephan said to me, "Then came the '60s, which was a time of 'throw it all out the window,' to be counter culture; the '70s came along and was about fast food and meals that were quick and easy. This was the standard of the day." But something happened in the 1980s to food and the way it was perceived in America. Stephan attributes part of the change in attitudes toward food to the role America's bicentennial celebration played in having the nation become more patriotic about everything, including food. Stephan also noted that during the early 1970s, the chefs in France were brewing a revolution in French cooking known as the French Nouvelle movement. This movement somewhat influenced American chefs such as Alice Waters, Wolfgang Puck, and Paul Prudhomme, who during the seventies were creating amazing food dishes using natural, seasonal, and organic food from the regions of America in which they lived and cooked. They were bringing good, quality food to America's dining tables. Chefs in the United States had become interested in food again! They had become intrigued by American-grown ingredients and began studying and learning about good food. This was all very American in Stephan's opinion and occurred well before people's social consciences were raised about what we were eating and where it came from—in today's language, our carbon footprint.

Another example of this revolution was trained chefs from or living in Texas beginning to question why they couldn't use ingredients that were indigenous to Texas. As Stephan shared with me, "I wanted to cook classic French food, but in the closet I was eating Texas food. I then asked myself, why can't I use French Buerre Blanc with cilantro and jalapeños?" This was the beginning of the creation known as southwest cuisine. A regional cuisine was being developed not only in Texas, but also in other parts of the country, such as Miami, the Pacific Northwest, and the Midwest. A new American cuisine was being created.

By the 1990s, the American restaurant industry was in full force but still fluctuating with the economy. And although the restaurant industry has become more casual in many ways, the American food and wine revolution that began in the late 1970s and early 1980s is here to stay. Restaurants became a place not only for dining but also for entertainment. The food was good, and dining out became an experience.

Stephan also believes that travel and the globalization of the world led Americans to become more comfortable with different combinations of food. To him, the boundaries have disappeared and wonderful opportunities are available to the chefs of America and the world.

As many people know, Stephan spent a portion of his career in Las Vegas developing restaurants. Although many people dismiss Las Vegas for various reasons, Stephan does not. He told me with much amusement that he believes one day, a millennium from now, when aliens come to Earth from far-away galaxies, they will go to Las Vegas and see the pyramids, the Eiffel Tower, and the good restaurants and think, "This is where it all started!" Meaning things in Las Vegas such as those listed above as well as the Brooklyn Bridge, would be thought to be replicated from Vegas to other parts of the world. Seriously, Stephan recognizes how Las Vegas reinvented itself by upping the concept of what it was.

Thinking back to his concept of "go with the flow," Stephan told the story of starting the Star Canyon restaurant and having a belief of how his company would look in one, two, and five years. In the end, his business looked nothing like he envisioned it but was much better. Not only did he have a national television program, two new cookbooks, a line of cooking products, and two new restaurants in the works, but also he had an offer from a large corporation to buy all his interests at what at the time was a staggering amount of money. So his philosophy today is to do what is in front of him, expect great things to happen, and not to have specific expectations.

Stephan shared with me that there is a saying in Texas, "Dance with the one that brung ya." He believes that when one gets involved with things that are outside of one's business brand, entrepreneurs can find themselves in trouble. Very few entrepreneurs can manage their businesses and successfully leverage that brand into other areas. For chefs, this would include canned products, sponsorships, and books. The list can go on and on and can cause problems if a focus is not maintained. Stephan thinks it is easy to be distracted and to have your business brand be watered down. This is especially true with young chefs. As Stephan says, "I'm guilty of some things, but have learned to not say 'yes' to everything. I am not Superman and that is something we must all learn."

Stephan sold his restaurants, with the transition being complete in 2000. Although he traveled and continued to learn, he realized that selling his business was painful in many ways. One of the unforeseen things it caused to happen was that he had to step aside from his charitable work.

If you haven't guessed, hunger is Stephan's charitable cause, the one he works to alleviate and solve. He says that philanthropy and doing philanthropic work teaches him constantly. By giving he receives. He never feels better than when he has pulled off a successful charitable event. To him, doing events for charity brings a level of awareness and causes change. In other words, you can make a difference.

Stephan recalls thinking that when he grew up in Big Spring, Texas, with a population of 20,000, nobody was homeless and therefore nobody was hungry. According to him, philanthropy, or rather charity, was done through the churches and focused primarily on bake sales, with the money being raised for missions and orphanages.

It should be noted that this great chef of American cuisine and founding father of the southwestern cuisine movement first studied music and wanted to be a musician, not a chef!

One of Stephan's first experiences of philanthropy occurred in 1987 at a celebration of the 50th anniversary of the March of Dimes, which took place in Washington, DC. The event had twenty chefs from across the country preparing a meal for 1,000 people. It was a multiple-course meal, with most of the chefs preparing appetizers. This was a very positive interaction with a nonprofit organization for Stephan.

A few years before this event, Stephan participated in a Citymeals-on-Wheels program in New York City that honored James Beard on his birthday. Citymeals-on-Wheels draws awareness to the homebound seniors and hunger in New York City.

According to the Citymeals-on-Wheels website, Gael Greene and James Beard founded Citymeals-on-Wheels in 1981 after reading a newspaper article about homebound elderly New Yorkers with nothing to eat on weekends and holidays. They rallied their friends in the restaurant community, raising private funds as a supplement to the government-funded weekday meal delivery program. Twenty-five years ago their first efforts brought a Christmas meal to 6,000 frail aged individuals.

It was during the March of Dimes event that Stephan was approached by Debbie Shore and Cathy Townsend of Share Our Strength to help the non-profit organization launch a huge outdoor meal feeding thousands of people. According to its website, Share Our Strength began in the basement of a row house on Capitol Hill in 1984, in the wake of the Ethiopian famine. Bill and Debbie Shore started the organization with the belief that everyone has a strength to share in the global fight against hunger and poverty, and that in these shared strengths lie sustainable solutions. Stephan agreed to help and remembers seeing many, many rotisserie grills as well as thousands of people passing by and stopping to watch when the event took place at Rockefeller Center in New York City. And although Share Our Strength paid air travel costs, as a chef Stephan donated his time and the food.

Stephan was very active in pulling together the chefs for the Taste of the Nation events during the first years. As he explained, the first one took place in 25 cities across the country on the same day, with the best chefs preparing samples for the attendees and the proceeds from each event benefiting the local food banks in the areas. There was lots of press and press opportunities; however, the first year was still painful to pull together. But as Stephan says, "Don't give up!" The next year will usually be better for events such as this, and usually the funds raised will increase.

In 1988, Share Our Strength pioneered what is still the nation's largest and finest culinary benefit: Share Our Strength's Taste of the Nation, presented by American Express. On a single day in April 1988, the best restaurants in 25 cities hosted food and wine tastings to raise funds for Share Our Strength grants. Corporate sponsorship from American Express ensured that the nonprofit organization could—and still does—grant 100% of the ticket sales from the events. Those 25 tastings raised nearly $250,000.

Taste of the Nation now spans 55 cities across North America, involves more than 10,000 chefs and restaurateurs, and has raised more than $70 million since that first quarter-of-a-million-dollar day. In addition to raising significant funds, Taste of the Nation has raised awareness of the invisible hunger that exists in our country at the local, state, and national levels and has built lasting partnerships among local anti-hunger programs, corporations, foodservice professionals, and concerned individuals.

Chefs truly have become a phenomenon in America; as a *New York Times* article stated, chefs have become the golden boys for charity. Having a chef at your charitable event is a great marketing opportunity, with the end result being lots of good press. Stephan shared that he receives numerous requests on a daily basis from nonprofit organizations or well-meaning supporters asking him to "close his restaurant" for a night for a charitable event. Or he gets asked to be an "auction item" for a charity's gala, meaning that he as a chef would donate his time and the food to cook dinner for 8 to 10 people in a person's home who was the highest bidder at the charitable event.

Stephan receives so many charitable appeals that one of his assistants daily goes through the stacks of mail discerning what is feasible and what is not. As he told me, his restaurant could conceivably be closed every night of the week and weekend for a charitable event because that is how numerous the requests are asking him for help. Stephan also noted that through his philanthropic and charitable work he has met some remarkable individuals, such as Jan Pruitt, CEO of the North Texas Food Bank, John Beckert, a Dallas humanitarian and philanthropist, and Kathryn Hall, the former ambassador to Austria under President Clinton.

Stephan readily points out that when he became involved in the hunger issue, one in eight children in Texas was hungry. Today, even after more than 20 years focusing on this issue, the situation has worsened, with one in four children in Texas at risk of hunger. Despite all the efforts, more children in Texas are hungry; Stephan believes that poverty is the real issue. According to Stephan, you can call it what you will, but the political programs to address poverty have failed. Despite all the prosperity experienced in this country recently, poverty has grown proportionally. Stephan has personally conducted mini-surveys asking those he meets whether they know how many children in the state of Texas are hungry. More than 90% do not realize that children in Texas and this country are hungry.

Stephan has no regrets about any of his activities on behalf of charities. He does, however, think that individuals need to make a difference and relate to a cause in order to become passionate about it and truly involved with it.

While hunger is a cause that speaks to Stephan's heart, it is not the only cause. He also chooses to be involved with the Dallas Opera as well as AIDS and cancer research organizations. The common thread, again, is meaningful engagement with a charitable effort that touches one's heart.

Stephan's Advice

- Do philanthropy in the sprit of community, knowing that it is the right thing to do and that it is needed.
- Find a charity that speaks to your business and employees and establish a long-term relationship.
- Conduct philanthropy astutely as you do your business; recognize that it is an opportunity for marketing, networking, general good will, and public perception of you and your business.

JOHN W. ROGERS, JR.

John W. Rogers, Jr., is founder, chairman, and chief executive officer of Ariel Investments, a Chicago-based money management firm that serves individual investors and 401(k) plans through its no-load mutual funds and manages separate accounts for institutional clients. In 1983, at the age of 24, John founded the firm with an investment philosophy grounded in patience, discipline, and independent thinking. More than 25 years later, his original philosophy still guides Ariel Investments. John is the lead portfolio manager of the Ariel Fund as well as its mid-cap counterpart, the Ariel Appreciation Fund. Additionally, as the firm's chief investment officer, he manages Ariel's small, small/mid, and mid-cap institutional portfolios.

John serves as a corporate board member of three public companies: Aon Corporation, Exelon Corporation, and McDonald's Corporation. Also dedicated to giving back to the community, his civic affiliations include serving as a director of the Chicago Urban League, a trustee of the University of Chicago, and a member of the John S. and James L. Knight Foundation. In addition, he is a past president of the board of the Chicago Park District. John received an AB in economics in 1980 from Princeton University, where he was also captain of the varsity basketball team. In 2008, John was awarded Princeton's highest honor, the Woodrow Wilson Award, bestowed annually on a graduate whose career embodies a commitment to national service. Following the election of President Barack Obama, John served as chair for the Presidential Inauguration Committee 2009.

His investment expertise has brought him to the forefront of media attention. He is a regular columnist in *Forbes* magazine and is frequently quoted in various news and business publications, including *USA Today, The New York Times, Black Enterprise, BusinessWeek,* and *SmartMoney.* In addition, he has made guest appearances on television shows ranging from CNBC to Fox News and has also spoken at many academic institutions.

Town + Coach = Philanthropy

When you meet John Rogers, you instantly realize you have met an extraordinary entrepreneur. John has always been a businessman in his own right, from his days of selling hot dogs, soft drinks, and peanuts at Comiskey Park to Chicago White Sox fans to today as he runs his own firm, Ariel Investments, which employs 74 individuals and is the largest investment firm owned by an African American in the country.

> John told me that currently there are no investment firms, hedge funds, or private equity groups that have a senior partner or manager who is African American. It is a missed opportunity for these firms.

During our interview, John shared that philanthropy, meaning looking out for others, was not part of his family's daily life or part of their regular family discussions. He did, however, learn this valuable lesson from Coach Pete Carril when John was playing basketball at Princeton University. According to John, Coach Carril taught him the meaning of looking out for others, an experience John did not have because he was an only child. Coach Carril taught John the value of a team and how to help others, which was especially important when John served as captain of Princeton's basketball team. John believes that the teachings of his collegiate basketball coach and his experiences looking out for his teammates forced him to think about things differently. He believes his awareness of and commitment to philanthropy, to giving back, began during his days on campus and his work with the basketball team.

John Rogers was born and raised in Chicago. It was always his plan to return to his hometown after graduation and work in the city he loved. However, as with most students upon reaching graduation day, John was now thinking of things differently. One of the first things he realized was that his "home team" was now double focused: one focus was the Chicago business world into which he was entering, and the second focus was the Chicago African American community of which he was already a part. Upon his return to Chicago, he was committed and determined to be involved with both "teams," offering his assistance, knowledge, skill set, and financial support as needed.

One of John's first philanthropic endeavors in the city of Chicago was to become involved as a member of the board of directors of Chicago Urban League. He stated that he was and is still very engaged and involved with this group, whose mission, according to its website, is to "support and advocate for economic, educational and social progress for African Americans through our agenda focused exclusively on economic empowerment as the key driver for social change."

The Chicago Urban League was established in 1916 by an interracial group of community leaders to help rural African Americans migrating from the South in unprecedented numbers adjust to urban living. The establishment of the Chicago chapter was viewed then as an important step in spreading the National Urban League's civil rights agenda across mid-America and parts of the West.

Throughout his career and life in Chicago, John has served in numerous capacities for various cultural and community nonprofit organizations, including the Adler Planetarium, the Field Museum, the Museum of Science and Industry, and WBEZ Chicago Public Radio. In addition, he is a past president of the board of the Chicago Park District. He also serves on corporate boards of directors for companies such as Aon, Exelon, and McDonald's.

John separates his philanthropy into two areas: company focused and personal focused. According to him, it is fairly easy to separate the requests that come in to determine which ones will receive philanthropic support from his company and which ones will receive funding from him personally. As an example, he told me that projects and programs receiving funding from his company include organizations such as Rush Presbyterian Hospital, the Chicago Symphony, and other civic-oriented projects. He says his company supports these opportunities because "it is the right thing to do." In other words, it is a continuation of his long-time commitment to supporting the home team.

During our interview, John shared that two of the first nonprofit organizations he became really involved with personally were his alma maters, the University of Chicago Laboratory "Lab" School and, as stated earlier, Princeton University. John is overall very committed to educational philanthropy. He believes in and supports the public school system and especially the small public schools. Education might even be the area that drives him the most in the philanthropic arena. As an example, in 2005 John established the Rogers Scholars program, which to date has allowed three students to attend a private high school of their choice for four years. This program allows those who might not have an opportunity to attend the high school of their choice because of financial means to do so. Occasionally, funding requests for nonprofit projects will be split between the company and personal, such as Chicago's Millennium Park and Ariel Educational Initiative.

John encourages his employees to be philanthropic by following their hearts. He further encourages his staff to look at the needs of the community and then at their own skill sets to determine where they would like to get involved. He opens doors for his employees by making calls to individuals who are making decisions about who will be asked to serve on nonprofit boards and committees. As part of this encouragement, Ariel Investments has a matching gift program that matches up to $1,500 annually per employee making donations to nonprofit organizations. According to John, this program has been a long-time benefit for the now 74 employees of the company.

John truly believes philanthropy is more than just giving money; it is about giving time. An example of how John lives this belief is his work with seventh- and eighth-grade students from the Ariel Community Academy during Analysts Day, a day dedicated to discussing how to pick stocks. John personally spends time with these young people, teaching them what he has learned over a long and successful career. He also mentors students not only at the Academy but also at Kenwood School and the Lab School.

Volunteering is an activity his employees also do. For example, 20 employees and friends of Ariel Investments volunteer every Saturday for two hours during five-week sessions tutoring 80 students from the Ariel Community Academy in math and reading.

Ariel Community Academy was established in 1996 and has been supported by the Ariel Education Initiative as well as by other funders. According to the 2007 Ariel Education Initiative annual report, "The model of the Academy is rooted in the understanding that family and community are vital ingredients in the social, physical, emotional and educational well-being of children. By doing so, students not only learn the importance of education, but also the value of being a part of community."

Classes are from pre-kindergarten to eighth grade, with a public school curriculum that has a unique and special focus on investment education. The Ariel Community Academy specifically is dedicated to providing low-income communities with opportunities to be both educationally and financially literate. To date, Ariel Community Academy has 440 students, with 43 students graduating and attending 14 different high schools.

Just as John leads by example at his company, so too he leads by example at home, which includes introducing his daughter to the world of philanthropy through showcasing the philanthropic and charitable endeavors being done by Ariel Investments, its employees, and himself. He proudly shares that she has been involved and included in the donations he has made to the University of Chicago Lab School as well as attending graduations at the Academy. John now sees his legacy carried forward as his daughter is giving back by serving as a volunteer tutoring individuals in prisons and homeless shelters.

John Rogers exemplifies his beliefs in many ways and one of them is in his offices. When you arrive at Ariel Investments, what you first notice are all the turtles. It seems that John's patient investment strategy has been equated with Aesop's fable of the hare and tortoise. The offices actually have a conference room named the Aesop Room.

In honor of the man who taught him much, including the importance of teamwork that was the foundation for John's philanthropic beliefs, there is a conference room named the Pete Carril Room, which is used for team building and has a round table so that everyone sitting at the table is viewed as members of the team.

The board room is named the Warren Buffett Room; as one might expect, Warren is a friend of John's and also has participated in volunteering and meeting with two students from the Ariel Community Academy.

The most touching part of the offices is the kitchen, which is named in honor of an Ariel Community Academy graduate, Travis Bergans, who worked in the offices. He died very young of an undetected heart ailment, but his memory and famous smile live on every time an employee says, "Let's go to the Travis Bergans kitchen."

When asked whether there is a difference between philanthropy and charity, John responded "Yes." He believes philanthropy is a sense of giving to programs and projects that have long-term viability and stability—that philanthropy is not a handout that helps perpetuate the existing situation. An example of this would be John's donation to the University of Chicago Lab School. He has pledged over $2 million as a challenge to other alumni to make donations to the Lab School to enable disadvantaged youth to attend. John believes it is important to recognize that this form of philanthropy goes beyond the person who graduates and is successful. It is also about giving back.

John shared that to him charity is a short-term solution. It is giving someone $1,000 to stay in school, which he recently did when he became aware that a graduate of the Ariel Community Academy was not going to be able to continue to attend a Catholic high school due to lack of funding. John further shared that nine out of ten times he will give someone the money when they ask if the story they share is what he terms "a great story."

John and his company have not had to set a budget for philanthropy and definitely do not let guilt drive their philanthropic decisions. However, given the recent economic conditions and the growing size of the requests, it is anticipated that a philanthropic budget will have to be established.

The entrepreneurs that John knows do not discuss philanthropy or, for that matter, charity. John believes that although this generation is lacking in this dimension, the prior African American generation of entrepreneurs did discuss it and did extraordinary things. To John, philanthropy hasn't been at the same level since the generation that produced John Johnson, George Johnson, and Ed Gardner. John stated that these men were giants and not only built great businesses but also were great philanthropists.

John H. Johnson was the founder of the Johnson Publishing Company, located in Chicago, Illinois, which published *Ebony, Jet, Fashion Fair Cosmetics*, and *EBONY Fashion Fair* magazines. George Johnson founded Johnson Products, which was an international cosmetics company also headquartered in Chicago, Illinois. Ed Gardner founded Soft Sheen Products, again located in Chicago, Illinois, which produced hair and beauty products for the African American market.

As a point in reference, John shared that when Dr. Martin Luther King, Jr., came to Chicago's Southside to raise money from local African American entrepreneurs for the Southern Christian Leadership Conference, he secured $60,000 in donations. John stated that "We [entrepreneurs] don't talk about [philanthropy] as much as we need to."

John's Advice

- Try to be focused; don't spread your donations too thin.
- Stay in areas where you understand the issues; give in the areas of your competence.
- Give where you can see the impact you are making.

John Rogers definitely followed this advice as he watched the students from the Ariel Community Academy recently hang out with Warren Buffett. He is living his philanthropic beliefs.

CIBELINE SARIANO

From Hong Kong to Los Angeles, Italy to New York, and now Boston, Cibeline Sariano has trained and traveled around the world, working with many fashion designers such as Richard Tyler, Calvin Klein, Liz Claiborne, Emmanuel Ungaro, Larke Intl. Limited, Kasper for ASL, Due per Due, and Sigrid Olsen.

Landing in Boston in 2002, Cibeline opened her namesake boutique in the hip Davis Square in Somerville, Massachusetts. Her premiere collection included tailored suits, sophisticated separates, and elegant cocktail dresses. Cibeline proudly supports local production of her garments and has all her designs made in New Bedford, Massachusetts. Over the past six years, the collection has evolved and grown, and so has the boutique. Cibeline relocated into the exclusive shopping district of Beacon Hill and set up shop on Charles Street in November 2008.

Cibeline's collection and custom one-of-a-kind designs have been featured on national television as well as red carpet events. Her designs have been seen on comedienne Lisa Lampanelli at the 2008 Grammy Awards, multiple appearances on *The Tonight Show with Jay Leno*, Lampanelli's one-hour HBO special in November 2008, and the Comedy Central special "Dirty Girl" in 2007. Swarovski Crystal Company commissioned Cibeline to design an original cocktail dress and featured her design in 105 Swarovski retail boutiques nationwide for its holiday 2006 window display.

Cibeline's collection of Barbie dolls and fashion coloring books when she was young were just the beginning. Growing up in New York in a creative environment (both her parents are professional artists), Cibeline had many influences and tools to cultivate her talent at a young age. She developed her ability to make the connection between art and fashion with her own imaginative nature. Cibeline is a graduate from Syracuse University with a BS in fashion design. Cibeline's 20 years' experience has given her a well-rounded view of the fashion industry, but most important the ability to conceptualize, design, and produce a designer collection from initial concept to finished product.

Cibeline's style is classic and tailored with a feminine twist. Her boutique is filled with looks for day (work) to evening (play) and incorporates vintage pieces into the mix of product. In the boutique there is an abundance of modern as well as vintage mixed in with the Cibeline Collection: such as must-have handbags, clutches, and jewels made by Boston-based designers as well as exquisite vintage pieces such as coats, hats, jewels, and stunning one-of-a-kind handbags and clutches. Cibeline builds wardrobes and designs clothes for women with curves, and a service is available to customize all of Cibeline's in-store collection garments to fit each individual body type perfectly.

Cibeline produces her exclusive collection locally in the state of Massachusetts and produces a very limited number of each style. In each season's collection, Cibeline only produces one to two garments in each size; when the design sells out it is no longer available, thus providing women the opportunity to have their own individual style and avoid seeing coworkers in the same look.

Additionally, Cibeline is available to shop for and consult women on how to wear certain styles, what fits their body types well, what styles to avoid for specific body types, colors that work well for each individual complexion, and to provide in-home consults on wardrobe and what should stay in one's closets and what should stay out.

Cibeline Boston is a lifestyle boutique where a woman can dress herself head to toe and walk away feeling and looking vibrant and beautiful. "It is exhilarating and terrifying at the same time to start your own business as well as a line of clothing. . . . My idea was to create a lifestyle boutique where women could shop for one-of-a-kind designer clothing, vintage as well as new fashion accessories and much more, albeit 'a one stop shopping experience' where the professional women could get herself a new look from head to toe, a gift for her friend, and a fabulous handbag! This has been extremely rewarding, my life-long dream becoming a reality!" according to Cibeline.

Fashion + Charity = Marketing Opportunities

When you meet Cibeline, you immediately recognize a woman on a mission. Her boutique, located on Charles Street in Boston, Massachusetts, is amazing, and she is larger than life in bringing creativity and fashion to the real-world woman.

Cibeline's first memory of philanthropy comes not from her mom and dad but from her aunt. Cibeline recalls her aunt working in a soup kitchen, especially during the fall when the holidays came around. Her aunt helped to ensure that everyone in her community had food to eat. While Cibeline was designing and creating clothing for her modern-day Barbie dolls, she was acutely aware of a greater need existing in her community.

Cibeline views philanthropic and charitable endeavors as an opportunity to combine business and a good cause. She sees an opportunity to align her brand with the recognition of a charity, and vice versa. To her, nonprofit activities provide avenues for exposure of her clothing line and boutique and perhaps even new clients. To Cibeline's great surprise, she has had both very positive and very negative experiences. While someone might think the latter was attributable to unrealistic expectations, it truly was, in her opinion, a lack of preparedness and readiness by the nonprofit organization to deal with business people becoming involved and their expectations.

An example Cibeline shared was that she approached a local Boston nonprofit organization, whose mission is to fight cancer in children and adults, and asked it to help sponsor her 2006 fashion show, in return for which she would raise money for this specific charity. Cibeline was thrilled to collaborate with this charity and raise donations; however, soon that excitement turned to frustration. This organization initially offered Cibeline support, but once they realized the monetary value she would be raising, there was no further support. They did not provide support staff at her event or any educational pamphlets for attendees, and, much to her dismay, only gave her unsharpened pencils. As she jokingly said to me, "What was I going to do with unsharpened pencils?" There was no support for her as a business person from the charity's community and Cibeline found herself trying to answer questions, sometimes very specific questions, which attendees were asking about the nonprofit organization. Remember, as stated earlier, she had received no educational information from the nonprofit organization.

Boston is a city that acts like a town; that said, Boston is a town that supports charities and charity events, according to Cibeline. However, she has discovered that people in Boston have a hard time justifying attending a fashion show unless the show or event has a charitable component. In

Cibeline's opinion, fashion shows for fashion show's sake may be seen as too frivolous by most people in her adopted city. She has seen evidence that if events, especially fashion shows, have a charitable component to them, they are much more successful in attendance than those that do not have a charitable component.

Cibeline was raised in New York City, where fashion shows are attended and celebrated on a regular basis, even if there is not a charitable component.

Cibeline does believe there is a difference between philanthropy and charity. To her, philanthropy is an event or an activity that is big in size and works to generate interest and support for a particular cause. Charity, on the other hand, is defined by her as giving money to a cause.

Cibeline's philanthropic activities are not limited to fashion. She trained for six months and ran a marathon for a leukemia and lymphoma nonprofit organization for which she agreed to fundraise $3,000. Initially it was hard for her to identify with the cause because at that time she did not know anyone who had been affected by the disease, but the nonprofit organization had an amazing way to connect participants. It assigned Cibeline a patient with which to correspond, and the two of them sent letters to each other. Cibeline felt this solidified her commitment to finishing what she set out to do, namely, fundraise for a great cause and get healthy doing so. Ironically, after she ran the marathon race, Cibeline's uncle was diagnosed with lymphoma.

She pondered this issue and realized that she would have been committed to raising even more money if someone she knew had been affected by the disease prior to her running the race. Cibeline believes this is true of most people who are fundraising for a charity, whether they are doing activities for breast cancer, Parkinson's disease, or any other disease. If you've been affected by it somehow, it can help drive you to achieve a financial commitment you made to yourself and to the charity of choice.

Cibeline views philanthropic and charitable work as more than just giving money. It is also about giving time. She sees it as an opportunity to "pay it forward." To live out her view, Cibeline regularly donates products and her time to events for nonprofit organizations. For example, she will donate a gift certificate to her store and include a two-hour fashion and beauty consult session for a fashion makeover to a nonprofit organization, often used as part of a silent or live auction to raise money on the night of an event. It's a feel-good donation for Cibeline, and all parties benefit.

Cibeline's Advice

- Marketing is most difficult for entrepreneurs; teaming up with a nonprofit organization or hosting an event for a nonprofit organization will always attract more participants.
- Find a charity that can provide you with the support you need, so you can be promoted and marketed as well as promoting and marketing the nonprofit organization.
- Learn to speak on behalf of the nonprofit organization.
- Choose nonprofit organizations and causes closest to your heart; it also helps if it is something you have experienced.
- Finally, find the right nonprofit organization to support; this means finding the cause that resonates with you.

PETER THOMAS

Peter started life from very humble beginnings, watching his single mother struggle to make a living as a nanny in London, England, during World War II. After the war, she remarried, and the new family immigrated to Canada, where Peter grew up on a remote farm outside Perryvale near Athabasca in northern Alberta. Peter was a happy kid who turned every situation, no matter how tough, into an opportunity. He heeded his mother's advice to be the best at whatever he wanted to be. Determined to make it on his own, Peter left home at age 15 to join the Canadian army. During his seven-year service, including a tour of duty in the Middle East and the Gaza Strip in 1961, Peter learned the importance of self-discipline, realizing that it would allow him to focus on a goal and achieve it. After leaving the army, Peter recognized his passion and strength in sales. He became a business visionary, a master salesman, a consummate dealmaker, and a goal-oriented achiever. Among the many ventures he led and was involved with, Peter is best known for founding Century 21 Real Estate Canada Ltd., which, by the time he sold his interests in 1987, had turned into a company with $9 billion in annual sales through 450 offices with over 8,000 sales agents. Peter went on to become one of Canada's top business leaders and was recognized as such when he was awarded the Ernst & Young Entrepreneur of the Year Award for the Pacific Region in 1998.

Throughout Peter's successful business career, he has always felt a strong commitment to support his community. He served under Premier Bill Vander Zalm as chairman of the BC Housing Commission and co-chairman of the Privatization Review Committee. In both these instances, Peter was a $1.00 per year man. Moreover, for the past 18 years, Peter has been the chairman of the board of trustees for the Thomas Foundation, which he funded and incorporated in 1990. Since the year 2000, the public foundation has distributed over $2 million to Canadian charitable causes that focus on children, education, and mental health.

The need to give back was intensified for Peter after tragedy hit his family in 2000 with the suicide of his only son, Todd. A gifted, spiritual young man, Todd lived a life of conflict and decided to end it by leaping to his death from the 14th floor of the New York Plaza Hotel. Todd had a severe sleeping disorder and over the years was diagnosed as manic depressive, bipolar, chemically imbalanced, and even schizophrenic. Struck by grief over the death of his son, Peter was determined to focus all his energy in a positive direction and decided to honor and celebrate Todd's life. He began this mission in two ways. First, he founded the Todd Thomas Foundation in 2000 to celebrate and honor his son and "[t]o help raise the awareness of the magnitude of mental illness and the effect it has on individuals as well as our society, to assist in decreasing the stigma associated with it, and to support research for effective treatments" (www.toddthomasfoundation.org). The foundation is a component fund of the Arizona Community Foundation in Phoenix, Arizona. (See Chapter 12 for working with Community Foundations.)

Second, Peter decided to use his method of values-based goal setting and share it with others through LifePilot, a British Columbia–based nonprofit organization that provides programs that empower and teach people from all walks of life to live in alignment with their values. Since LifePilot's inception in 2002, Peter has spent countless hours traveling the world to touch as many lives with his message as possible. To date, LifePilot has inspired over 5,000 individuals, ranging from business leaders, students, and families to prison inmates. Peter is committed to have net profits from LifePilot flow to LifePilot community outreach programs such as the University and Prison Series (www.lifepilot.org).

Peter is passionate about sharing his experience and wisdom with young entrepreneurs and our leaders of tomorrow. As such, he has served on the board of the Entrepreneurs' Organization (EO; www.eonetwork.org) for 20 years. As one of the founding members of this organization, Peter has been recognized as chairman emeritus of the EO advisory board. In addition, Peter dedicated his time to be the chairman of the 2008 Global Student Entrepreneur Awards (GSEA) Judges Committee. The EO-led GSEA is the premier global competition for undergraduate students who own and operate businesses while attending college or a university (www.gsea.org).

In the fall of 2007, Peter was inducted into the CEO Entrepreneurship Hall of Fame and received the Lifetime Achievement Award from the Collegiate Entrepreneurs' Organization (www.c-e-o.org) of which he is now the vice chairman. Furthermore, in keeping with his message of values-based living and leadership, Peter wants to instill values-based leadership in young leaders and organizations. With this objective, Peter made a gift to the Royal Roads University Foundation in Victoria, British Columbia, in December of 2006, to create the Todd Thomas Institute for Values-Based Leadership (www.royalroads.ca/tti). Founded with a commitment to global leadership for social, environmental, and economic sustainability, the institute was launched in the summer of 2008 to advance the theory and practice of values-based leadership through applied research with partners in the workplaces and communities.

At age 70, Peter continues to pursue ways of providing support for the causes that he holds dear. He is a role model and values-based leader who has made a major impact both in the business community and in the lives of the many people he has met and touched throughout his illustrious life. An entrepreneur at heart, Peter's life has taken him from serial entrepreneurship to social entrepreneurship, a vocation that he will continue to passionately pursue to enrich the lives of others.

Turning Grief into a Charitable Mission

I will always remember when I first encountered Peter Thomas. It was in 2006 and I was meeting with his friend, Alfredo Molina. During our conversation, Alfredo said, "You have to meet Peter," and with that he picked up the phone and told Peter to come to his offices immediately to meet me. About 15 minutes later, Peter came bounding into Alfredo's offices exuding an unbelievable amount of energy. It was clear that he was on fire about life, embracing it fully. He was excited and eager to meet and ready to share his philanthropic views.

As his biography indicates, Peter did not grow up in a wealthy family and did not come from a family of philanthropists. But he learned to give back along the way. When I talked to Peter about his first philanthropic experience, he shared that it was volunteering to go on the board of St. Michael's University School, the private school his son and daughter attended. As he tells the story, it was not long before the board decided that he should be involved in the fundraising activities. It is here that Peter says he learned about giving and contributing. He saw that it was important not only to give money but that nonprofit organizations also needed skill sets he had as an entrepreneur. This occurred when Peter was in his early 30s, and as he states, "It is a formula I have followed ever since." For those who can and who have the opportunity, Peter advises they should give both their time and their money. As he says, "It is needed and it is very rewarding in a feel-good way."

I asked Peter what causes move his heart and to what nonprofit organizations he makes his philanthropic donations. Peter responded that among the various community causes he supports, he focused primarily on initiatives that foster values-based living and leadership, such as LifePilot and the Todd Thomas Institute, and entrepreneurial education initiatives because he believes they align with his values. He is very supportive of the Collegiate Entrepreneurs' Organization and the Global Student Entrepreneur Awards spearheaded by the Entrepreneurs' Organization.

CEO, the Collegiate Entrepreneurs' Organization, is the premier global entrepreneurship network that serves 30,000 students through 400 chapters and affiliated student organizations at colleges and universities. Its mission is to inform, support, and inspire college students to be entrepreneurial and seek opportunity through enterprise creation.

Global Student Entrepreneur Awards (GSEA) is the premier global competition for undergraduate students who own and operate businesses while attending college or a university. Nominees compete against their peers from around the world. Founded by St. Louis University in 1988, the GSEA is now an Entrepreneurs' Organization program, held in partnership with Mercedes-Benz Financial.

Peter and I discussed why he gives and he stated that he does it because it feels good and is the right thing to do. He also gives because he has the ability to do so, having both the business acumen as well as the funding of resources at his disposal. Given his skills set and the financial resources he has available, he feels it is an honor and almost an obligation to give.

He and his wife, Rita, do not set an annual budget, but on average they give 10% of what they make annually. Some years it is more when, as Peter puts it, there is a windfall, and other years it might not be as much depending on the resources available. They do, however, look at every request that comes in, and Peter noted that the Thomas Foundation board has an outline it follows in making decisions usually allocating two-thirds to their key pillars and one-third to causes that are dearly needed in the community or that are close to the hearts of family and friends.

Because Peter is Canadian, I asked him whether he saw any difference between philanthropy and charity in Canada and the United States. He said no. What really made the difference to Peter was his son Todd. When Todd died, Peter realized that we are not immortal, and in honor and celebration of Todd's life, Peter began his philanthropic and charitable efforts in earnest. He readily states that he was motivated to give because of Todd.

Peter does see a difference between philanthropy and charity. Philanthropy, according to Peter, is substantial and long term, whereas charity is more about giving to need. Peter's financial contributions go more toward philanthropy, with an approximate split of 75% directed toward philanthropic endeavors and 25% toward charitable requests.

Peter has never been disappointed by his involvement with the philanthropic and charitable worlds and plans to stay just as involved, if not more so, in the future!

Peter's Advice

- Become socially involved. Entrepreneurs need to get involved in their community, be it the school board, the mayor's office, city councils, churches; you need to get these groups thinking differently and outside the box.
- Get involved as early as you can.
- The planet needs to be improved; get involved in the green movement with the focus on a triple bottom line of enhancing the economic engine, social engine, and the environmental engine.

ART VELASQUEZ

Arthur R. Velasquez is a founder of Azteca Corn Products Corporation, Chicago (in 1970), and served as its president and chief executive officer from that time through May 1987. The Pillsbury Company acquired Azteca, one of the largest Mexican food manufacturing companies in the Midwest, in 1984. Azteca Foods Inc. was formed in early 1989 to acquire Azteca from Pillsbury. Mr. Velasquez resumed his position of chairman, president, and chief executive officer.

Art received his BS in electrical engineering from the University of Notre Dame in 1960 and his MBA from the University of Chicago in 1967. He is active in business, civic, and service groups locally and on the regional and national scenes. A trustee of the University of Illinois from 1974 through 1980, Art was the first Hispanic elected to a statewide office in Illinois.

He is currently a director of the Museum of Science and Industry, the Catholic Charities of Chicago, the Big Shoulders Fund, the board of trustees of the University of Notre Dame, the Alford Group, and the advisory board of the Nogales Fund, Boys Town of Chicago, and Cook County Forest Preserve Foundation. He also is a member of the Civic Committee of the Commercial Club of Chicago and the Chicago 2016 Olympic Advisory Committee.

Art Velasquez has been involved in the Pilsen–Little Village Communities for many years. He has been able not only to generously provide his resources to the community but also to take leadership roles in three important institutions during their critical development years. He was chairman of the first two capital campaigns for the Mexican Fine Arts Center. These funds were used for the refurbishing of the Park BoatHouse. He was co-chair of the $7 million capital campaign for the museum's recent major building expansion. He also served as chairman of the board of trustees for two years.

Art was chairman of the $2.5 million capital campaign to raise funds to build the first Alivio Medical Center on 25th and Western Avenue. He worked closely with Carmen Velasquez, his sister. He was co-chair of the $7 million capital campaign to raise funds for the second Alivio Medical

Center on Cullerton. He was also co-chair of El Valor's capital campaign to build the El Valor Early Child Center on 19th and Damen. Through Art's generous giving of his time, resources, and leadership, the community can be proud of three major institutions serving thousands of residents of Pilsen–Little Village.

Art's past activities include the following: director or trustee of LaSalle Bank N.A., Peoples Energy Corporation, the Mexican Fine Arts Center Museum, Maryville City of Youth; United Way of Chicago; Arvin Industries; General Trustee of the Lincoln Academy of Illinois; commissioner, Chicago Economic Development Commission; co-chair of Chicago United; the Mexican-American Legal Defense and Education Fund (MALDEF); Illinois Bell; the Executive Committee of the Chicago Community Trust; trustee, St. Xavier University; the Tortilla Industry Association and the Chicago Plan Commission. Mr. Velasquez was awarded an honorary doctorate from St. Xavier University and Governors State University.

He and his wife, Joanne, reside in Palos Hills, Illinois. They have six children and eleven grandchildren.

From Wanting a Bicycle to Being a Philanthropist

When you say the name Art Velasquez in Chicago, you get a knowing smile from individuals. Art has been a part of the Chicago community his entire life and is not only a successful business man but also a community leader and philanthropist. I first met Art during my work at the University of Illinois at Chicago's College of Business Administration. He was supportive of this university as well as his alma mater, the University of Notre Dame. But Art does more than support educational institutions. Art makes a difference on a daily basis to thousands of people. This is evident by what I saw when I walked into his conference room waiting for our interview to begin. On the bookshelves were awards and recognition items from numerous nonprofit organizations, including El Valor, the United Way of Metropolitan Chicago, the University of Notre Dame, Chicago Commons, and the University of Illinois at Chicago to name a few.

It all began when Art was 10 years old and wanted a bicycle. Yes, a bicycle. Art grew up living across the street from Hull House in an Italian neighborhood. His home was a three-room apartment with no hot water. Art and his sister, Carmen, shared a room, his parents slept on a pull-out couch in another room, and there was a kitchen. Art recalls going across the street to Hull House to take a shower.

One day Art was made aware of a raffle held to raise funds for Villa Scalabrini, a nursing home located in Northlake, Illinois, that many of his neighbors went to when they became too old or ill to live on their own. The prize for the person who sold the most tickets, or chances as Art refers to them, was a bicycle. Art believed—or as he says, knew—that the only way he was going to get a bicycle was to sell the most tickets. And that is what he did. Art and his father "hustled nickel chances," and he won the bicycle. It was one of his first fundraising efforts. Through this effort and his parents' example, Art got the philanthropy bug. Another early fundraising effort for Art was tied to his childhood church, St. Francis of Assisi, located on Roosevelt Road in Chicago. Art, along with his family, would raise money for the church and the nuns. Art also shared that in his high school year book there is a picture of him when he was a junior handing over a check for the mission collection. Art remembers gleaning donations from his high school classmates for that initiative.

When I asked Art why he was philanthropic, he responded that it is part of his values that he learned from his religion (he is Catholic) and his attendance of the University of Notre Dame. Today, his passion is his business, and he believes that if you are successful at what you do then you have to give back time and resources to the community in order to help others. Philanthropy and helping others are part of the values his parents instilled in him.

As an example of their parents' influence, Art noted that his sister, Carmen, started the Alivio Medical Center, which is a bilingual, bicultural organization committed to providing access to quality cost-effective health care to the Latino community, the uninsured, and underinsured, but not to the exclusion of other cultures and races. Art helps and supports his sister's endeavor to give back. Alivio Medical Center just celebrated its 20th anniversary.

Art told me that even when he was dating his wife, Joanne, fundraising was part of their lives. They met when Art was 16 years old and Joanne was 14, and as Art said, "There was always a dinner or a fundraiser each weekend and given our families' involvement it was what we planned our dates around." According to the 2006 annual report of the Chicago Community Trust, Joanne said, "There were times when we were young that we would have seven charity dinners in a week." According to Art, charity and philanthropy were part of his and his wife's growing-up experience, be it a dinner, fundraiser, or raffle. Also, by virtue of having six children attending

Catholic schools, raising money was a never-ending proposition. There was always a fundraiser or something to sell to benefit the schools. It was part of Art and Joanne's culture that they stood for community and for giving to those who did not have anything.

Art says he understands what it is to have nothing. Art is passionate about giving back. He grew up with the understanding that if you received blessings, you should show appreciation for those blessings. For Art and his family, both his parents and now his children, this appreciation was shown through giving back. If you grow your business and it leads to a growth in your resources, it is your responsibility to give more. This is a credo by which Art lives his life. By doing this, Art believes one will see his or her community grow. He also believes it is important to give financially to those organizations and projects with which you are involved. As Art bluntly states, "If you go on a board, you need to realize you need to make donations financially."

As is apparent from his bio, Art was always involved with his community. He was recruited to serve on the boards of the Chicago Community Trust, where he served on the Executive Committee, and the United Way of Metropolitan Chicago.

Art's company is a United Way participant and has been one for 20 years. It is also not uncommon from his staff to bring an issue or a situation to his attention and ask for help.

After being involved with these two groups, Art noted that his perspective on giving became bigger. He saw communities that were growing and communities that struggled against what was perceived to be in the mainstream. And he saw communities who were left out. In addition by becoming involved with Chicago United, Art worked with corporate CEOs, which he says was important because he was able to see how big business was involved and not involved in certain communities.

Through his work with the Chicago Community Trust, Art worked to champion building a future for Latino nonprofit organizations. As articulated in the 2006 annual report of the Chicago Community Trust, "Creating institutional support for the Latino community is so important because 52% of the Latino population is now in the suburbs, which is an astounding number and really throws people for a loop." Art further shares, "It is our future and it is important to grow philanthropy in the Latino community." With that knowledge, Art worked with Latino community leaders and the Trust to create Nuestro Futuro, an initiative to support and promote strategic charitable giving from Latinos living in the Chicago area through the Chicago Community Trust. The fund's goal is $6 million.

Art believes his involvement in philanthropy helps his business, but indirectly. He believes it gives the business a sense of being bigger and of being a leader in the community. In the end, according to Art, philanthropy demonstrates that a business cares.

I asked Art of which philanthropic endeavor he was most proud. His immediate response was that there were too many to choose from, but upon a minute's reflection he mentioned his sister's nonprofit organization. He was proud of working with his sister to pull off her dream to help others. He also acknowledges his work with the National Museum of Mexican Art (formerly known as the Mexican Museum of Fine Arts). He is also proud of his work with educational organizations from high schools to colleges and universities, sharing that both he and Joanne have given back to their high schools.

Art shared with me that in 1974 he received a call from Mayor Richard J. Daley asking him to become a trustee for the University of Illinois. Art's immediate response was negative because he was only 36 years old, had six children, and was building his business. However, when Mayor Daley told him that there were only 20 to 24 Latino students in the class of 6,000 entering freshmen, Art knew he had to say yes. He gave his time and thus changed a situation that to date has affected thousands of lives. Art Velasquez knows how to make a difference!

Overall, Art is pleased that he was and is able to connect people and resources. Through his efforts, charitable foundations and big businesses have become aware of and involved with the Hispanic community. Today, Art spends about 30% to 40% of his time on charitable and philanthropic endeavors. On the day I met with him, he told me about the eight interactions with nonprofit organizations that had occurred since 8 am. Now that's philanthropy in action!

Art notes that all six of his children are philanthropic minded, serving on numerous boards. One of his sons took a lesson from his dad to heart. Art readily admits that at one time he was overly involved and committed. His son learned from him and now limits his involvement to two or three non-profit boards at a time (see Chapter 2 for more recommendations on this).

Currently, Art and his family donate 30% to 40% of their charitable budgets to approximately six areas, primarily focusing on education, including high schools, colleges, and capital campaigns. Art readily confesses that it is hard for a new nonprofit organization or cause to secure funding from the Velasquez family or company because one of the current projects would have to be reduced or removed. Although Art is beginning to turn over his philanthropic activities to his children, he showed me an award he received in 1993 from the then-named National Society of Fundraising Executives. In that year, he was named Outstanding Volunteer of the Year. This is a truly outstanding accomplishment from a man who began his commitment to philanthropy and giving back by wanting a bicycle.

Art's Advice

- You need to be passionate to be successful both in business and in philanthropy. Art recommends reading the book *The Answer*, by John Assaraf and Murray Smith. This book states that you can grow your business, achieve financial freedom, and live an extraordinary life. Art shared that if you make money and have a high net worth, you begin thinking what do I do with it? Giving back is the answer in terms of time, effort, and financial resources.
- If philanthropy is not part of your goals when growing your business, then what is it all about? Art believes that making money is not what it is all about.
- Incorporate philanthropy into your work while you are building your business. You don't have to wait until you have all the money; start small and grow.
- Lock in a percentage that you will give to charity always.
- When you sit back one day and say, "What legacy did I hand to my children?" what will your answer be? Art believes it should be that you were very involved in philanthropy and giving of your time. Your children should understand that is it about a culture of caring and community.

DAVID WEINBERG

David Weinberg lives and works in Chicago, Illinois, where he was born. His mother was a successful commercial potter; David helped her carry and display her pottery at art markets and shows. His father operated a sculpture center and art gallery in California for 10 years and maintained a private collection. He inherited from them a love of art and an admiration for artists that expressed itself in a talent for photography. He spent his spare time learning the technical skills needed for landscape photography, photojournalism, portraiture, and photo silkscreening.

But David inherited more than a love of art. For generations, his family ran Fel-Pro Inc., a gasket manufacturing company in Skokie, Illinois. The company was famous for its generous benefits and even-handed treatment of employees. Additionally, Fel-Pro was recognized as one of the top 10 companies to work for in the United States. David and his family attributed the company's remarkable success in the marketplace to the good morale among their workers. David rose to the position of co-chair of the company and went on to teach his personnel methods to graduate students at the University of Illinois, as well as lecturing at numerous universities and governmental agencies.

Rewarding as the work was, David was ready for new challenges in his life. He saw in photography a chance to share and communicate with others on a higher level. Focusing himself on the task, he rededicated himself to photography. Two journeys inspired him: a trip to a rural farmhouse in Wisconsin and a trip to a similar farmhouse in Tuscany. He planned a series of photographs contrasting and comparing the landscapes and the form and function of local tools, but once at the farmhouses, he found himself drawn to the scrap heaps. He was fascinated by how exposure to the elements transformed man-made objects into complicated new creations. His photographs from those trips were the first step toward his photo-abstract style.

One of David's first series, "Reflections on a City," a study in visual abstraction and a showcase of modern architecture, is featured in the book *Towering Mirrors, Mirroring Towers, Photographs of Urban Reflections*. The book, published in September 2006 by Glitterati Inc., is prefaced by Carol A. Willis, founder and curator of the Skyscraper Museum in New York, and forwarded by Rod Slemmons, director of the Museum of Contemporary Photography in Chicago. The collection features an incredible variety of magnificent buildings, making interesting subjects of the ordinary places where people work and live.

David's newest series continues his signature style of documenting natural visual abstraction. Shot largely on the waters of Lake Geneva, this body of work features infrared photographs of the real, but unseen, effects of light wavelengths as they are absorbed or reflected from organic material. Sharply contrasted and evocative of litho prints or ink washes, the unique format urges viewers to deeply contemplate David's meditative compositions.

Doing Philanthropy Right

I remember meeting David Weinberg. It was my first day on the job at the University of Illinois Chicago, and I was stopping by a board meeting for the Center for Urban Business. David immediately got up and came over to introduce himself to me, stating that he was looking forward to the lunch we were having the next day. At that lunch, I knew we would be friends forever because I could not make up my mind whether to have a Caesar salad with calamari or the risotto, two of my favorite dishes. David saw my dilemma and suggested we order both and share. We became fast friends!

In his official capacity with the University of Illinois at Chicago, David served as the chair of the advisory council for the College of Business Administration. At the time I met him, David served on almost two dozen boards, both nonprofit and corporate. David was in a transition period of his life because he had just sold his family business, Fel-Pro, in 1997 to Federal Mogul. At Fel-Pro he served as the co-chair of the company with his cousin. Now he was a successful entrepreneur and businessman looking to make a difference.

During that first lunch David shared his frustration with the College of Business Administration and the advisory council. He told me that the meetings were unorganized, there was no follow-up on any of the items discussed, and, most important, he was frustrated. He was ready to give the new dean, Tony Rucci, a chance, but if things did not change, he was going to change by leaving the organization as a volunteer. I knew I had my work cut out for me. With David's help we turned around the advisory council, making it truly a significant asset to the College of Business Administration as well as the University of Illinois at Chicago.

I once asked David what made him care so much about philanthropy, and without hesitation he said his mother. His mom was always doing something for her community that was either charitable or civic-oriented. David recalled one of his first philanthropic volunteer experiences. He was still in junior high and was asked to volunteer to work a crowd in his hometown of Winnetka, Illinois, because Martin Luther King, Jr., was coming to give a speech. Young people had been recruited to go through the crowd and be spotters of suspicious-looking individuals. Although David cannot recall what Martin Luther King, Jr., spoke about that day, he does readily remember that the work he was doing and his participation was important to the civil rights movement as well as his community.

> David once shared with me that when he was young he did not understand why his mother was often not at home, like his friends' mothers. It was only later that he realized that she was often away participating in the civil rights movement and had actually marched in Selma, Alabama.

David believes that his first experience with charity was at temple because his participation fulfilled the laws of tzedukah. Tzedukah reminds the giver that it is not only giving charity that is significant, but also the manner in which we offer it, by not humiliating or demeaning those who receive it. David recalls that although he had no idea where the money went, he knew it was really important that he give. Today he believes it is equally important to give but to also know where the dollars are going.

Fel-Pro was started by his maternal grandfather as a company that sold felt blankets to the cavalry. David worked for Fel-Pro for 23 years, and when he began, the charitable arm of the company was already operating. Funded by the company, the Mecklenberg Foundation was the charitable aspect of Fel-Pro, and it grew considerably; when the company was profitable, the Foundation received larger contributions from the company.

Fel-Pro started a program through the Mecklenberg Foundation in which employees could request funding for nonprofit organizations, including churches, with which they were involved. An employee would complete a form, secure the signature of an executive at the nonprofit organization, and then present it to the Mecklenberg Foundation. David recalls that 9 out of 10 times, the request was granted. Although the limit was $5,000, David believes it afforded someone who was not wealthy to participate in the process and still deliver a sizeable charitable donation through his or her efforts.

David and his family sold Fel-Pro in 1997, and since that time David has done many things, including ramping up his philanthropic activities while reigniting his passion in photography. I reminded David of a story he once shared with me when I worked with him as the chair of the Business Advisory Council at the University of Illinois at Chicago. During a conversation, David had told me that he was involved with 25 organizations, both nonprofits and start-up businesses. He told me that annually he would sit down and review all his volunteer activities and decide which ones he would stay involved with and which ones he was going to stop his involvement. David laughed and said, "That's right; I use my Passion-O-Meter."

The "Passion-O-Meter" is a very simple tool. He sits down once a year with a piece of paper and a pen. He draws a straight horizontal line on the paper and at one end of the line writes the words "Not So Passionate" and at the other end of the line "Very Passionate," as shown here.

Not So Passionate_____ Very Passionate

Then, without thinking, he begins plotting on the line the organizations, both nonprofit and for-profit, with which he is involved. He simply puts a dot and the organization's name on the line according to how he feels. The example he shared is that when he thought about the organization, he would check his passion for it, meaning whether he was excited to attend meetings, liked the people he was serving with on the board, attended events, and so on. Once he completed the plotting, he looked at the organizations that were at the "Not So Passionate" end and knew he had to disengage from working with them. To be clear, he was not passionate about them.

When David shared with me how he annually analyzed the groups with which he was involved, I made it my personal mission to see that the University of Illinois at Chicago, the group for which I worked, was not deleted from the list. One day when he was showing me his new office, he shared that I was number three on his office phone speed dial. Incredulous because this seemed improbable, I asked him rhetorically, "Who puts a fundraiser on their speed dial?" At that moment I was fairly sure the University of Illinois Chicago was on the high end of his Passion-O-Meter.

Today, David is very passionate about the charter school movement and after-school programs. He continues to serve on a couple of start-up, entrepreneurial companies, but finds his passion in the world of photography and his art gallery (www.davidweinberggallery.com). David chooses to make a difference these days in three or four areas. He believes that by limiting his involvement, it leaves a little room for those unexpected requests from out-standing organizations and causes.

When I asked David whether he and his wife, Jerry Newton, set an annual budget, he shared with me that although they have no fancy formula, they do have a system. He stated they know what they earn, what they spend an-nually on their expenses (including taxes), and how much they can and do give away to charitable activities. They meet annually with their advisors, in-cluding an attorney, accountant, banker, and estate planner, to review their upcoming year's spending plan. David said that he and his wife are together in their thinking about charitable donations, believing that when you make a contribution to a nonprofit organization, you really must be actively en-gaged—preferably, playing a major role. By doing this you are assured of al-ways knowing where the financial contribution is going, and it feels great. David shared that often he and Jerry make gifts anonymously.

Additionally, David's immediate family has a family foundation called the Relations Foundation. The members of the Relations Foundation are David, his sister, and their spouses. (It should be noted that David has a brother who lives in Montana, so they split the Relations Foundation three ways, allocating one-third of it to a foundation in Montana that David's brother operates.) The Relations Foundation was started by David's mother, her husband, Joe, and his father. The Relations Foundation gives away what the corpus earns annually and makes no multiyear pledges. The family is also teaching their children, as the foundation has a budget from which the next generation makes charitable donations too.

David's Advice

- Give money where you can follow it by serving as a board member or board chair; you need to know exactly how the donation you made is being used.
- Give responsibly, meaning don't give more than your business can afford; a number of entrepreneurs can find themselves in a difficult situation if they are giving beyond their financial means.
- Teach your children how to do philanthropy well. David remembers his mom was an amazing teacher of philanthropy and how she taught was simply by doing it. At her death, she gave away 95% of her wealth. That definitely is teaching and leading by example.

CHAD WILLIS

As president and director of Texas Energy Holdings Inc., Chad Willis leads the strategic development of the company's investment portfolio. He is also responsible for the selection, negotiation, well operation, evaluation, and field operational management of oil and gas drilling prospects. With a focus on conservative operations and a proven investment strategy, he has enabled Texas Energy Holdings to consistently surpass internal benchmarks for assets under management. In August 2008, *Inc.* magazine ranked Texas Energy Holdings in the top 10 percent of fastest-growing private companies in the nation. Chad Willis has been featured in numerous media publications, including *Oil & Gas Investor* magazine, *Dallas CEO* magazine, the *Dallas Morning News*, and the *Fort Worth Star Telegram*. He is a frequent lecturer at financial industry events and is a member of many industry organizations, including the Texas Alliance of Energy Producers, the Dallas Petroleum Club, the Tenant-In-Common Association, and Athletes & Executives.

Chad is actively involved in local and national philanthropic and nonprofit organizations, including Dallas-based alley's house, the New York Rescue Workers Detoxification Project, and Big Brothers Big Sisters.

What You Give Comes Back to You Tenfold

Chad Willis describes his childhood as very middle class. His mother was a school teacher, and his father was a school maintenance engineer. Chad's family did not have time or money to donate to charity, but what it did have, he says, was unconditional love. He watched his parents share unconditional love and support, and this is where he learned the power of investing in people; he calls it "a natural investment of love." Taking what he learned from his parents, Chad began his journey into philanthropy by honoring his family: he paid off his grandmother's house, and he purchased a home for a disabled uncle. Chad says his parents' never-ending investment of love and support in him instilled a sense of compassion, honor, and altruism that guides him every day. Chad believes it is easy to overlook the people who are closest to you and those whose story you already know when thinking about philanthropy, but it is important to help them. According to him, doing things such as paying for a sibling's college education and helping friends by providing a job, even though every person would advise you against it, is philanthropy.

An early cause that touched Chad's heart was Alzheimer's disease when his grandfather was diagnosed with it. He worked with his family to ensure that his grandparents could relocate near his mother's home so that the entire family could provide care and help to his grandfather.

It was after this incident that Chad began looking for avenues to become more charitably involved, but he knew he wanted to stay away from the large nonprofit organizations. He thought if he selected nonprofit organizations that were smaller and more localized, he could see the results of his actions and interactions. One of his first endeavors began with the local Big Brothers Big Sisters organization, volunteering to serve as a big brother. However, Chad quickly realized that his lifestyle, with two small children and ever-increasing business demands, were such that he did not have enough time to dedicate to the program. Instead, he found himself simply writing a check and he did not feel really connected to the organization. Through this experience, however, he discovered that nonprofit organizations need both financial donations and expertise. He knew he could provide both if he found the right charitable cause.

As luck or fate would have it, Chad found himself invited by a friend to an event for alley's house, located in Dallas, Texas. Alley's house is a nonprofit organization that exists to break the generational, economic, and social impact of teen pregnancy in the Dallas community. He quickly learned that the nonprofit organization was started by Allison "Alley" Whitehead while she was working full time. Chad was impressed and soon became, as he puts it, "crazy for the company."

When I was talking with Chad, he repeatedly referred to nonprofit organizations as companies. When I asked him why he uses this language, he immediately replied that he sees nonprofit organizations as companies, operating much like a small business, with marketing, sales, and infrastructure.

Chad also fell in love with Allison's passion for what she was doing and became a student of the teen pregnancy problem. For example, he learned that when teenagers become pregnant, 70% of them drop out of high school, and the majority of these young girls end up on government assistance, sometimes for their entire life. He also learned that alley's house was and is committed to breaking this cycle in its community and attacking the situation at its root, which is poverty.

Chad became so enthused about the nonprofit organization that during the event, which was a wine and art event, and his first event for alley's house, he alone bought about 80% of the artwork available. He also noticed that the people in the room were not purchasing art or even bidding on it. As a businessperson, Chad was able to detect what the problem was. The attendees at this event were a nice group of people but not the right audience. In other words, these individuals were not capable of purchasing the art that was being auctioned and available. As he attended a few more events for alley's house, Chad continued to notice this problem, seeing the same thing happen again and again, mainly because of the wrong audience being in the room. It was at this point in time that he decided something needed to change. He began suggesting a number of marketing programs to Allison for their special events to ensure that the right individuals were attending and capable of making donations through purchasing whatever was being sold.

Allison soon realized she had a committed supporter to the nonprofit organization and the cause. However, Chad was very candid and honest with Allison and told her what he had told the Big Brothers Big Sisters group; namely, that he did not have time to serve on a board of directors. But he did make a commitment to continually challenge the board as he offered both his time, financial contributions, and skill sets. His first example of this commitment was to initially provide 30% of the nonprofit organization's budget annually through his charitable donations. He also challenged the board to think differently, because according to him they were fairly pessimistic and not necessarily thinking productively about what was possible for alley's house. The result of Chad's involvement is a nonprofit organization that is in a much better place, both financially and in terms of opportunities now seized, than it was before Chad's involvement.

When I asked Chad to share some of his thoughts about the philanthropic world for entrepreneurs, he told me he believes that by becoming philanthropically involved with a nonprofit organization you can change someone's life, but that most entrepreneurs do not know the best places to begin. They do not know how to find a nonprofit organization or vet it, or even how to start the process. He also believes that if people had seen what he has seen, meaning the need in the world, they would be giving three times the amount they currently are donating.

When asked whether he sees a difference between philanthropy and charity, his response was that he thinks they are both the same and that philanthropy is just a fancy word for charity. Like other entrepreneurs, he believes that philanthropy is not just making a financial donation, but also doing things such as serving as a mentor, volunteering, and so on.

Chad has one regret about his work in the philanthropic world and that is that he did not start sooner. During our meeting, he laughingly shared that he had actually spent more time learning to ride a bicycle in his youth than time spent learning about philanthropy. To him, this is his major regret.

Chad is planning to start the Texas Energy Holdings Charitable Foundation through his company. He views it as a mutual fund of charity, anticipating to give much to charities throughout the country. Watch for this exciting new grant-making organization to begin soon!

Chad's Advice

- Respect the word success. Everyone defines it differently, but take one step to help others succeed, however you define it.
- Pick something that you think you can provide tremendous help; it is better to provide a large amount of time or dollars to a few nonprofit organizations.
- Be smart with the way you give away money.
- Be creative in your charitable efforts; try to challenge the board by giving them the tools to fish.
- Involve other people, especially coworkers and employees, in charitable efforts. As an employer, give credit and incentives to employees to get them involved; challenge them to push themselves further into the charitable world.

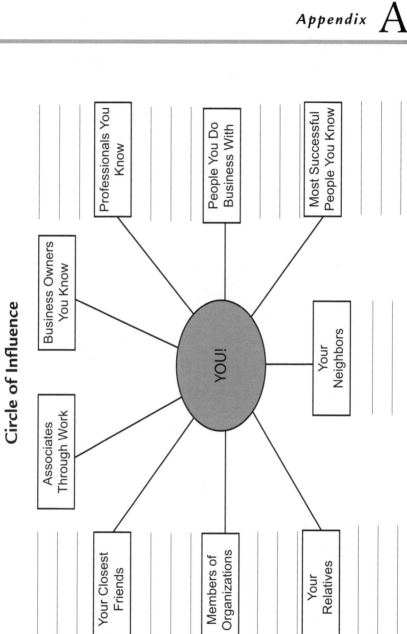

Circle of Influence

- Professionals You Know
- People You Do Business With
- Most Successful People You Know
- Business Owners You Know
- YOU!
- Your Neighbors
- Associates Through Work
- Your Closest Friends
- Members of Organizations
- Your Relatives

New Industries to Consider

10,000 baby boomers are turning 60 every day, and they have needs; entrepreneurs are responding by creating businesses and having encore careers in these areas. There are also sectors that do well in tough economic times, a time when entrepreneurism often thrives.

- Alternative energy firms (e.g., wind, solar, nuclear)
- Appearance-enhancing services
  - Botox
  - LASIK eye surgery
  - Teeth whitening companies or companies that produce the products
- Bankruptcy law firms
- Collection companies
- Computer technology
- Diabetes treatment companies
- Education
- Environmental companies
- Eye clinics
- Green cleaning services
- Green companies
- Green home remodeling
- Grocery stores, especially organic focused stores
- Health companies (e.g., fitness gyms)
- Healthcare companies
- Infrastructure companies (e.g., roads, bridges)
- Asphalt companies

- Low-water landscaping companies
- Military contractors
- Natural pet treats companies
- Obesity treatment companies
- Oil and gas companies
- Organic food companies
- Pharmaceutical companies and/or medical supply companies
- Pizza companies
- Recession-proof industries
  - Coffins/caskets
  - Funeral homes
  - Garbage pick-up/disposal
  - HVAC
  - Paper products companies (e.g., diapers, toilet paper, facial tissues)
  - Plumbers
- Recycling companies
- Safes for the home
- Salt companies (e.g., for cities to salt roads)
- Security (ports)
- Security and safety companies
- Seed companies
- Specialty/gourmet food companies
- Technology industry
  - Cellular phone companies
  - Music playing devices
- Wine companies

Sample Congratulations Letter

Date

Name
Title
Company/Organization
Address, Suite
City, State, Zip Code

Dear Name:

Greetings from Organization!

Congratulations on your appearance in the article titled "Name of Article" in *Name of Publication* dated Month, day, year.

I enjoyed reading the article and the wisdom/information/material that you shared. I look forward to connecting with you as our paths have not crossed since we met through/during *person or event*. Rest assured I will be in touch. Until then, I can be reached at (###) ### - #### or via email at *email address*. Again, congratulations!

With kind regards.

Sincerely,

Name
Position

Gift Agreement Template

The gift agreement is completed after a pledge agreement or if there is no pledge period, meaning that the donor contributes the gift in one donation. The gift agreement sets out specific criteria for how the nonprofit organization will utilize the donor's gift, reinforces the payment plan of the gift (if there is a pledge period), specifies how the donor will be recognized, deals with privacy issues, and contains a legal binding (or nonbinding, upon a donor's request) statement. The document ensures the gift will always be used exactly as the donor intended. Additionally, the document sets out alternative uses for the gift should it become impossible or impractical for the nonprofit organization to carry out the donor's original intentions.

At least two copies of the gift agreement should be created and signed. One copy will be for the nonprofit organization's record keeping and the other will be for the donor's record keeping.

USE OF GIFT AGREEMENTS

Gift agreements should be used in the following cases:

- Upon receipt of a pledge agreement or verbal commitment to make a donation at the $10,000 level or above, the nonprofit organization will send a gift agreement to the donor
- When gifts or pledges require a specific designation to a specific project or fund for the nonprofit organization
- Any ongoing or multiyear obligation between a donor and the nonprofit organization
- Any project that is a significant new undertaking for the nonprofit organization

Gift agreements should not be used when gifts are the following:

- Gifts made to the annual fund
- Current use or cash gifts
- Gifts under $10,000

SAMPLE GIFT AGREEMENT

Gift Agreement

Between

Nonprofit Organization and Donor Name

Date

This AGREEMENT is made and entered into this _____ day of _____, YEAR, between DONOR NAME (hereinafter called the "Donor") and the NONPROFIT ORGANIZATION NAME.

A. Acknowledgment and Gift

The nonprofit organization, in acknowledgment of the fact that the Donor intends to make a gift of $XX,XXX [INCLUDE PERIOD OF TIME IF NECESSARY] for the purposes described herein, agrees to hold, administer, and distribute the funds received as a result of said gifts as provided herein. The gifts shall be designated on the books and records of the nonprofit organization as having been received from the Donor, and recognition as decided and agreed between the Donor and the nonprofit organization.

B. Use of Gift

Describe the purpose of the gift, the area(s) within the nonprofit organization it will benefit, such as specific projects/areas of the organization, or whether it is unrestricted. It is strongly suggested to use words that reserve maximum flexibility for the nonprofit organization, such as *prefer* in place of *will be*.

C. Schedule of Contributions

A schedule of payments is required, although it may take more than one form. The timing of the initial gift should be included (often it is sent by the donor with the signed gift agreement), as well as future payments, either listing individual payments or simply affirming that the promise to give will be paid in full by a specific date.

D. Recognition

If the donor would like to be recognized, provide an outline describing how the donor will be acknowledged through the use of internal newsletters, emails, website postings, annual publications, promotional opportunities, use of logo, and other ideas discussed with the donor.

E. Representatives and Successors Bound

It is preferable for the nonprofit organization to seek as a first choice to enter into gift agreements with donors. Whereas the nonprofit organizaton prefers this form of agreement in all instances, the nonprofit organization understands that some donors may not want to potentially bind their estates in the agreement. Should a donor direct the nonprofit organization to create a nonbinding agreement, it will be necessary to discuss the implications before moving forward.

Suggested Language for Legal Binding
This Agreement shall be binding upon and inure to the benefit of the parties hereto, their heirs, executors, administrators, legal representatives, successors, and assigns.

F. Alternate-Use Clause

This section builds in flexibility in the event that at some time in the future the original purposes of the fund cannot be fulfilled. The alternate-use clause is not usually needed for current-use funds. There may be a situation in which a gift to support a capital project that is dependent on future funding requires a paragraph to describe what will happen to the gifts if they cannot be used for the original purpose. The donor should understand that in such circumstances, without this language as part of the agreement, the nonprofit organization could be prevented from fulfilling the donor's purpose or might have to go to court in order to get a judge's permission to revise the purpose of the fund in cases where the donor is no longer alive.

G. <u>Privacy</u>

This is also a good opportunity to capture the donor's wishes regarding issues of privacy and/or anonymity. It is important to determine whether the donor does or does not have specific requests regarding his or her privacy.

Suggested Language Regarding Privacy
"I/we expect the nonprofit organization to maintain my/our privacy with regard to this gift (except for listings in internal newsletters, website or other publicity internal to the nonprofit organization, or annual reports which may have limited distribution) to the extent provided by law, except with our express permission to do so otherwise." If a donor wishes to be anonymous, that should be clearly noted.

H. Attachments (if applicable)

IN WITNESS WHEREOF, the parties have caused this Agreement to be executed the day and year herein above written.

The Nonprofit Organization   Donor

_____   _____
Executive Director/President Date   Donor Name   Date

WITNESS

_____
Name   Date

Pledge Agreement Template

The pledge agreement form is used to record a pledged gift by a donor and to document the amount, designation, and preferred time frame for the gift. A pledge agreement should be completed immediately after a verbal commitment to a pledge has been made.

Using best practices, the nonprofit organization will need a signed pledge agreement on hand before counting the pledge or recording the pledge as a gift to be received.

The donor and the executive director/president of the nonprofit organization will sign two original copies of the pledge agreement form—one for the nonprofit organization's recordkeeping and one for the donor's recordkeeping.

Depending on the donor's wishes, the nonprofit organization may not need to utilize a pledge agreement before moving forward with a gift agreement. At times, the pledge agreement serves as a document to allow the donor to become more comfortable and confident with the donation while providing the nonprofit organization with a signed document for recording purposes.

SAMPLE PLEDGE AGREEMENT

Pledge Agreement

Between

Nonprofit Organization and Donor Name

Date

This pledge agreement is made and entered into this ⎯⎯⎯ day of ⎯⎯⎯⎯, YEAR, between DONOR NAME (hereinafter called the "Donor") and the NONPROFIT ORGANIZATION NAME.

A. <u>Acknowledgment of Pledge</u>

Nonprofit Organization, in acknowledgment of the fact that the donor made a pledge of $X in MONTH, YEAR, to be paid over TIME FRAME in the AMOUNTS OF $X for the purposes described herein, agrees to hold, administer, and distribute the property received as a result of said gifts as provided herein. The pledge has been designated on the books and records of Nonprofit Organization as having been received from the donor, and will be publicly recognized in this way.

B. <u>Use of Gift</u>

The payments and net income, if any, of the pledge shall be directed toward FILL IN AS APPROPRIATE. The Executive Director/President, or designee, shall determine the timing of the release of funds to the project or program.

C. <u>Representatives and Successors Bound</u>

This Agreement shall be binding upon and inure to the benefit of the parties hereto, their heirs, executors, administrators, legal representatives, successors, and assigns.

IN WITNESS WHEREOF, the parties have caused this Agreement to be executed the day and year herein above written.

The Nonprofit Organization   Donor

_____   _____
Executive Director/President   Donor Name

_____   _____
Date   Date

Individual Philanthropic Audit

lisa m dietlin & associates
TRANSFORMATIONAL PHILANTHROPY

About this Questionnaire

This questionnaire is for the sole purpose of evaluating your philanthropic belief systems, charitable priorities, and potential availability.

The information supplied on this questionnaire does not oblige you to any charitable commitments.

Please contact us if you have any questions regarding this application.

Part I.
Internal Reflection

While this portion of the questionnaire will provide you and us initial focus, we fully understand that the philanthropic variables we ask to self-evaluate and disclose here are subject to change.

Personal Interests can include sporting activities, hobbies, art, collecting, entertainment, etc.

Questionnaire For Individuals

Name

Contact Information

ADDRESS 1

ADDRESS 2

CITY   STATE   ZIP

PHONE/FAX   CELLPHONE   EMAIL

Professional organizations with which you are affiliated
Advisory Boards, Governing Boards, etc.

Community organizations with which you are affiliated
Advisory Boards, Governing Boards, Volunteer, Donor, etc.

Personal Interests

☐ GOLF   ☐ PAINT   ☐ SKI

☐ RUN   ☐ PERFORM   ☐ OTHER

&associates
TRANSFORMATIONAL PHILANTHROPY

Philanthropic Values
*are broken into the seven basic
areas of philanthropy. Examples
of each are given. We ask you to
make an initial prioritized listing,
from 1 to 7, of your current
support (if any) of these values.*

Specific Beliefs and Causes
*We ask that you either write
or verbally dictate to the interviewer
an expansion of the following
specific categories. This may
include the following:*

*1) organizations worked with
or interested in working with
2) specific issues of interest
3) personal stances and beliefs*

Philanthropic Values
PRIORITIZE FROM 1 (HIGHEST PRIORITY)
THROUGH 7 (LEAST PRIORITY)

☐ REDUCE HUMAN SUFFERING
health care, human services,
and international relief

☐ ENHANCE HUMAN POTENTIAL
religion, education, the arts,
culture and humanities, public and
social benefit, environment,
and international efforts

☐ PROMOTE EQUITY AND JUSTICE
human services and advocacy on
behalf of those who cannot speak
for themselves, helping to build a
more just society

☐ PROVIDE HUMAN FULFILLMENT
the opportunity to become that best
image we have of ourselves;
self-realization

☐ SUPPORT EXPERIMENTATION
AND CHANGE
improve society, take risks, explore
areas that the larger community or
market sector may be unwilling to
enter, looking for alternative or
new solutions

☐ FOSTER PLURALISM
challenges the status quo and goes
beyond the interests of the majority
allowing for multiple responses

☐ BUILD COMMUNITY
giving back to the community
(the common experience)

Animals

Arts and Humanities

Children

Community

lisa m dietlin & associates
TRANSFORMATIONAL PHILANTHROPY

Specific Beliefs and Causes
(continued)

We ask that you either to write
or verbally dictate to the interviewer
an expansion of the following
specific categories. This may include
the following:

1) organizations worked with
*   or interested in working with*
2) specific issues of interest
3) personal stances and beliefs

Education Kindergarten through 12th Grade, Collegiate, Adult Learners, etc.

Family

Health and Disease Related Issues

History

Human Suffering Hunger, Disaster Relief, etc.

International Focus and Causes

**lisa m
dietlin
& associates**
TRANSFORMATIONAL PHILANTHROPY

*Specific Beliefs and Causes
(continued)*

*We ask that you either write
or verbally dictate to the interviewer
an expansion of the following
specific categories. This may include
the following:*

*1) organizations worked with
    or interested in working with
2) specific issues of interest
3) personal stances and beliefs*

Part II.
Individual
Philanthropic Audit

*This portion reviews your
current participation in various,
causes, charities, or nonprofit
organizations (not necessarily
in a financial way).*

*Lisa M. Dietlin and Associates, Inc.
will help evaluate the consistency
related to your Internal Reflection
comments.*

Research

Safety and Security

Other

What causes and/or organizations do you currently support?

Why do you support philanthropic causes, charities or nonprofit organizations?

What do you hope to "gain" from these interactions?

What is your top charitable cause? Top three?

lisa m dietlin & associates
TRANSFORMATIONAL PHILANTHROPY

Part III.
Board Service

Part IV.
Charitable Financial
Contributions

This portion reviews your current financial donation practices in those charities, or organizations listed in the Individual Philanthropic Audit.

Are you available for Board Service? ☐ YES ☐ NO

What is your availability for Board Meetings?
☐ MONTHLY   ☐ BI-MONTHLY
☐ 4 TIMES PER YEAR ☐ 1 TIME PER YEAR

What are your areas of expertise?
☐ FUNDRAISING   ☐ LEGAL
☐ FINANCIAL   ☐ MARKETING
☐ PUBLIC RELATIONS ☐ OTHER

Are you currently participating financially with any nonprofit organization? ☐ YES ☐ NO

Would you like to share this information?

What, if any, additional causes/organizations would you like to support?

lisa m
dietlin
&associates

TRANSFORMATIONAL PHILANTHROPY

*If you are currently honoring
a pledge or proposal, please provide
us with details such as:*

1) amount pledged and remainder
2) current proposals considered
3) duration of the pledge

*Regarding your potential
or current contribution(s), what
financial usage factors are most
important. Some items to
consider may or may not be:*

1) organization size and structure
2) specific aspects of the donation use
*3) acknowledgement / anonymity
    factors*
4) differences / changes strived for
5) well established organizations
*6) new and emerging organizations
    and issues*

Part V.
Next Steps

*This portion reviews your future
philanthropic possibilities and
methods in which to proceed
effectively.*

Are you currently paying on any financial
pledges or have any proposals currently being
considered for a financial donation? ⬜ YES ⬜ NO

Do you want to share this information?

Regarding philanthropy financially, what is most important to you?

What philanthropic endeavors (events, outings, causes, etc.)
are you already committed to this year?

**lisa m
dietlin
&associates**
TRANSFORMATIONAL PHILANTHROPY

What additional philanthropic endeavors are you willing to add or subtract from the list above. Name organizations and causes.

What are you willing to consider to commit philanthropically this year?

TIME COMMITMENTS

SERVICE COMMITMENTS

FINANCIAL COMMITMENTS

*Thank you for taking the time
to fill out this questionnaire.*

Donor Bill of Rights

Philanthropy is based on voluntary action for the common good. It is a tradition of giving and sharing that is primary to the quality of life. To ensure that philanthropy merits the respect and trust of the general public, and that donors and prospective donors can have full confidence in the nonprofit organizations and causes they are asked to support, we declare that all donors have these rights:

I   To be informed of the organization's mission, of the way the organization intends to use donated resources, and of its capacity to use donations effectively for their intended purposes.

II   To be informed of the identity of those serving on the organization's governing board, and to expect the board to exercise prudent judgment in its stewardship responsibilities.

III   To have access to the organization's most recent financial statements.

IV   To be assured their gifts will be used for the purposes for which they were given.

V   To receive appropriate acknowledgement and recognition.

VI   To be assured that information about their donation is handled with respect and with confidentiality to the extent provided by law.

VII   To expect that all relationships with individuals representing organizations of interest to the donor will be professional in nature.

VIII   To be informed whether those seeking donations are volunteers, employees of the organization, or hired solicitors.

IX To have the opportunity for their names to be deleted from mailing lists that an organization may intend to share.

X To feel free to ask questions when making a donation and to receive prompt, truthful, and forthright answers.

The Donor Bill of Rights was created by the American Association of Fund Raising Counsel (AAFRC), the Association for Healthcare Philanthropy (AHP), the Association of Fundraising Professionals (AFP), and the Council for Advancement and Support of Education (CASE). It has been endorsed by numerous organizations.

Resources

BOOKS

Alexander, Scott. *Rhinoceros Success*. Laguna Hills, CA: Rhino's Press, 2003.

Bremmer, Robert H. *American Philanthropy*. 2nd ed. Chicago, IL: University of Chicago Press, 1988.

Clinton, Bill. *Giving*. New York: Alfred A. Knopf, 2007.

Collier, Charles W. *Wealth in Families*. Boston: Harvard University, 2003.

Collins, Jim. *Good to Great and the Social Sectors* [sound recording]. New York: HarperAudio, 2005.

Graham, Stedman. *You Can Make It Happen*. New York: Simon & Schuster, 1997.

Prince, Russ Alan, and Karen Maru File. The *Seven Faces of Philanthropy*. San Francisco: Jossey-Bass, 1994.

Salamon, Julie. *Rambam's Ladder*. New York: Workman Publishing, 2003.

Shaw, Sondra C., and Martha A. Taylor. *Reinventing Fundraising: Realizing the Potential of Women's Philanthropy*. San Francisco: Jossey-Bass, 1995.

Stanley, Thomas J. *Millionaire Women Next Door*. Kansas City, MO: Andrews McMeel, 2004.

Stanley, Thomas J., and William D. Danko. The *Millionaire Next Door*. Atlanta, GA: Longstreet Press, 1996.

WEBSITES

Association of Fundraising Professionals: www.afpnet.org

Association of Small Foundations: www.smallfoundations.org

Better Business Bureau Wise Giving Alliance: www.bbb.org/charity

Charity Navigator: www.charitynavigator.org
The *Chronicle of Philanthropy*: www.philanthropy.com
The Council on Foundations: www.cof.org
Great Nonprofits: www.greatnonprofits.org
GuideStar: www.guidestar.org
Idealist.org: www.idealist.org

Bibliography

CHAPTER 1

Bank of America. (2007, March). *The Bank of America study of high net-worth philanthropy*. Indianapolis, IN: The Center on Philanthropy at Indiana University.

Bianco, R. (2008, February 28). 'Oprah's Big Give' puts good works in a bad light [electronic version]. *USA Today*.

Busse, M., & Pascal-Joiner, S. (2008). It's not what you think: dispelling some common misconceptions about nonprofit work. In *The Idealist guide to nonprofit careers for first-time job seekers* (pp. 193–203). Portland, OR: Action Without Borders. Retrieved June 10, 2008, from http://www.idealist.org/media/pdf/career/guide/ChapterThirteen_f.pdf

Busse, M., & Pascal-Joiner, S. (2008). What exactly is a nonprofit? (The answer will surprise you). In *The Idealist guide to nonprofit careers for first-time job seekers* (pp. 15–26). Portland, OR: Action Without Borders. Retrieved June 10, 2008, from http://www.idealist.org/media/pdf/career/guide/ChapterOne_f.pdf

Dietlin, L. M. (2006, June). *Timing the major gift ask*. Presentation made at the National Alliance for Grieving Children's 10th Annual Symposium, Chicago, IL.

Friedman, R. A. (2005, December 21). Behind each donation, a tangle of reasons. *The New York Times*. Retrieved June 8, 2008, from http://www.nytimes.com/2005/11/14/giving/14rfriedman.html

National Women's Business Council. (2007, July). Women business owners and their enterprises. Retrieved June 10, 2008, from http://www.nwbc.gov/ResearchPublications/documents/KeyFactsWBOandtheirEnterprises.pdf

Stanley, T. J. (2004). *Millionaire women next door*. Kansas City: Andrews McMeel Publishing.

CHAPTER 2

Alleyne, S. (2008, June). Oprah means business. *Black Enterprise*, 117–126.

Andrew Carnegie. (2008, June 27). Retrieved June 29, 2008, from Wikipedia: http://en.wikipedia.org/wiki/Andrew_Carnegie

Bentz Whaley Flessner. (1996, Summer). Raising funds in the era of the entrepreneur. *Occasional Papers, IV,* 3.

Caring and sharing [Electronic version]. (2005, December 7). *The Arizona Republic.*

Dell, Inc. (2008). Consolidated statements of income: Form 10-K for the fiscal year ending February 1, 2008. Retrieved November 10, 2008, from Securities and Exchange Commission: http://www.sec.gov/Archives/edgar/data/826083/000095013408005718/d55156e10vk.htm

Di Mento, M., & Lewis, N. (2008, January 24). A big year for big giving [electronic version]. *The Chronicle of Philanthropy.* Retrieved from http://philanthropy.com/free/articles/v20/i07/07000601.htm

Di Mento, M., & Lewis, N. (2008, January 24). 23 donors claimed spots on both '06 and '07 most-generous lists [electronic version]. *The Chronicle of Philanthropy.*

Dorsey, K. (2008, June 29). Bill Gates: Life after a legend finally logs off. *Business.Scotsman.com.* Retrieved June 29, 2008, from http://business.scotsman.com/ business/Bill-Gates-Life-after-a.4233788.jp

Ehrlich, S. G. (2008). Create philanthropic culture to attract transformational gifts. *Major Gifts Report, 10*(9), 1.

George Soros. (2008, June 28). Retrieved June 29, 2008, from Wikipedia: http://en.wikipedia.org/wiki/George_Soros

Joan B. Kroc. (2008, May 25). Retrieved June 29, 2008, from Wikipedia: http://en.wikipedia.org/wiki/Joan_B_Kroc

John D. Rockefeller. (2008, June 26). Retrieved June 29, 2008, from Wikipedia: http://en.wikipedia.org/wiki/John_D._Rockefeller

Joseph, A., Lapidos, J., Shen Rastogi, N., Rubin, J., & Wilson, C. (2008, February 11). The 2007 *Slate* 60: Donations. *Slate.* Retrieved June 30, 2008, from http://www.slate.com/id/2184056/

Kelly, K. S. (1998). *Effective fund-raising management.* Mawah, NJ: Lawrence Erlbaum Associates.

Krull, L. (Ed.). (March 5, 2008). The world's billionaires: Special report [Electronic version]. *Forbes.* Retrieved from http://www.forbes.com/2008/03/05/richest-people-billionaires-billionaires08-cx_lk_0305billie_land.html

Landis, J., & Butler, J. (2008). Fast Draw: Philanthropy [Video]. In R. Morrison (Executive Producer), *The Early Show.* New York: CBS Broadcasting Company.

Lansdowne, D. (1999). *Fundraising realities every board member must face.* Medfield, MA: Emerson & Church.

Lewis, M., Jr. (2003, November). Chef executive. *Smart Business* [Chicago]. Retrieved June 29, 2008, from http://www.sbnonline.com/Local/Article/5459/68/0/Chef_executive.aspx.

Mason Kiefer, H. (2004, November 9). Who's the boss? Teens would like to be. *Gallup.com.* Retrieved November 15, 2008, from http://www.gallup.com/poll/13993/Whos-Boss-Teens-Would-Like.aspx

McLoone, S. (2008, November 21). Growth of minority-owned firms sky-rockets. *Washingtonpost.com.* Retrieved November 22, 2008, from http://voices.washingtonpost.com/small business/2008/11/growth_of_minority_women-owned_1.html

The philanthropy 50: Americans who gave the most in 2007 [electronic version]. (2008). *The Chronicle of Philanthropy.* Retrieved from http://philanthropy.com/philanthropy50/gifts.php?view=topdonors&year=2007

Shaw, S. C., & Taylor, M. A. (1995). *Reinventing fundraising: Realizing the potential of women's philanthropy.* San Francisco: Jossey-Bass.

Slate 60 appearances by Doris Christopher. (2007). Retrieved June 29, 2008, from *Slate:* http://specials.slate.com/slate60/donors/doris-christopher/

Small Business Administration. (2007). What is a small business? Retrieved November 10, 2008, from http://www.sba.gov/advo/stats/sbfaq.txt

The University of Chicago. (2008). About the university. Retrieved June 29, 2008, from http://www.uchicago.edu/about/

CHAPTER 3

FedEx. (2008, June 29). Retrieved June 29, 2008, from Wikipedia: http://en.wikipedia.org/wiki/FedEx

Frederick W. Smith. (2008, June 24). Retrieved June 29, 2008, from Wikipedia: http://en.wikipedia.org/wiki/Frederick_W._Smith

Giving USA Foundation. (2008). *Giving USA 2008: The annual report on philanthropy for the year 2007* [electronic version]. Indianapolis, IN: The Center for Philanthropy at Indiana University.

Kessler, E., & Boyd, B. (2008, Summer). *7 questions for effective philanthropists.* Chicago: Arabella Philanthropic Investment Advisors.

Preston, C. (2008, October 16). Making a big difference: Small businesses want to offer cash and services to charities. *The Chronicle of Philanthropy,* 17–22.

CHAPTER 4

Ingram, V. K. (1999, July). *Navigating the white water: The evolution of small nonprofit organizations.* Unpublished master's thesis, St. Mary's University of Minnesota, Winona, MN.

Robert F. Kennedy. (2008, July 13). Retrieved July 14, 2008, from Wikipedia: http://en.wikipedia.org/wiki/Robert_F._Kennedy

CHAPTER 6

American Red Cross. (2006). The American Red Cross 2005: Highlights and statistics. Retrieved November 12, 2008, from http://www.redcross.org/special/printer/0,1203,0_0_5017,00.html

American Red Cross. (2006, December). *Tsunami recovery program strategic plan 2006–2010.* Retrieved November 12, 2008, from http://www.redcross.org/news/in/tsunamis/strategicplan_dec2006.pdf

American Red Cross Liberty Disaster Relief Fund. (2007). Semi-annual report, October 1, 2006, through March 31, 2007. Retrieved November 11, 2008, from https://americanredcross.com/images/pdfs/911Semi-AnnualReport.pdf

Internal Revenue Service. (2008). Exemption requirements. Retrieved August 2, 2008, from http://www.irs.gov/charities/charitable/article/0,,id=96099,00.html

Miller, M., & Greenberg, D. (2008, September 17). The 400 richest Americans [electronic version]. *Forbes.*

Preston, C. (2008, June 12). The long view: Ted Turner's plans include goading other donors to join his campaign to save the world [electronic version]. *The Chronicle of Philanthropy.*

September 11 donations: How much charities have raised and distributed [Electronic version]. (2003, September 4, 2003). *The Chronicle of Philanthropy.*

Ted Turner donates $1 billion to 'U.N. causes' [electronic version]. (1997, September 19). CNN.

United Nations Foundation. (2006, October 10). Ted Turner's United Nations Foundation delivers $1 billion to UN causes; foundation makes new comitment to leverage another $1 billion [Press release]. Retrieved August 2, 2008, from http://www.unfoundation.org/media_center/press/ 2006pr_101006.asp

Warren Buffet. (2008, August 2). Retrieved August 2, 2008, from Wikipedia: http://en.wikipedia.org/wiki/Warren_Buffet

Whelan, D. (2008, October 6). Club generosity. *Forbes,* 39.

CHAPTER 7

Bellis, M. (2008). Automobile history: The history of cars and engines. Retrieved August 3, 2008, from http://inventors.about.com/od/cstartinventions/a/Car_History.htm

Gose, B. (2009, January 15). A Bitter End: Settlement resolves dispute between Princeton U. and the donors' heirs [Electronic version]. *The Chronicle of Philanthropy.*

Gose, B. (2008, March 20). Golden rule: A family's $70 million gift forces Oral Roberts U. to transform its management [Electronic version]. *The Chronicle of Philanthropy.*

Gose, B. (2007, March 22). Princeton University returns small part of donation ensnared in court battle [Electronic version]. *The Chronicle of Philanthropy.*

Gose, B. (2007, August 23). Settlement requires animal charity to return $4 million in Katrina gifts [Electronic version]. *The Chronicle of Philanthropy.*

Kean, S. (2007, December 13). A Zagat's for charities: A new online venue allows charity clients, volunteers, and others to post guidebook-style 'reviews' [Electronic version]. *The Chronicle of Philanthropy.*

Lipman, H. (2006, January 12). Donors say intentions are key [Electronic version]. *The Chronicle of Philanthropy.*

Stamp, T. (2006, August 17). Charities must heed the lessons from Hurricane Katrina [Electronic version]. *The Chronicle of Philanthropy.*

US National BBB.org. (2008). About BBB Wise Giving Alliance. Retrieved August 10, 2008, from http://us.bbb.org/WWWRoot/SitePage.aspx?site=113&id=cf401757-e890-4352-8d73-829eb595de21

Wilhelm, I. (2006, April 20). Michigan Asks Ford Foundation to show it is following donor's intentions [electronic version]. *The Chronicle of Philanthropy.*

CHAPTER 8

Bank of America. (2008, November 24). The 2008 Bank of America Study of High Net-Worth Philanthropy. Indianapolis, IN: The Center on Philanthropy at Indiana University.

Collins, J. C., & Porras, J. I. (1996, October). Building your company's vision. *Harvard Business Review, 65*, 13–16. Retrieved September 5, 2008, from http://faculty.washington.edu/janegf/buildingvision.html

Prince, R. A., & File, K. M. (1994). *The seven faces of philanthropy*. San Francisco: Jossey-Bass.

CHAPTER 9

Six degrees of Kevin Bacon. (2008, September 25). Retrieved September 28, 2008, from Wikipedia: http://en.wikipedia.org/wiki/Six_Degrees_of_Kevin_Bacon

CHAPTER 10

Ashoka International. (2005). What is a social entrepreneur? Retrieved October 11, 2008, from http://www.ashoka.org/fellows/social_entrepreneur.cfm

Delancey Street Foundation. (2007). Our enterprises: Social entrepreneurship. Retrieved October 12, 2008, from http://www.delanceystreet foundation.org/enterprises.php

Gaffin, A. (2003). Boston's Emerald Necklace. *Boston Online*. Retrieved October 12, 2008, from http://www.boston-online.com/emerald.html

Gill, D. (2008, July 14). Can you make money and do good? [electronic version]. *Crain's Chicago Business.*

Kemp, J., & Crane, C. (2003, August 26). Compassionate capitalism: Entrepreneurship can lift the third world out of poverty. Retrieved October 12, 2008, from http://www.freedomworks.org/informed/issues_template.php?issue_id=2019

Opportunity International. (2007). History: Who we are. Retrieved October 11, 2008, from http://www.opportunity.org/Page.aspx?pid=204

Oregon Public Broadcasting. (2005). Meet the new heroes: Albina Ruiz. Retrieved October 11, 2008, from http://www.pbs.org/opb/thenewheroes/meet/ruiz.html

Oregon Public Broadcasting. (2005). Meet the new heroes: Dr. Govindappa Venkataswamy ("Dr. V.") & David Green. Retrieved October 11, 2008, from http://www.pbs.org/opb/thenewheroes/meet/green.html

Oregon Public Broadcasting. (2005). Meet the new heroes: Mimi Silbert. Retrieved October 11, 2008, from http://www.pbs.org/opb/thenewheroes/meet/silbert.html

Oregon Public Broadcasting. (2005). Meet the new heroes: Muhammad Yunus. Retrieved October 11, 2008, from http://www.pbs.org/opb/thenewheroes/meet/yunus.html

Oregon Public Broadcasting. (2005). The new heroes. Retrieved October 11, 2008, from http://www.pbs.org/opb/thenewheroes/meet/

Oregon Public Broadcasting. (2005). What is social entrepreneurship? Retrieved October 11, 2008, from http://www.pbs.org/opb/thenewheroes/whatis/

Oregon Public Broadcasting. (2005). Who were the first social entrepreneurs? Retrieved October 11, 2008, from http://www.pbs.org/opb/thenewheroes/whatis/whatis_ss_1.html

Oregon Public Broadcasting. (2005). Who were the first social entrepreneurs? Florence Nightingale. Retrieved October 11, 2008, from http://www.pbs.org/opb/thenewheroes/whatis/whatis_ss_6.html

Oregon Public Broadcasting. (2005). Who were the first social entrepreneurs? Frederick Law Olmstead. Retrieved October 11, 2008, from http://www.pbs.org/opb/thenewheroes/whatis/whatis_ss_5.html

Oregon Public Broadcasting. (2005). Who were the first social entrepreneurs? John Muir. Retrieved October 11, 2008, from http://www.pbs.org/opb/thenewheroes/whatis/whatis_ss_3.html

Oregon Public Broadcasting. (2005). Who were the first social entrepreneurs? Dr. Maria Montessori. Retrieved October 11, 2008, from http://www.pbs.org/opb/thenewheroes/whatis/whatis_ss_4.html

Oregon Public Broadcasting. (2005). Who were the first social entrepreneurs? Susan B. Anthony. Retrieved October 11, 2008, from http://www.pbs.org/opb/thenewheroes/whatis/whatis_ss_2.html

U.S. National Park Service. (2008). Yosemite National Park: People. Retrieved October 12, 2008, from http://www.nps.gov/yose/historyculture/people.htm

CHAPTER 11

Ballard, S. (2007, December 25). Sharing the wealth: Pro athletes, teams try to give back to the communities that support them [Electronic version]. *Indianapolis Star.*

Knecht, G. B. (2007, April 28). Big players in charity [electronic version]. *The Wall Street Journal.*

Newman's Own. (2008). $250 million for the common good. Retrieved October 18, 2008, from http://www.newmansown.com/commongood.aspx

Ricketts, C., & Knecht, G. B. (2007, April). What athletes are giving [electronic version]. *The Wall Street Journal.*

USC College of Letters, Arts and Sciences. (2008). USC Shoah Foundation Institute: History. Retrieved October 18, 2008, from http://college.usc.edu/vhi/history.php

CHAPTER 12

Chicago Community Trust and Affiliates. (2008). Giving vehicles: Types of funds. Retrieved October 19, 2008, from http://www.cct.org/page27931.cfm

Chicago Community Trust and Affiliates. (2008). Partnering with the Trust. Retrieved October 19, 2008, from http://www.cct.org/page27928.cfm

Cleveland Foundation. (2008). About the Cleveland Foundation. Retrieved November 16, 2008, from http://www.clevelandfoundation.org/About/

Collinson, S. (2006, June 27). Buffett-Gates merger creates $60bn charity giant. *Mail & Guardian Online*. Retrieved October 19, 2008, from http://www.mg.co.za/article/2006-06-27-buffettgates-merger-creates-60bn-charity-giant

Council on Foundations. (2008). History of the Council on Foundations. Retrieved October 19, 2008, from http://www.cof.org/council/content.cfm?ItemNumber=746&navItemNumber+2137

Exclusive: Buffet kids react to Dad's donation. (2006, June 29). *ABC News*. Retrieved October 19, 2008, from http://abcnews.go.com/print?id=2133209

Loomis, C. J. (2006, June 25). Warren Buffett gives away his fortune [electronic version]. *Fortune*.

Russell, I. (2006, April). Our story: A history of the Santa Fe Community Foundation.

Santa Fe Community Foundation. (2008). For donors: Types of funds. Retrieved November 1, 2008, from http://www.santafecf.org/donors/typesoffunds.php

Glossary

charity: The active effort to alleviate human suffering and promote human welfare; it is usually done on a short-term basis to help an immediate and particular situation.

community foundation: A nonprofit organization that exists to benefit community residents in a specific geographic region.

cultivation: The third step in the Moves Management process; cultivation involves working with the individual or individuals to have them become more familiar and supportive of the nonprofit organization.

donor: An individual who makes a charitable donation to a nonprofit organization; it can also refer to an entity such as a corporation or foundation that makes a charitable donation.

encore career: A second career in a person's life; something usually totally different than what was done previously with more and more individuals looking to the nonprofit world as a possible place to serve.

entrepreneur: An individual who identifies a niche in the marketplace that is not currently being filled and works to build a business to address it. An entrepreneur is also willing to bring all his or her resources to the situation in order to succeed.

fundraiser: An individual who is responsible for the task of raising funds for a nonprofit organization. A fundraiser can be either a paid staff person or a volunteer. At times, the word *fundraiser* is used to reference an event that is raising money for a nonprofit organization.

gift agreement: A signed and dated agreement by both the donor and the nonprofit organization that recognizes the gift being made and specifies for what it is being designated.

identification: The first step in the Moves Management process; identifying through discussions, research, benchmarking, and analysis individuals who might be prospective supporters or donors of the nonprofit organization.

independent sector: Wording used at times to describe the nonprofit sector to differentiate it from the government (public) sector or the corporate (public) sector.

Moves Management: A five-step process of moving a prospective donor along a path from being identified to making a gift, and then actively stewarding the donor.

nonprofit organization: A corporation that has received a ruling from the Internal Revenue Service, usually a 501(c) (3)–designated status, that provides a tax-exempt status. It is sometimes referred to as a not-for-profit organization.

philanthropist: This term can be applied to anyone who is a donor, but in society it is usually used in reference to wealthy individuals making significant seven- or eight-figure gifts to a nonprofit organization.

philanthropy: The active effort to promote the human welfare; it is usually focused on the long term and allows for sustainable change to occur.

pledge agreement: A signed and dated agreement by both the donor and the nonprofit organization that outlines the details of the gift to be made, including the amount of the gift, the number of years for it to be paid, the amount of each payment, and for what it will be designated. On occasion, information about the recognition of the gift will also be included.

private foundation: A 501(c) (3)–designated organization that secures its funding from one source and provides grants (i.e., gifts) to nonprofit organizations.

public charity: A 501(c) (3)–designated organization that is publicly supported by securing at least one-third of its funding from donations and other sources that are qualified.

qualification: The second step in the Moves Management process; usually done through meetings or conversations. Qualification seeks to determine whether the individual is interested in the nonprofit organization and would like to learn more by becoming involved.

social entrepreneur: Social entrepreneurs are change agents for their communities and society as a whole. They focus on opportunities others overlook or even miss by improving approaches and developing solutions to potentially insurmountable or large-scale problems.

solicitation: The fourth step in the Moves Management process; solicitation involves asking for a financial contribution to the nonprofit organization. The request is usually made in a face-to-face setting.

stewardship: The fifth and most overlooked step in the Moves Management process; stewardship is the process of not only thanking the donor but also ensuring that the donation is properly used in the manner for which it was intended or designated.

Photo Credits

Julie Azuma, Courtesy of Kenji Azuma

Suzy Bogguss, Courtesy of Amy Dickerson

John and Rita Canning, Courtesy of Northwest Community
Hospital Foundation

Lisa Dietlin, Courtesy of Lisa Crosby Photography

Richard Driehaus, Courtesy of Bill Zbaren

Garth Fundis, Courtesy of Ben Fundis

Carolyn Gable, Courtesy of Eddie Arrossi

Deborah Gibson, Courtesy of Diane Gibson

Leticia Herrera, Courtesy of Lynda Guillu Photography

Bill Imada, Courtesy of Ken Matsui

Al Johnson, Photo by Eugene Wood

Suzanne Jurva, Courtesy of Suzanna Jurva

Janet Katowitz, Courtesy of Carole Mundy

Marsha McVicker, Courtesy of Marsha McVicker

Alfredo J. Molina, Courtesy of Alfredo J. Molina

Carole Mundy, Courtesy of Carole Mundy

Stephan Pyles, Courtesy of Steve Foxall Photography

John W. Rogers, Jr., Courtesy of Andy Goodwin

Cibeline Sariano, Courtesy of Lisa Crosby Photography

Peter Thomas, Courtesy of Relne Mihtla

Art Valasquez, Courtesy of Art Valasquez

David Weinberg, Courtesy of Cassandra Ott

Chad Willis, Photo by Jennifer Browning

Vote Logo (crop circle), p. 225, Courtesy of Todd Johnson

Index

Note: Italicized page locators indicate a figure; tables are noted with a *t*.